By the same author:

Outside the Gate

BUSTLING INTERMEDDLER?

The Life and Work of

CHARLES JAMES BLOMFIELD

Dedicated to the memory of
Dr Patrick Welch

BUSTLING INTERMEDDLER?

The Life and Work of
CHARLES JAMES BLOMFIELD

Malcolm Johnson

GRACEWING

First published in 2001

Gracewing
2 Southern Avenue
Leominster
Herefordshire HR6 0QF

ISBN 0 85244 546 6

Typesetting by
Action Publishing Technology Ltd, Gloucester, GL1 5SR

Printed in England by MPG Books Ltd,
Bodmin PL31 1EG

Contents

Half title page illustration:

Charles James Blomfield, Bishop of Chester (artist unknown). Reproduced by kind
permission of the National Portrait Gallery, London.

Acknowledgements

The Church Commissioners have helped financially with this biography and I am immensely grateful for their generosity. Mr Howell Harris Hughes, their Secretary, has taken a close interest in the publication of this book.

I owe an enormous debt of gratitude to Dr Patrick Welch who in the 1960s loaned me his unpublished doctoral thesis on Blomfield, and then gave me much advice and help until he died in March 1995, aged 80. I was privileged to take his funeral. He was the perfect gentleman, a good friend, and, until retirement was a lecturer at Paddington Technical College. His widow, Joy, now living in Coulsdon, has graciously allowed me to dedicate this book to him.

Owen Chadwick's magisterial work on the Victorian Church has been a huge help as has Soloway's *Prelates and People* and Peter Virgin's two recent books.

I am indebted to the librarians at Lambeth Palace and also to Christopher Lloyd, Surveyor of the Queen's pictures, who took me to see the paintings at Windsor Castle and Buckingham Palace which include the Bishop. Michael Rutland, the Administrator at the Royal Foundation of Saint Katharine, has lovingly typed the text and I am so very grateful. He is now an expert on nineteenth-century ecclesiastical history, as is my friend, Robert Wilson who has patiently listened to all the chapters in the book – several times.

The five bishops of London I have known have all been admirers of Blomfield. When in 1967 I went in my best suit to see Robert Stopford at Fulham Palace, Blomfield gazed down at me from above the study fireplace. Gerald Ellison at his enthronement laid a wreath on the tomb in Saint Paul's as he had followed Blomfield at Bishopsgate, Chester and London. The official painting presided over Graham Leonard's first-floor meeting room in Barton Street where I and my fellow area deans used to gather; David Hope also admired the Bishop, but my special thanks go to Richard Chartres for writing the foreword to this book and, with Caroline, giving me so much encouragement and help over the last few years. I shall always be grateful. Miranda Poliakoff, curator of Fulham Palace Museum, has enthusiastically helped with the launch of this book.

The Blomfield family, particularly Mr David Blomfield at Kew, have been immensely supportive. I hope that they feel I have done their distinguished ancestor justice at last.

Being published by Gracewing is like marrying a duchess; the honour is almost greater than the pleasure. Tom Longford and Jo Ashworth have treated me gently and kindly.

Malcolm Johnson

Foreword

by the Rt Revd and Rt Hon Dr Richard Chartres, Bishop of London

Blomfield, thou art needed in this hour! This is a very timely biography as the Church of England faces a financial and administrative revolution.

Charles James Blomfield, a pioneer in so many ways, was the first Bishop of London to enter pensionable retirement, although it took an Act of Parliament to secure his pension of £6,000 per annum, which in today's money is not far short of a quarter of a million pounds. This is very topical since it is the cost of honouring past pension promises which has so drastically reduced the Church Commissioners' capacity to support other forms of active ministry. Today's Diocese of London is shouldering its share of the transfer of £92m per annum in costs, principally stipends, from central provision to Dioceses and Parishes.

This transfer will bring about a revolution in the structure of the church which Blomfield in his day did so much to shape. In a time of change it is always prudent to take counsel from the muniment room where there are records of so many schemes and debates which throw light on the challenges which face us now.

This biography reveals a Bishop who was awesome in his industry, and who proposed bold remedies for the Church's financial and structural distempers without being impeded by any craving to be loved. It may be as Disraeli hinted that Blomfield was one of those leaders who was not much of a spiritual guide but his achievements laid the foundations for the huge contributions of the Victorian Church in education, in social provision and in the mission field.

He was sometimes wrong and came to see, in the light of the Gorham Judgement, that his support for transferring the appellate function in Ecclesiastical Causes from the High Court of Delegates to the Privy Council was a mistake. It is a mistake that still awaits rectification. Occasional errors were inevitable since he was involved in so many causes and had a passion for detail even down to pronouncing on the species of soap to be used in public bathhouses. As his epigone, I constantly encounter his spoor, whether in the many churches he caused to be built or in institutions like the London Guildhall University. The Bishop of London is still proud to be connected to this and other bodies by virtue of Blomfield's endeavours on behalf of the education of working people.

Malcolm Johnson tells the story with admirable clarity and wit. This is an enjoyable book but also one in which justice has been done to one of the great reformers of the nineteenth century.

Blomfield sits above me in his portrait as I write these words. The Complutensian Bible is beside him on the table but firmly gripped in his hand is some legal document or possibly a Parliamentary Bill. Administration is also a spiritual gift.

'I can read poetry and plays, and things of that sort, and do not dislike travels,' [said Catherine Morland to Eleanor Tilney,] 'but history, real solemn history, I cannot be interested in. Can you?'

'Yes, I am fond of history.'

'I wish I were too, I read it a little as a duty; but it tells me nothing that does not either vex or weary me. The quarrels of popes and kings, with wars or pestilences, in every page; the men all so good for nothing, and hardly any women at all, it is very tiresome; and yet I often think it odd it should be so dull, for a great deal of it must be invention. The speeches that are put into the heroes' mouths, their thoughts and designs; the chief of all this must be invention, and invention is what delights me in other books.'

'Historians, you think,' said Miss Tilney, 'are not happy in their flights of fancy. They display imagination without raising interest. I am fond of history, and am very well contented to take the false with the true. In principal facts they have sources of intelligence in former histories and records, which may be as much depended on, I conclude, as anything that does not actually pass under one's own observation; and as for the little embellishments you speak of, they are embellishments, and I like them as such.'

Jane Austen, Northanger Abbey

Introduction

I have lived with Bishop Blomfield for forty years. We were introduced during the church history lectures at Cuddesdon given by the vice-principal, the Revd John Brooks who was manfully attempting to hold the college together during the 1960 interregnum, after the departure of the severe Edward Knapp-Fisher to be Bishop of Pretoria and before the arrival of the newly-married Robert Runcie. John enlivened his lectures by regular quotes from Sydney Smith but he also challenged me to look into the life of the neglected Bishop of London who had reformed the Church of England in the early nineteenth century. I took up the gauntlet and during my curacy at St Mark, Portsea, spent every Tuesday morning in the front room of Mrs Purkiss of Balfour Road writing an MA thesis for Durham University. The University rewarded me with the degree, and she rewarded me with home-made cakes at 11 am and a delicious lunch at 1 pm.

I am grateful to John for asking me to find out why Blomfield has received no biography since the tombstone one written by his son in 1863 which was described by his grandson Reginald as 'A lamentably serious book ... unrelieved by a flash of humour from cover to cover.' Dr Biber, the other biographer, reports he had had little contact with the Bishop or his family so his book (1857) 'is free from bias'. Sir John Wheeler Bennett, biographer of King George VI, who was one of Cuddesdon's Governors and local squires, has said that no one should undertake a biography inadvisedly, lightly or wantonly but reverently, discreetly and in the fear of God. However, the delay in my attempting this book has not been because of his advice but because I have been a busy parish priest over the last thirty-eight years. Now, thanks to the present Bishop of London, Richard Chartres, also an admirer of Blomfield, I have been given time and space to complete the task. The reforms which Blomfield and his co-worker Robert Peel (Prime Minister 1834–5 and 1841–46) pushed through Church and Parliament alienated many clergy because their stipends were shared out more fairly, each was made to live in his parish, and each found he could be incumbent of only one living. As clergy usually write church history and biographies of bishops it is not surprising that no one attempted to assess Blomfield's contribution to the Anglican Communion, despite the fact Sydney Smith called him 'The Church of England here on earth'. Owen Chadwick remarks, 'No English bishop of 1835 could claim to be so generally unpopular as Blomfield. He was said to be high-handed, sarcastic, meddlesome, hasty, overbearing. Even when he smiled he smiled episcopally – always conscious of his dignity. He commanded neither the art of charm nor the virtue of tact'.[1]

Charles James Blomfield lived at a time when two different eras met – eighteenth-century rural England, and early Victorian urban England – so he is a transitional figure. The world into which he was born on 29 May 1786 resembles in many ways the Indian sub-continent today. The vast majority of the population had one goal in life – to keep alive and avoid starvation. If your parents died you lived on the streets and survived as best as you could. If you stole anything worth more than £5 you could be hanged or transported to a penal colony; if it was under £5 you were sent to prison and lived in unspeakable conditions. If you went into service you worked eighteen hours a day, six and a half days a week. The majority of the population lived in the countryside and worked, if they were lucky, on the land. The Bible claimed that the poor went to heaven, so the rich felt justified in keeping the poor in poverty. No-one's health was good – TB affected a sizeable proportion of the population. London with its population of 900,000 was the seat of government and home to the ruling classes but it contained a great deal of poverty – a town of contrasts, as is Washington DC in America today. Marriages were arranged and lasted for ever – there were only 250 divorces in England between 1650 and 1850. In London there were 70,000 prostitutes out of the total female population of 475,000. To read the novels of the time – particularly those of Jane Austen, who was born eleven years earlier than Blomfield – you would never realise how horrid life was; novels then as now provided an escape from real life. Death was a well-known visitor to most households: 50% of all babies would die before the age of two, and one baby in four would be stillborn. Some children were abandoned or put out to fostering. The vicar of Steventon, Hampshire, Jane Austen's father, sent his second son, an epileptic, away to a parish clerk's family to be brought up in poverty and never mentioned again.

English countryside at this time was particularly beautiful, for there were no railways, motorways or aeroplanes to cause noise and filth. The rural idyll was marred by the human population which suffered from malnutrition, ignorance and disease.

In 1800 of a population of approximately 11 million there were 18,000 clergy of the Established churches in England and Scotland, and 14,000 dissenting clergy. Today the population has increased five times and the number of clergy has dropped by a third.

In Blomfield's lifetime the population of England and Wales increased considerably, because in 1851 it stood at 17,927,609.[2] London's population expanded from 958,863 to 2,362,236 during the first half of the century, and by the middle of the nineteenth century over half the population lived in urban areas. In 1851 of 3,336,000 people over the age of 20 living in the 62 largest cities of England and Wales only 1,337,000 had been born there.

Like most of the upper classes and most of the men who were to become bishops in Victoria's reign Blomfield was an eighteenth-century man with ingrained rationalistic assumptions about human nature and social harmony. Only seventeen of the 104 bishops who reigned during his lifetime had held an urban living, so most were out of touch with the day-to-day life of the population. None of the 104 were truly great leaders whose prophetic vision would inspire Church or nation – there was no Laud, Temple, Newman or Ramsey to excite their times. Bishop Bagot of Bristol probably spoke for most of the bench when in 1783 he said God desired order and harmony in society with all the 'various distributions of rank, wealth and power and all the extensive circumstances of life'.[3] Society was as much a divine creation as the Newtonian universe itself. Periodic imbalances in society were inevitable, but charitable relief would alleviate suffering until the balance was restored.

I am advised by the Bank of England that, using the Retail Price Index, £1 in 1800 is valued at £28 today, in 1830 £38 today, and in 1850 £45 today. In the text I have given both yesterday and today's approximate figures, so when Blomfield was enthroned in 1828 his income was in the region of £21,000 p. a. (£798,000 p. a.) and when he retired he asked for a pension of £6,000 p. a. (£270,000 p. a.). In his early life he set aside one-fifth of his income for charity, but in later life this became one-third. The church of St Stephen, Hammersmith, cost £30,000 (£1,250,000) and was built and endowed solely at the Bishop's expense.

In all but name Blomfield was the Archbishop of Canterbury, as Howley was pleasant but ineffective, and Vernon Harcourt of York was an insignificant and reticent prelate. When Howley was seriously ill in 1842 Peel offered the archbishopric to Blomfield, but Howley recovered. By the time he died six years later Blomfield himself was in poor health and past his prime. At London, however, he was able to achieve more than any other church leader of his time.

Chapter One

The challenge of London

The Diocese of London ought to be a pattern of order and discipline to the whole nation as it abounds with persons of greater learning, knowledge and experience than any other diocese.
Edmund Gibson, Bishop of London 1723–1748

It was disgraceful and unseemly. St Paul's was used to ugly scenes outside its walls, particularly at nearby Newgate on public hanging days, but inside the cathedral was a different matter. A large crowd had assembled under the dome on this cold January day in 1829 because several newspapers had announced that the infrequent ceremony of a bishop being enthroned would take place that morning. The new diocesan, Charles James Blomfield, formerly Bishop of Chester, was known to some, as he had been an archdeacon (of Colchester) in the London diocese, a former bishop's chaplain and, until the previous year, rector of St Botolph Bishopsgate in the City of London, a post he kept whilst at Chester. Now aged forty-two, he was a man of boundless enthusiasm and ability, round-faced, 5 feet 8 inches tall, large head too big for his body, eyes large, full and blue, pale complexion, skin and hair fine and soft. His walk was determined, firm and rapid. Abrupt. When he spoke to you he faced you squarely.[1] Like most bishops he was a classicist rather than a theologian, having had a brilliant career as an undergraduate and then as a Fellow of Trinity College, Cambridge.

The artist George Richmond, a close friend of the Blomfields, was able to observe the Bishop closely and has left us a careful description.

His limbs were well knit and shapely, and the hands and feet small. The mouth, though small, was decided and full of character, and the lips had some of the characteristics of infancy in their delicate rounding and shapeliness; while the whole mouth was tremulous with sensibility and humour ... The nostrils were well marked and expressed great energy and quiet feeling. The eyes were large and full, and the upper eyelid falling into one line over part of the eye, gave great vigour and vivacity to the look; and yet the expression of the eye, itself of a violet-blue tint, such as I have rarely seen, was full of humanity, of tenderness, and pity ... Like the face of childhood, it was a transparent mirror of the life within.

The baby-faced pugnacity of a Winston Churchill is thus joined with the patrician presence and authority of Archbishop Geoffrey Fisher or Bishop Gerald Ellison who was to follow Blomfield at Bishopsgate, Chester and London.

Accompanied by the Dean, Dr Copleston, the canons, prebendaries and the chancellor of the diocese, Dr Lushington, he had already arrived from the Chapter House through the great west doors and taken his seat. Edward Copleston had been Dean of Chester so he knew the Bishop well. Appointed to St Paul's the year before, combining it with the bishopric of Llandaff, he was, according to his biographer, the last man in England to be robbed by a highwayman – near Uxbridge in 1799.

The Lord Mayor, Mr Alderman Venables, arrived in state, with his officers carrying the sword and mace before him. 'There was however some difficulty in clearing a road through the crowd ... and the City officers only succeeded in obtaining them a small passage by promising that the gates to the choir should be opened to the public as soon as they had placed the Lord Mayor in his seat' – opposite the new bishop.

This promise was not kept to the letter and the crowd became rather riotous in consequence of hearing the ceremony proceeding without them being present to witness it. A call was made upon the officers to open the gates and as it was not immediately complied with, cries of 'Shame, shame – you've broken faith with the public' were set up by several individuals. The officers told the clamourers that, if they persisted in such unbecoming uproar, they should be obliged to lock them up, but finding that silence was not obtained by this threat they wisely gave up the point and let the multitude in. The pressure under the organ loft was immense and several ladies had their veils and bonnets torn from them before they obtained entrance into the choir.[2]

Morning Service continued to the end of the first lesson when the Dean, the Bishop of Llandaff, stood before the throne and read a paper to his lordship, 'the contents of which were inaudible except to those immediately around the throne'. Perhaps he was reminding the new Bishop of the immensity of his task, because the diocese comprised the whole of the metropolis north of the Thames, all of Middlesex and Essex, a considerable part of Hertfordshire and four parishes in Buckinghamshire. There was no other bishop to assist him and on top of these duties he was expected to be 'Bishop of the Empire' for he had pastoral care over all British possessions overseas which had no bishop of their own. There were in fact only five colonial bishoprics in 1829.

Blomfield was duly placed in his episcopal throne and the Dean blessed him, saying, 'Mayest thou remain in justice and sanctity and adorn the place thou art delegated to by God. God is powerful and may He increase your grace.' The new Bishop said a prayer, then Morning Prayer continued and after the liturgy the procession returned to the Chapter House, where the Bishop thanked everyone for their attendance and went home to Fulham. There is no mention of refreshments.

The clergy witnessing the service would have included a good number of Evangelicals, including the thirty-year-old Revd and Hon. Baptist Noel, perhaps the most influential gospel minister of his generation, co-founder of the Evangelical Alliance and an eminent preacher, who for the past twelve months had been minister of St John's Chapel, Bedford Row, Holborn, where he was to remain until he left the Church of England in twenty years' time. Other Evangelicals would have included Henry Watkins, rector of St Swithin, London Stone, for forty-four years, and Daniel Wilson, famous vicar of Islington, who was successfully mixing his new and old parishioners by introducing Sunday evening services and early morning communion on saints' days. He hated the 'gross popish impostures' of the Tractarians and his biographer reflected that 'things were said many times that might have been better left unsaid but though men might smile they never slept'. In 1832 he became Bishop of Calcutta, and Blomfield assisted at his consecration. R. W. Church in his book on the Oxford Movement published later in the century said that Blomfield introduced many Evangelicals into the diocese. In fact they were already there, and in 1829 others would have included James Haldane Stewart of the Percy Chapel, Tottenham Court Road, who left to build his own chapel of St Bride in Liverpool, Isaac Saunders, rector of St Andrew-by-the-Wardrobe in the City, and Henry Melvill, minister of the Camden Chapel where not even standing room was available during services. He was later rewarded with a residentiary canonry of St Paul's. Henry Blunt of

Holy Trinity, Sloane Street, who also preached to a packed church, was the first incumbent there. In his three years he 'drew around him what was perhaps the most influential congregation in London.'[3] He enjoyed publishing counterblasts to the *Tracts for the Times* and died in 1843, aged only forty-nine. Josiah Pratt, another prominent Evangelical, was vicar of St Stephen, Coleman Street, in the City, 1826–44; he built galleries in his church to accommodate the large number of worshippers and opened an infant school in the parish. He was one of the founders of the City of London School in 1834, helped to found the Church Pastoral Aid Society, and compiled a psalm- and hymn-book which sold 52,000 copies. The City was blessed with several Evangelical clergy, one of the foremost of whom, Samuel Crowther, died in 1829 after being vicar of Christ Church, Newgate, and lecturer of St Botolph, Bishopsgate for twenty-nine years. His 'suavity of manners and sanctity of life impressed many, he was a firm upholder of evangelical truth, and the famous African missionary bishop was named after him'.[4]

Also witnessing the enthronement would have been Henry Hutton who was to be at St Botolph, Aldgate, for 42 years, Thomas White at the Welbeck Chapel for 47 years and Richard Yates, Chaplain of Chelsea Hospital, who having married 'a modest heiress' was able to turn down several benefices, continuing to write pompous articles about church reform for many years. Not much changes in the London diocese, for in 1998 there were seven clergy whose length of service totalled 288 years – Gordon Taylor at St Giles-in-the-Fields since 1949; Chad Varah, founder of the Samaritans, at St Stephen Walbrook since 1954; William Atkins, St George, Hanover Square (1955); two Hackney clerics, Donald Pateman (1956), and Fred Preston appointed in 1961 by Henry Montgomery Campbell, who told him he would do no harm and might do some good. The others are Dick Lucas, St Helen, Bishopsgate (1961) and Brian Kirk Duncan, Archdeacon of Conakry, St Mary at Hill (1962).

Two prominent laymen were probably in the congregation at the enthronement – William Cotton, a high official in the Bank of England who was to provide advice, money and support for the Bishop's church building programme, and Joshua Watson, a wealthy City businessman who helped the Bishop build hundreds of schools and who became one of the Blomfield's closest friends: 'I never differed from the Bishop in matters of minor importance (for on questions of moment there was no difference between us) without mistrusting my own conclusions'.[5] Watson was a leader of the High Church 'Hackney Phalanx', which met at the rectory of his brother John in Hackney, who would have been at the service as he was one of the diocesan archdeacons (of St Albans) and vicar of Hackney for over forty years. In poor health, he left parish administration to his curate Henry Norris who was wealthy enough not to ask for a stipend. The Archdeacon had much influence with Lord Liverpool, Prime Minister 1812–27, and was probably his chief adviser on ecclesiastical appointments. His church was well attended considering the surrounding poverty, as was nearby Shoreditch which had nine Anglican churches in its parish with an average morning congregation of 400; Stepney had eleven churches with an average morning congregation of 500.[6]

Other incumbents present in the Cathedral would have included the rector of St Clement Danes in the Strand which had many of London's brothels in its parish and a 'frightful amount of infidelity', and the rector of St Anne, Soho, whose gravedigger had recently been discovered playing skittles with the skulls in the crypt.

Blomfield had a daunting task ahead but he was the right person in the right place at the right time, although *The Times* and the *Christian Observer* had suggested that Kaye, Bishop of Lincoln would have been a better choice for London, 'distinguished for learning, consistency, liberality, mildness and purity', rather than 'the meddling, worldly and pugnacious' Blomfield. Kaye, however, had moved to Lincoln from Bristol only the year before, so remained there as 'an able, energetic improver of his diocese and influential member of the bench'.[7]

In some ways Blomfield was a surprising choice as he had opposed the Tory government on Catholic Emancipation and on amendments to the Corn Bill. Wellington, the Prime Minister, was in no doubt and acted quickly. He had obviously made up his mind long before Manners Sutton, the Archbishop of Canterbury 'without genius or learning to make him angular or unpleasant', died on 21 July 1828. Immediately Howley was offered Canterbury, and on 24 July a letter was sent to Chester offering Blomfield London. A week later he kissed hands, was sworn in as a Privy Councillor and on 15 August royal letters authorising the election of a Diocesan went to the Dean and Chapter of St Paul's accompanied by a recommendation that the Bishop of Chester be elected. This happened five days later and was confirmed at St Mary le Bow on 23 August. In less than five weeks a new Archbishop and a new Bishop of London were appointed. Such things take longer today.

Life in London

Blomfield came to the capital when life was squalid and unpleasant for most of its inhabitants. Things had changed considerably since

1802 when Wordsworth rattled across Westminster Bridge in his coach on the way to Dover, writing

> Earth has not anything to show more fair:
>> Dull would he be of soul who could pass by
>> A sight so touching in its majesty:
> This City now doth, like a garment, wear
> The beauty of the morning; silent, bare,
>> Ships, towers, domes, theatres, and temples lie
>> Open unto the fields, and to the sky;
> All bright and glittering in the smokeless air.

At that time London was approximately five miles long and three miles wide, with Park Lane and Edgware Road the western boundary, Marylebone and City Roads the northern boundary, and the docks the eastern boundary. The population was around a million, a tenth of that of England and Wales. Now, in 1828, London was stretching outwards and there was extensive building in Bloomsbury, Islington, St John's Wood and Paddington. The population was increasing at a rapid rate due to the decrease in the death rate, the increase in the birth rate and a considerable movement of people from country to town to find employment. Amongst these was the young Charles Dickens, who moved from Chatham with his parents in 1822 when he was ten. He was sent to work a twelve-hour day at Warren's Boot Blacking Factory at Hungerford Stairs near the Strand for six shillings a week, and had to walk a considerable distance to and from his home every day. Migrants from the country had to live in squalid lodging houses.

> When a man arrives he is directed to Whitechapel or St Giles and journeys through tight avenues of glittering fish and rotten vegetables with doorways or alleys gaping on either side – which if they be not choked with squalid garments or sickly children, lead the eye through an almost interminable vista of filth and distress ... The pavement where there is any, ragged and broken, is bespatted with dirt of every hue, ancient enough to rank with the fossils, but offensive as the most recent deposits. The houses, small, low and mournful present no one part, in windows, door posts or brickwork that seems fitted to stand for another week – rags stuff up the panes.[8]

By 1845 the London air was laden with smoke from steam vessels, gaswork furnaces and industry. New locomotives were hissing at Waterloo Station, and the newly built Victoria Embankment had confined the Thames. Beneath was an underground railway and two tunnels, one for sewage. A new Palace of Westminster gleamed in the sun and more bridges had been built, including those at Vauxhall and Waterloo. A crust of 'unutterable grime' covered everything, so most of the wealthy had decided to move out. London had become a centre of service industries, but had no stable manufacturing industry of its own. Communications became easier as roads were improved. In 1821 a new express chaise service, London to Manchester, achieved an average speed of eleven miles an hour. The new macadam roads meant faster travel by coach – there were twelve coaches a day between Leicester and London, and one could travel the 170 miles to Exeter in 21 hours including halts. Edinburgh to London took 40 hours, weather permitting. Short-stage coaches plied between the centre of London and the outer parts, and in 1825 six hundred coaches made 1,800 journeys daily with four to six passengers inside and up to seven outside. They were not allowed to pick up passengers on the way as this was the privilege of the 1,250 hackney cabs in the capital.

Until the arrival of the railways most people had not travelled beyond their own village. In 1802 Richard Trevithick built a steam coach which reached 9 miles an hour, then blew up, but two years later he designed a train which carried 70 men at nearly 5 miles an hour for nine and a half miles. In 1808 he astonished Londoners with his mini train which ran round a circular track in north London at 15 miles an hour. The ride cost one shilling but most people were terrified of this iron horse. How could it replace the real thing?[9] In 1822 the first public railway, Stockton to Darlington, was opened and Sydney Smith was most impressed: 'The early Scotchman scratches himself in the morning mists of the North and has his porridge in Piccadilly before the setting sun.' New horizons opened up but were often clouded by danger and discomfort. Travelling by train was hazardous. Hot ash and embers emitted from the engine furnaces were an ever-present fire risk, and steam boilers were liable to explode. Passengers were advised that they should seat themselves as far from the engine as possible and have their backs to it. Those who travelled second or third class had to make do with open trucks and hard wooden benches, until 1844 when the Government legislated to protect them from the elements. Even in first class there was no heating or sanitation. The London to Birmingham Railway was built 1833–8 and by the time of Blomfield's death the framework of a national railway system had been built. A steam-powered railway opened in London on 14 December 1836 to convey passengers to Deptford; two years later it was extended to Greenwich.

Life in the inner city could be dangerous. In the 1820s Londoners were protected by some 5,500 men under the control of local vestries. Each ward had its beadles, constables and watchmen, with unpaid constables helping out. In the daytime citizens were expected to protect themselves, but as dusk fell these men came on duty. A centralised police force was opposed because it might limit individual liberty, freedom of speech and movement. In 1829 Robert Peel, the Home Secretary, began the long process of eliminating the riot and disorder which were such a part of everyday life, and by 1833 he employed 3,389 men under a central authority. The City of London was exempt, and today still has its own Commissioner and police force. In 1851 the Square Mile had a population of 129,128, so such a bid for independence is understandable, but today with a population a tenth of that number it seems an anachronism.

Early nineteenth-century men and women took their pleasures in a boisterous and full-blooded way on the Turf, at bull- and bearfights – suppressed in 1835 – or cockfights and prizefights. Hotly contested elections and public hangings provided amusements and drew large crowds. A racecourse existed at Ladbroke Square, Notting Hill, and prize fights were held in Holborn, St Martin's Street and other venues. Grimaldi the clown kept audiences laughing at Sadlers Wells and Mrs Siddons and Edmund Kean showed off their talents at Drury Lane. Song and Supper rooms spread out from Covent Garden, then in the 1850s came the music halls. Rowlandson and Cruikshank portrayed London life in their cartoons showing the great divide between rich and poor, from the man described in Henry Mayhew's *London Labour and the London Poor* (1851) who searched the sewers for saleable objects ('the smell's nothing') to the wealthy in Belgravia off for an afternoon's 'wide in Wotton Wow'.

The growing middle classes ate at home and entertained there, because chophouses and coffee-houses were unsuitable for ladies, and very few restaurants had been opened. Shops were small and inde-pendent, open all hours like today's Mr Patel's corner shop. Street hawkers – 13,000 of them according to Mayhew – and street markets abounded but much merchandise was delivered to the door. During the first half of the century drapers and haberdashers sold materials so that sewing and needlework could be done at home. Large stores only opened in the second half of the century.

The Victorians had a great interest in matters religious, even those who were not regular worshippers themselves. Towards the end of Blomfield's episcopate the census of 1851 revealed that in London less than a quarter of the total population attended Church of England services.[10] Today the figure is around $2\frac{1}{2}\%$. 276,885 people filled the Established Church pews on a Sunday; today the figure hovers around 55,000. It also revealed the strength of the Dissenters – 186,321 Londoners attended their Sunday worship. Civil disabilities had been removed so the Independents and the Congregationalists, the largest groups, had 161 places of worship in London. The Wesleyan Methodists had 154 chapels and the Baptists 130 congregations. The Quakers had nine Meeting Houses.[11] There was a small number of Roman Catholics, most of whom had arrived after the 1846–7 famine in Ireland, so only 36,000 heard Sunday Mass in thirty-five London churches. The census revealed that approximately a third of Londoners attended a place of worship: so two-thirds stayed away. Mayhew asked a costermonger what St Paul's was. 'A church, sir, so I've heard. I never was in church.'[12]

Sir C. C. Eastlake describes the cold, classic churches of the time:

Who does not remember the grim respectability which pervaded the modern town church of a certain type with its bleak portico, its portentous beadle, the muffin-capped charity boys. Enter and notice the tall neatly-grouped witness and jury boxes in which the faithful are empanelled; the three-decker pulpit placed in the centre of the building, the lumbering gallery which is carried round three sides of the interior on iron railings; the wizen-faced pew-opener eager for stray shillings; the earnest penitent who is inspecting the inside of his hat; the patent warming apparatus; the velvet cushions which profane the altar; the hassocks which no one kneels on; the poor box which is always empty.[13]

In *Dombey and Son*, Dickens paints a similar picture describing Mrs Miff the pew-opener, and Mr Sownds the Beadle who hovers around Dombey's wedding, then sits on the steps counting the cash after the ceremony.

London presented Blomfield with a difficult, almost unsurmountable challenge but his four years at Chester had provided him with an excellent apprenticeship.

Chapter Two

Preparation for power

I mean to be a bishop.

The young C. J. Blomfield

Political upheaval and unrest had surrounded the birth of the future Bishop, who was three when the French Revolution sent shock waves through Europe. George III was in Windsor Great Park addressing trees as the King of Prussia, and his Tory Prime Minister, William Pitt, was attempting to resist the verbal assaults of the Whigs led by the redoubtable, lazy, clever Fox who, because he was descended from the Merry Monarch, bore the same names as the new member of the Blomfield family, Charles James. The baby received these names because the first was his father's and the second his grandfather's. The political scene was changing; the resounding defeat of the Whigs in the 1784 election had been due to the royal control of rotten boroughs: all the 44 Cornish and all the 45 Scottish seats were at the King's disposal. Fox felt that the constitutional gains of 1642 and 1688 were being reversed but his attempt to stop it was frustrated by the 1789 French Revolution, which led to conservatism at home and a war against France which lasted nearly twenty years. Intelligent men and women asked why England should be involved, particularly as the ruling classes were all francophile.

All this seemed far removed from Hatter Street, Bury St Edmunds where Charles James Blomfield was born on 29 May 1786, 'a small delicate boy full of high spirits and quick intelligence adored by his brothers and sisters, full of invention and fancy'. Even today the town possesses much of its eighteenth-century charm, and seems aware of its historical and architectural distinction. It makes its living as it always has done, as a market centre of an area rich in agriculture, and big in beer and sugar. The town is set out on a grid laid down in the late eleventh century, when its Abbey attracted thousands of pilgrims to see the mummified remains of St Edmund. 'Its ruins, now containing two hard tennis courts, resemble less a monastery garden than a part of Torquay seafront. However, few historic towns have more skilfully married the demands and opportunities of the present with the fragile fabric of the past.'[1]

The Blomfields were a well-known East Anglian family. In the middle of the seventeenth century when the Revd Matthias Candler drew up his pedigrees, the Blomfields were county gentlemen, merchants and farmers, owning much property and land. Four members of the family feature in a 1670 list of gentry. The family became keen Puritans and increased greatly in the eighteenth century, becoming small farmers and tradesmen. John Kirby who surveyed the county of Suffolk in 1732–4 notes that Stonham Parva near Stowmarket 'is of note for the residence of the ancient family of the Blomfield's or Blondevilles, an ancient family near as old as the conquest'.[2]

For forty-three years the future Bishop's father Charles kept a school at the corner of Lower Baxter Street and Looms Lane in Bury, in which Charles James received his first education. The building has been demolished and replaced by Blomfield House, now a medical centre. Father was a much-loved schoolmaster, a prominent member of the Corporation and Justice of the Peace, 'impartial, anxious not to punish the guilty but rather to reclaim the sinner, not merely by good advice but often by pecuniary assistance when most needed'. He himself was fond of riding and 'wasting his substance in altering his house',[3] a keen gardener, wise, gentle and courteous – too courteous, because he was to die after falling when giving up his seat to a lady at an oratorio in Norwich. At his funeral an anonymous writer suggested he had bought 'unfading honours' for his son, but also wrote:

> Behold the sun before whose dazzling blaze
> Newton's bright halo rapidly decays;
> Behold the sage whose unexampled lore
> Hath taught his boys that two and two make four.

Hester, his wife, the daughter of a local grocer, bore him ten children, four of whom died in childhood. Edward, two years younger than Charles James, went to school with him, then to Gonville and Caius College, and then became a Fellow of Emmanuel College where he died and was buried in the chapel. Anna, his sister, only lived eleven years, dying 'of fright in a thunderstorm'.

The home was a happy one with younger brothers and sisters, all enjoying summer holidays at Cromer. There were plays to act and an electric machine to make. Well educated at home, Charles James entered the local grammar school when he was eight and enjoyed for ten years the tuition of the Revd Michael Becher, Headmaster 1799–1809, and Fellow of King's College, Cambridge. He gained a scholarship to Eton but his stay there was short, probably because his father realised a better education could be gained locally. Eton held no examinations and seemed to despise learning. Charles Simeon, the great Evangelical preacher, thought the place so profligate that he would murder his son rather than send him there[4] and the teaching of Christianity was not much in evidence.[5]

Ordination

In 1804 Dr Becher was delighted when Charles James won an Open Scholarship to Trinity College, Cambridge. The University at this time was unkempt and its buildings were shabby. His lodgings were above a tailor's cutting room and he complained of the noise from the girls' school kept by the tailor's wife. He read for fourteen hours a day, which may explain why his health suffered. He won Browne's prize for a Latin ode in 1805 and presented himself as a candidate for the Craven scholarship. Porson, the examiner, pronounced him a 'very pretty scholar' and awarded him the prize.

Earlier Blomfield had declared 'I mean to be a bishop', and circumstances seemed favourable, as he possessed many of the necessary qualities. Later in the nineteenth century Anthony Trollope considered that there were four ladders to the episcopate in 1800: a good acquaintance with Greek; to be a tutor to a noble pupil; to charm a royal ear; and to publish a pamphlet. Added to these the young Charles James had the support of Archbishop Howley, so a seat on the bench seemed certain, particularly as the early nineteenth-century bishops were not known for their theological attainment. Greek, not theology, remained Blomfield's first love, and at Cambridge as well as collecting a gold medal for Latin verse he was awarded another for his Greek ode on the death of Nelson. In 1808 he took his BA as Third Wrangler and First Chancellor's Medallist, which earned him the lifelong resentment of the runner-up, Thomas Barnes, who was later to become editor of *The Times*. He attributed his failure to the fact that the examiners preferred Blomfield's straitlaced habits to his own 'laxity of conduct'. This explains why *The Times* rarely gave the future Bishop a favourable review. Blomfield did not endear himself to senior scholars by writing criticisms of Samuel Butler and Dr Valpy in erudite classical journals. Many thought him too arrogant. He was elected a Fellow of Trinity College and it seemed that an academic career would be suitable, but in

March 1810 he was made deacon, and in June ordained priest, to serve a few miles east of Cambridge in the parish of Chesterford, then in the diocese of London. The new curate protested to the Jockey Club that Easter Monday was not a suitable day to begin racing nearby at Newmarket. He disliked the fact that racegoers from London would change horses on Easter Sunday and take refreshment at an inn near the village, then patronise the Easter Fair, entertaining his rustic parishioners by playing whist in their carriages, displaying their fashionable costumes and regaling them with tales of the great city. With the help of his neighbour, Lord Braybrooke, he did eventually persuade the Jockey Club to move the first day of racing to Tuesday. All this foreshadowed his complaints about day trippers on the Thames when he was Bishop of London and residing in Fulham Palace.

The rector was non-resident, so Charles James lived in the rectory. Probably, like many other men at the time, he took his ordination lightly. Promotion was a gamble, the glittery prizes few: of 10,840 benefices 3,528 had an income of less than £130 (£4,000) per annum. He was able to continue his studies, so that two years later he published an edition of *Prometheus Vinctus* which earned praise from Sydney Smith and the *Edinburgh Review*. This was followed by his *Persae* of Aeschylus, which sold 700 copies in a few weeks despite one German critic saying it had 'a dogmatical tone'. It appears that the future Bishop's self-assurance earned him much unpopularity amongst his fellow scholars. T. S. Hughes, a fellow of St John's, thought that Blomfield's presumption and arrogance arose from the flattery and excessive attention devoted to him in his undergraduate days. Meanwhile, Lord Bristol had presented him to the living of Quarrington in Lincolnshire, and in November of that year (1810) he married Anna Maria, daughter of W. Heath of Hemblington in Norfolk.

Blomfield never lived at Quarrington, so he became and remained until 1828 one of a class which in later life he was bent on exterminating – that of non-resident incumbents. Now only twenty-five, he was made Rector of Dunton in Buckinghamshire, which looks across the Vale of Aylesbury to the Chilterns, so he left Chesterford and moved there, where he remained amongst his 72 parishioners for six years. It was here that he began his theological reading, whilst at the same time tutoring several sons of local nobility, and he was able to increase his fees from £150 (£4,500) to £400 (£12,000) p. a. Life at Dunton had few problems although the parish clerk, a septuagenarian, was found guilty of taking the communion plate to the nearest pawnbroker. Unable to read, she did not realise that the name of the parish was inscribed on the chalice. He became a commissioner of turnpikes and a magistrate like most of his fellow clergy (only 7 out of 59 Lincolnshire magistrates were laymen), and seemed to be unaware that by doing so he appeared to working people to be an agent of a repressive government.

As the new incumbent moved into Dunton Vicarage, news came of civil disturbance just as the Regency began. The Luddite riots, protesting against the new machinery, were to last for several years. Strikes broke out all over England. According to one estimate only two million men were employed at this time and a quarter of these were living on just over £1 (£30) a week. The London mob was particularly menacing and mischievous, and everyone feared they would cause scenes of horror similar to those in Paris twenty-five years earlier. Abroad, Wellington was crossing the Pyrenees and in March 1814 the Allies arrived in Paris, exiling Napoleon to Elba. Perhaps one or two Dunton parishioners travelled to London that year to witness the visit of the Tsar of Russia, the King of Prussia and the newly restored Louis XVIII of France. Sadly the royals were dressed so plainly that no one could see who they were. 'I wish they would all go about ticketed', said one onlooker.

In 1815 Blomfield preached a charity sermon for the Society for Promoting Christian Knowledge, and this led to an invitation to return to Aylesbury to preach at the Triennial Visitation of the Bishop of Lincoln. He thought of preaching on the usefulness of learning to the clergy, but decided against it, as it would be like praising a fair complexion to a party of negresses. Instead he preached on 'The Responsibleness of Pastoral Office'. St Paul, he said distinguished between instructors and hearers: Hearers may certainly edify one another, but should look up with superior deference and respect to those invested with the sacred office of spiritual guides. Instructors must answer for their charges and no one could be responsible if he were not regularly ordained or if he exchanged 'workshop or plough for the pulpit of the Conventicle'. Enthusiasm without the learning and judgement necessary to present parts of the Bible in clearer light was 'a fire which burns but to delude'. Pastors should 'confine themselves to the safe and strait line of instruction, marked out in the formularies of the Church.' The sermon concluded with a warning against deviating into the byways of doubt or fanaticism.

One wonders what the assembled clergy made of it all. Many of them were ignorant, and if they had any education it was usually pursued in any subject except theology. Bishops paid little attention to choosing fit men for the ministry, and stories of interviews on cricket fields or whilst shaving are too regular to be discounted. Bishops were often uninterested in their diocese. Bishop Watson of

Llandaff was a great scholar but never lived in his diocese, and spent his evening years in Westmorland where he actively employed himself in rural decorations and agricultural improvements. Similar stories abound.

Blomfield's reputation as a preacher now stood high: he preached before Cambridge University at Great St Mary's and was invited to give the Address at the Visitation of that picturesque survival of the eighteenth century Bishop Bathurst of Norwich. In June 1815 Dunton with the rest of England was thrilled by the news of the victory at Waterloo. The Prince Regent was attending a party in St James's Square when Major the Honourable Henry Percy, still bloodstained and dusty, arrived with Wellington's dispatch. 'I congratulate you, Colonel Percy', said the Regent; then as he read on, tears coursed down. Fifteen thousand of Wellington's men had died. 'It is a glorious victory and we must rejoice at it', said the Prince, 'but the loss of life has been fearful and I have lost many friends'. One of the last French cannon to be fired had narrowly missed Wellington, passing over the neck of his horse and hitting Lord Uxbridge. 'By God, Sir' exclaimed the officer, 'I've lost my leg'. 'By God, Sir, you have', said Wellington, taking a telescope from his eye.[6]

In the summer of 1817 Blomfield returned to Chesterford where he now held the incumbency in plurality with Tuddenham in Suffolk. Death was a constant visitor to most Victorian households, and the rectories of Dunton and Chesterford were no exception. Charles and Anna's firstborn, Charles William, was baptised by his father on 9 August 1815 and died three months later. The second child, Edward Thomas, lived four years but three others of their children, Anna, Charles James and Charles James died soon after birth. No wonder the portrait painter George Richmond detected in Blomfield 'a touch of sadness underlying all that revealed itself when the face was in repose'. Only one child lived to adulthood – Maria, who was to marry the Revd Henry Brown, rector of Woolwich. After eight years of marriage Anna herself died in Chesterford in 1818. Her memorial tablet states:

> In the pure and virtuous tenour of her life,
> In Charity and Meekness and Patience
> She followed the footsteps of her Blessed Saviour
> In this faith she departed and now rests in hope.

Charles James was married again a year later on 29 May 1819 at St George's, Hanover Square, London, to Dorothy Kent, a young attractive widow, daughter of Charles Cox, brewer of Kingston upon

Thames. She is immortalised in G. H. Harlow's famous painting *The Proposal*, which shows three young ladies discussing a letter held by one of them, and the girl on the left is Dorothy. She already had one son by her previous marriage, Thomas Fassett Kent, who was to become a barrister and be one of the future Bishop's executors. He made his home with the Blomfields, which was a large household because Dorothy and Charles James had eleven children, only one of whom died in infancy at Chesterford. Of their children Frederick, friend of Matthew Arnold, became rector of St Andrew Undershaft in the City, Henry became an Admiral, Alfred, whilst he was vicar of Saint Philip, Stepney, wrote a memoir of his father: later he became suffragan bishop of Colchester, and Arthur was a church architect. Charles went to Canada, and Frank was drowned at sea attempting to save someone's life. Dorothy married Gerald Gurney, the author of 'O Perfect Love' and the poem 'God's Garden', the fourth verse of which is rather worn by repetition:

> The kiss of the sun for pardon
> The song of the birds for mirth
> One is nearer God's heart in a garden
> Than anywhere else on earth.

Isabella, the fourth child, had a son who later wrote about his grandmother, Dorothy, 'a shrewd rather hard old lady', and of his aunts and uncles, 'they were a clever family and witty but the massive ability of their father did not descend to that generation ... It was also an unfortunate tradition of our family for each branch of it to go off on its own at the earliest opportunity.[7]

In 1818 a friendship began between Blomfield and Bishop William Howley of London, who made him one of his chaplains, and in that July he preached at the Bishop's Visitation in Saffron Walden on 'The Duty of a Canonical Adherence to the Ritual of the Church', and in it he called for the Church to have 'a certain external splendour corresponding to her inward holiness'. He condemned private prayer meetings which detract from public worship, and deprecated the use of 'coarse or colloquial language' by the minister. Ceremonies should be 'simple yet dignified, easy to be understood yet not inspiring contempt ... grave yet decent, majestic'. We are told that Mr Blomfield spoke with authority, had an impressive delivery and a clear musical voice. Obviously he was bound for preferment. The young incumbent had little time for the Evangelical party who were still a minority in church life; this is surprising as his Whiggishness might have made him sympathetic to a party which campaigned for the abolition of the slave trade. Neither did he ally himself with the High Church party, centred on the Hackney Phalanx, which tried to promote missionary and educational projects. He remained detached.

City incumbent and archdeacon

William Howley's senior appointments were all High Church – a rather elastic term used to describe those who held elevated views of sacramental grace both in the Eucharist and Baptism and who were anti-Roman Catholic and pro-Establishment. Clive Dewey has described Howley's patronage networks after he was enthroned in London in 1813.[8] Somewhat surprisingly, Howley was fourth choice for London. George Tomline of Lincoln, Cornewall of Worcester and Cyril Jackson, not yet a bishop, all refused it. The new bishop liked his new chaplain, and in future years was to rely heavily on his judgement although, as G. K. Best remarked, he 'was not just a puppet pulled by Blomfield's strings'. It was not surprising, therefore, when in May 1820 Howley appointed Blomfield to the living of St Botolph, Bishopsgate in the City of London, left vacant by the departure of Doctor R. Mant to be Bishop of Killaloe. St Botolph's was an ecclesiastical plum worth over £2,000 p. a. (£60,000). Another cleric had turned the living down when he discovered that the rectory was at the mercy of an 'irremediable nuisance of rats' who brought in bones from the neighbouring graveyard. Howley wrote to Lord Liverpool, the Prime Minister, that he had a very high opinion of the young priest who is 'without comparison', and the first classical scholar in Cambridge, a very sound and able divine. Blomfield decided to keep the living at Chesterford which had a curate and as St Botolph's had two curates it would mean he could travel between the two places for, as Howley remarked, it was 'desirable that an incumbent of a popular parish in London should have a place of retirement in hot weather'. The parishioners of Bishopsgate pointed out that their rectors were usually Doctors of Divinity so, obligingly, Blomfield received this degree by Royal Letter from his old university in 1820.

Being in London meant that the young rector could have a high profile in church affairs, so he became an active member of both the Society for the Propagation of the Gospel and the Society for Promoting Christian Knowledge. He took a great interest in education, and was a supporter of the National Society which had been formed in 1811. He realised that many were apprehensive about teaching the children of the poor – it might give them ideas above their station, and some wanted a restricted curriculum. Hannah More drew the line at science, and many suspected that teaching handwriting might make for an epidemic of forgeries.

For three months each year he lived in Chesterford, but at other times the curate sent a report to London tucked in the grocery basket. By all accounts Blomfield was a diligent parish priest, winning the support of dissenters and regularly visiting the squalid houses clustered around St Botolph's. One of his parishioners said she had 'never seen so infant a face for a doctor of divinity'.

In 1821 Earl Spencer proposed and Lord Liverpool seconded his election to the Literary Club, founded by Doctor Johnson and Sir Joshua Reynolds. There were only thirty-five members and Howley was the only other cleric. Influential and important friendships were being forged.

A year later Howley appointed him Archdeacon of Colchester, and Charles James told the clergy he would be prompt in delivering unto the bishop all ecclesiastical irregularities. His only Charge to them, delivered in May 1823, contained a long explanation of the powers of an archdeacon, which most think concern only downpipes and guttering. Archdeacons, he said, had the power of visitation 'and with the right of enquiry they obtained the right of correction'. Duties are placed upon them by ecclesiastical law but

> it is a matter of discretion with the person who fills the office to determine which of its branches he shall execute according to the letter of his instructions, and which he shall suffer to sleep in desuetude, from a regard to the spirit of his commission, and to the ends of all ecclesiastical authority, the good order and well being of the Church.

He agreed he should be the eyes of the bishop, but promised he would execute his functions in a spirit of brotherly kindness and conciliation. He had little time to do this, as he was already being looked at as a possible bishop. Many thought he would take the place of the eighty-year-old Bishop of Norwich, but Bathurst confounded everyone by holding the 'Dead See' for another fourteen years.

Bishop of Chester

In 1824 Dr Law of Chester was translated to Bath and Wells (his predecessor went to Ely) so this episcopal stepping stone was offered to the 38-year-old Archdeacon of Colchester, who accepted and was consecrated on 20 June 1824 by Vernon Harcourt, Archbishop of

York, the sermon being preached by a future bishop of Lichfield, John Lonsdale, who described him as 'High in talent and rich in learning'.

The comparative financial hardship of accepting an episcopal stipend of £1,400 p. a. (£53,000 p. a.) was ameliorated by the new Bishop keeping the living at Bishopsgate. Lady Spencer thought that present ruin would bring future affluence and, after all, the Metropolitan would not last much longer to judge by his looks, so Howley would move to Canterbury, leaving London for Blomfield.

The appointment, almost certainly engineered by Howley, was popular; the press was kind and tributes were made to the new Bishop's character, learning and commitment to the Establishment. George IV was always ready to hear Howley's recommendations, particularly as he had been supportive over the King's problems with his consort, Queen Caroline. Caroline had been estranged from George since 1796, and in 1813 went to the Continent and found herself a lover, Bartolomeo Bergami. In 1820 she had become Queen, but George directed that her name be omitted from the State Prayers. She returned to England, but Lord Liverpool, supported by Howley, had introduced into Parliament a Bill of Pains and Penalties to deprive her of her titles. Later in 1828, when Manners Sutton died, George IV rewarded Howley by appointing him to Canterbury and he was enthroned by proxy as were his two predecessors – to save money. His income was reckoned at £28,000 p. a. (£1,000,000 p. a.).

Howley in London was delighted to have his former chaplain at Chester, as was one of the new Bishop's young friends who wrote:

> Through Chesterford to Bishopsgate
> Did Blomfield safely wade
> Then leaving ford and gate behind
> He's Chester's bishop made.

Blomfield joined a bench of bishops who were certainly not popular – Jeremy Bentham described them as 'those sitting and walking pageants', and Thomas Carlyle called them 'Stupid fetid animals in cauliflower wigs and clean lawn sleeves, parading between man's eyes and the eternal light of heaven'. Sydney Smith lamented that a clergyman suddenly elevated was 'flattered by chaplains and surrounded by little people'. It seemed inevitable he would lose his head.

Blomfield had no intention of losing his head – he relished the challenge provided by his new diocese, which was 100 miles long and covered the counties of Cheshire and Lancashire, part of Wales and large chunks of Yorkshire, Cumberland and Westmorland. A previous bishop told Blomfield he had once confirmed 8,000 schoolchildren at Manchester in one day. When it was founded in 1541, the diocese had been given the endowments and jurisdiction of Richmond. A commissary, not necessarily a priest, was usually appointed to fulfil the duties in Yorkshire, so Blomfield appointed the Revd John Headlam, giving him once again his archidiaconal functions.

Chester was an excellent training ground for more important dioceses, but frequent episcopal changes meant that there was a lack of continuity and planning – there had been six bishops of Chester in fifty years. Many of their diocesan clergy were ill-educated Irishmen who had fled across the water, and Roman Catholics were numerous, particularly around Liverpool. Blomfield was alarmed at the growing number of Dissenters in the diocese and learned that of 59 new places of worship opened in Manchester and Salford between 1741 and 1820, only 18 had been built for the Established Church.

The standard of clergy in the Chester diocese was abysmally low, mostly due to very small stipends and poor ordination training. Blomfield sought to reform both of these, writing to his close friend Joshua Watson,

> There is a sad want of spirit here on matters connected with religion which I fear I shall not do much towards supplying. I am wading through business with my seven league boots on, but there is a great dreary tract of country life before me. Discipline is sadly relaxed here. The things which want rectifying are numberless ... An explosion or two in the course of the process must be looked for ... there is no personal energy or activity.[9]

He was unable to do much about clergy stipends – this had to wait until he sat on the Ecclesiastical Commission ten years later. He knew that the average stipend in his diocese was only £100 (£3,000). The incumbent of Well received £30 p. a., Eastham £25, Cowton £32, Coniston £35, so naturally men of low calibre were often the only clergy allocated to the diocese. The Bishop was able, however, to tighten up clergy training, although the Universities were giving little help – there was no Oxford Honours School till 1868 and no Cambridge Theological Tripos until 1874. There were no theological colleges until 1839 – except for St Bees' College, founded for non-graduates in 1817 by Blomfield's predecessor, Bishop Law.

On arrival at Chester, Blomfield directed that ordination candidates must in future give three months' notice of their intention, and he would then interview each one personally. Except in very special cases he said he would not ordain non-graduates – he considered St Bees a 'special case'. He also disliked ordaining men who had recently left the Navy or Army, as he suspected that they only wanted a house to live in and a place to retire to. He said that in his diocese he would expect candidates to have a knowledge of the historical books of the Old Testament, the prophetical books relating to Christ, the four Gospels and Acts, and the Articles and liturgy of the Church. If a candidate was unable to write 'correct Latin and construe the Greek Testament' at the age of 23, he was 'either greatly deficient in diligence and seriousness or not qualified by natural endowment for the office of an expositor of God's Word'. The Bishop closed the door to a large number of Irish ordinands who were flooding the diocese, one of whom went to the Bishop of Norwich who ordained him. He promptly returned to Chester and exercised his priestly office. Blomfield complained to Howley, who pointed out to Bishop Bathurst the impropriety of his conduct. The press liked Bathurst because he was a supporter of Roman Catholic emancipation, and they attacked the new Bishop of Chester for his attitude. *The Times* even condemned him for informing against his brother of Norwich for playing cards! Bathurst agreed that cards were his only resource on a winter's evening and said he had no intention of giving up his favourite pastime.

Blomfield's strictness was not appreciated in Chester, but a firm hand was needed. He strongly expressed his disapproval of clergy doing secular work – one parish priest in the diocese was the town's postmaster, and another hoped soon to become Mayor of Macclesfield. Drunkenness was common: one parson was so drunk whilst waiting for a funeral that he fell into the grave, and another one remonstrated with the Bishop saying, 'But my Lord, I never was drunk on duty'.

The Bishop's zeal, strictness and efficiency made him very unpopular, especially amongst the slacker clergy, but most clergy respected his efforts to reform the diocese. The Revd. H. V. Bayley, afterwards Archdeacon of Stow, wrote to Joshua Watson in 1825, 'The great secret of his success is his manliness; speaking with authority and trusting to the character of his office and to the truth of his arguments he convinces and influences all who hear him. With the utmost firmness, openness and decision he joins a manner of conciliation and a tone of persuasion quite irresistible'.[10] In the first autumn of his episcopate he visited the great manufacturing towns and preached to 6,000 people in Manchester. He travelled 200 miles in ten days confirming nearly 8,000 children. The following year he repeated his progress and there were the same number of confirmands.

In his 1825 Charge to the Chester clergy he discussed the parson's job, and in passing he referred to many reforms which later he was to help bring about. He said the most convincing criterion of the Church is its usefulness. The effect the clergy have on society depends upon the influence they exert, and this influence is 'commensurate with their character and example ... Members of the sacred profession are ... to exercise great caution in the choice of their pursuits and amusements.' He strongly objected to card-playing, hunting and dancing, and because of this many thought him a Puritan. In fact, he only objected to these pursuits if they interfered with a clergyman's pastoral work. Sydney Smith unkindly parodied the Bishop's Charge in writing,

> Hunt not, fish not, shoot not;
> Dance not, fiddle not, flute not;
> But before all things it's my particular desire
> That once at least in every week
> You take your dinner with the Squire.

The Bishop also asked the clergy to pay closer attention to the rubrics and canons of the Church. They must be obeyed for 'we are no more at liberty to vary the mode of performing any part of public worship than we are to preach doctrines at variance with the Articles of Religion'. He forbade baptisms to be held in private and expressed his disapproval of the non-residence of the clergy. Soon after his consecration he suggested his newly-painted portrait should be dedicated to his non-resident clergy as it depicted him with a frown. He also directed that a gown should be worn whilst preaching and not a surplice, week-day services should be discouraged as they detract from Sunday services; he expressed his dislike of CMS, and said that the revival of an active Convocation would be inexpedient. Later he was to change all these four views.

The Bishop did not resign his living at Bishopsgate but continued his work there as best he could. He began to take an interest in local affairs at Chester, but also accepted invitations in London to sit on several committees of important church societies such as the Church Building Society, the SPCK, the Bounty Board, the SPG, and the Negro Conversion Society, and he agreed to become a Governor of King's College London. He took a close interest in the business and commercial life of the nation and metropolis and in 1826 he championed the cause of the London weavers who had fallen on hard times, knowing about this at first hand, as the weavers lived in Spitalfields close to St Botolph's. These Huguenot families had fled from France after the Revocation of the Edict of Nantes in 1685, and were welcomed because they brought with them many skills and talents amongst which was silk weaving. Soon the brocades, damasks and velvets of Spitalfields were much sought after.

In the eighteenth century there were sixteen Huguenot churches in the area, serving 15,000 people. Unfortunately business had decreased and in the early nineteenth century the spread of the power loom meant that wages fell to starvation level. Protective duties were reduced in 1824, and many weavers left East London or tried to take other jobs in the nearby docks. Blomfield became chairman of a committee formed in 1826 to help distressed weavers, and a charity ball was held in Covent Garden raising £3,750 (£142,000). The King sent a further £1,000 (£38,000). Sadly, there were not sufficient funds to keep a dying industry on its feet; only legislation could do that, so Blomfield asked Peel to intervene. He declined, however, saying it would make the price of silk artificially high, so the trade continued to decline.

House of Lords

The Bishop of Chester now began to speak on a variety of religious subjects in the Lords. Bishop Copleston wrote 'As a public speaker he is the best I have ever heard. For he is ready, fluent, correct, always addressing himself to the point, never seeking admiration by sarcasm and rhetorical flourishes. He is above all that.' David Webster, a lawyer and politician from America, said there was no speaker in Great Britain who could rival Blomfield. On 28 February 1825 he made his first speech in the Lords and realised it had been a great success, for he wrote to a friend saying that he hoped God would keep him humble, removing conceit and making him dependent for strength on Christ alone.

The controversial issue at this time was Roman Catholic emancipation, and Blomfield often had to rise to his feet in the Lords to defend the Established Church in England and Ireland. Just after his appointment to Chester he had earned praise by replying firmly to Mr Charles Butler, who thought Anglican clergy and laity sat lightly to the doctrines of the Trinity, the Incarnation, the Divinity of Christ and the Atonement. Do the clergy 'not sign the Thirty-Nine Articles with a sigh or a smile?', he asked. The new Bishop in a letter indignantly rebuked him and dwelt upon the obnoxious and anti-social doctrines of the Roman Catholic Church. Why should people who believe such heresy receive relief from their civil disqualification? By 1825 he had shown himself to be an opponent of any relief being given to Roman Catholics, admitting he had at one time thought that they ought to have the same rights as everyone else, but now he had changed his mind after becoming 'more thoroughly acquainted with the doctrines and constitution of the Roman Church'.

His maiden speech in the House of Lords was hasty and ill-prepared, but he could not resist an attack on the Romish priests who 'made no scruple to say that the churches of this Kingdom had been theirs once', and he returned to the subject when the Roman Catholic Relief Bill was received in the Lords from the Commons. This time his speech, carefully prepared and argued, suggested that every community has a right to exclude from offices of power those who hold opinions subversive of its constitution and dangerous to its welfare. The Church of Rome if allowed by this Bill would make sure its members were elected to the Commons where they could do great damage to the Established Church. He agreed he had at one time supported Roman Catholic claims, but now he had changed his mind and particularly regretted the sarcastic remarks made about the bishops and clergy of the Established Church. Such missiles were not parliamentary and if anyone thought they were, then the rules of Parliament should be changed. Blomfield spoke longer than Bishop Bathurst of Norwich who supported the Bill, and the only other bishop to speak was the inaudible Van Mildert of Durham. Despite the Commons having passed it by 21 votes the Lords rejected the Bill by a majority of 48, three archbishops and eighteen bishops voting against. *The Times* lamented Blomfield's speech, calling it intolerant and angry.[11] In a meeting of Roman Catholics at the Anchor Tavern, O'Connell accused Blomfield of breaking the ninth commandment: 'I shall say nothing of you, Bishop of Chester, you do not belong to us and I am not sorry for it'.

Many of his enemies, especially in the liberal press, and the *Edinburgh Review* said he had spoken thus to ingratiate himself with the Government who were at this time opposed to Roman Catholic emancipation. 'A forwardness of obsequiousness distinguishes him from other bishops', said one writer. The Earl of Bristol and his son, Lord Hervey, told him they were shocked by these remarks, but many Protestants in England applauded his stand and one living in Cheshire sent him a large cheese weighing 160lb as a thank-offering.

In 1828 he spoke again this time in favour of the Corporation and Test Acts Repeal Bill. This seems a volte-face, but he said he felt the Bills had been injurious to the Church. They led 'directly to a profanation and abuse of the most holy ordinance of our religion', because they compel 'the clergy of our Church to administer the holy sacrament to persons whom by the spirit, if not by the letter, of their ministerial instructions they may be directed to repel. It imposes an intolerable burden on clergy conscience'. He thought both Acts were only a political security and in themselves could not support and maintain true religion. 'It was for the Established Church now to look to the purity of its doctrines and to the discipline of its forms, which ages had already supported'.[12] Quoting Lord Kenyon's letter to George III, he said he felt that 'any ease given to sectaries would not be a threat to the Church or England or to the royal coronation oath or to the Act of Union'.[13] It would be better he thought, if their Lordships paid attention to institutions of education which were being founded with the express purpose of excluding religion. No names were mentioned but he was obviously referring to the foundation of University College London.

Whilst at Chester the Bishop made sure he and the family enjoyed regular holidays, and wrote in 1827 to William Wordsworth asking where he should stay in the Lake District – he would be accompanied by his wife, four children and eight servants. He visited Dr Samuel Butler, the headmaster at Shrewsbury, and remonstrated with him for sharpening a pencil before morning chapel was over. Regular visits were paid to St Botolph's, where large congregations listened to his sermons which were described as pastoral and unambitious with a sedate, earnest and affectionate exposition of Scripture. In June 1828 in a sermon on a Christian's duty towards criminals he lamented that there was little emphasis on the reformation of the offender. 'Retaliation and revenge' were 'utterly to be reprobated'.

The four years spent at Chester were a good episcopal apprentice-ship for higher things, and the diocese was sad to see Blomfield leave, its Dean describing him as 'by far the ablest man on the Bench, the only very good speaker ... He is distinguished by ability, learning, firmness, disinterestedness, independence of mind ... beyond any man I have ever met with', and one of his archdeacons wrote to remind him that when St Romuald tried to leave Chester his people considered killing him to secure his relics.

It was now time for the earnest forty-two year old to step on to the centre of the ecclesiastical stage.

Chapter Three

Early days in London

In company Blomfield possessed an agreeable streak of caustic
humour and anecdote. At desk he was plain and sober, wanted the
church to be pastorally efficient, worked many hours a day,
could note the answer to thirty letters whilst travelling across
London in a carriage, talked about the Church and the beauty
of her holy usefulness.

Owen Chadwick, *The Victorian Church*.[1]

The new Bishop visited his predecessors before they moved out of
Fulham Palace. Mrs Howley was a hospitable hostess who had entertained 970 people to dinner during the previous year, 1827. She told
him her annual housekeeping bill which included coal, linen and
washing was only £1,800 (£68,000) and that she had spent £800
(£30,000) on staff wages. The family clothes bill amounted to £1,000
(£38,000). The majority of households in England at this time had to
exist on an annual budget of £50 (£1,900) or less, which was well
below the poverty line. However, a young upper-class couple living
modestly had to budget for £2,200 (£83,600) per annum, which
included employing six house servants and a coachman. The middle
classes had to manage on much less. According to Isabella Thorpe in
Northanger Abbey, £400 (£15,200) per annum as a parson's wife was
'an income hardly enough to find one in the common necessaries of
life', and the thought of living on such a paltry sum was enough to
make her switch suitors at once.

Mrs Howley spent £900 p. a. (£34,000) on carriages. *The*
Traveller's Oracle published in 1827 estimated the cost of keeping a
horse in London inclusive of stabling and groom at approximately
£120 p. a.; the family carriage would cost £400 and a two-wheeler
with horse, the sports car of the day, would cost £150 p. a. (£6,000).
Often the food for the horses cost more than that for the groom,[2] but
to put on a display he would need several coats with brass buttons,

breeches, hats etc at a cost of £20, so Mrs Howley's bill suggests that the Bishop kept two coaches and several coachmen.

Blomfield then went on to visit another of his residences, London House in St James's Square, which he thought less satisfactory than the St Botolph Rectory in Devonshire Square. London House had been bought from Lord Warwick in 1770 as a town house for Richard Terrick, 100th Bishop of London. Howley was allowed to have it rebuilt on the condition he did not sublet and that he insured it for £10,000 (£300,000) – the cost of rebuilding – and it still stands today at the south-east side of the Square, with mitres emblazoned on its drainpipes. Blomfield preferred for much of the year to live at Fulham, as did his successors except Tait, so No. 32 fell into disrepair until Mandell Creighton brought it back to life in 1897. His successor, Arthur Foley Winnington-Ingram, a bachelor, did not seem troubled at having seventeen bedrooms and several grand reception rooms, soon filling them with parties and conferences, until the house was leased to the Caledonian Club in 1921. It finally passed out of church ownership in 1939.[3] As a London residence it was completely outclassed by No. 21 which became a social and ecclesiastical powerhouse during the long reign, 1827–69, of the Bishop of Winchester, Charles Sumner, brother of the Archbishop. He had been a chaplain to George IV who towards the end of his life paid more attention to religious matters, well summed up in W. M. Praed's verse on him:

> And drinking homilies and gin,
> And chewing pork and adulation,
> And looking backwards upon sin
> And looking forwards to salvation.

Sumner persuaded the King to have family prayers and to take Communion with his household instead of, as previously, alone. He generally attended Communion fasting at 10 am but on one occasion sent a servant to St James's Square to ask Sumner to begin at 9 am. The servant forgot to deliver the message. At 10 am Sumner arrived to find the King boiling with pre-breakfast rage, so refused to administer the sacrament as George was not 'in charity with all men'. Later the King thanked his chaplain for his decision.[4]

Howley told Blomfield that he should be able to live on £8,000 p. a. (£304,000) which would leave him £13,000 (£0.5 m) for his own use. When he died Howley's estate amounted to £120,000 (£5.5 m) all of which had come from his ecclesiastical income so, unlike the 'inferior clergy', he was able to save considerable sums from his income. No wonder Trevelyan in his *English Social History* describes bishops and cathedral clergy as the 'enjoying class'.

The Bishop paid income tax at two shillings in the pound which was not a hardship, but indirect taxation could be considerable, as many of the necessities of life were taxed. Canon Sydney Smith had decided views on the subject.

> Every article which enters into the mouth, or covers the back, or is placed under the foot – taxes upon everything which is pleasant to see, hear, feel, smell or taste – taxes upon warmth, light and loco-motion – taxes upon everything on earth and the waters under the earth. The dying Englishman pouring his medicine which has paid seven percent into a spoon that has paid fifteen percent, flings himself back on his bed which has paid twenty two percent and expires in the arms of an apothecary who has paid a licence of one hundred pounds for the privilege of putting him to death. His whole property is then immediately taxed from two to ten percent.

Fulham Palace with its thirty-two bedrooms was a drain on the epis-copal finances, but the gardens and the nine cows meant that a daily basket of vegetables, fruit and cream etc could be sent to St James's Square. So much cream was consumed by the Bishop and his friends that extra butter had to be bought in.[5]

The Bishop relished his new appointment and hoped he would be able to 'do greater good to the cause of religion and the Church'. Opinions of press and people about his translation had been mainly favourable although an editorial in *The Times* attacked Blomfield for being 'stiff and somewhat eager in debate, a strong and unflinching controversialist, a willing ministerial servant'. Bishop Lloyd of Oxford, perhaps a trifle jealous, thought Blomfield 'does not suffi-ciently take advice of his brethren' and Peel should teach him 'more delicacy and tact'. Sydney Smith liked his humanity but thought he lacked discretion. The new job was certainly a difficult one from any point of view, for the diocese was huge, covering a vast, thickly populated area. Until 1845 it comprised the whole of the metropolis north of the Thames (except for various Peculiars), all of Middlesex and Essex, a considerable part of Hertfordshire and four parishes in Buckinghamshire. Until 1831 the diocese contained the archdeacon-ries of St Albans and Chelmsford. Many of its 608 benefices had only one church to serve the parish for, despite a large increase in population, few new churches had been built. The population of Middlesex had increased by half during the first thirty years of the century but it was difficult to build new parish churches because an

Act of Parliament was needed. In 1801 Paddington's population was 1,881; by 1830 it had risen to 14,540. St Pancras parish had increased during the same period from 31,779 to 103,548. Chapels were erected in the wealthier areas – the Tavistock, Bedford, Fitzroy, Portman and Quebec Chapels were well-appointed but had no places for the poor. In 1809 and the following years Parliament voted £100,000 to augment and endow the income of the benefices in populous districts, and in 1818 they allocated £1m to be spent by the newly formed Church Building Society which also received £500,000 in 1828. Grants could only be a quarter of estimated costs, so local parishioners had to find the rest. The Society itself raised little money, but after twelve years 134 'Waterloo' churches had been built, one of which was St Pancras. Blomfield was anxious to cut down the size of parishes, build more churches and increase clerical stipends. He was appalled that an average beneficed London cleric received only £399 p. a. (£15,000), and London's 355 curates only received £98 p. a. (£3,500). There was much to do.

Roman Catholic emancipation

Soon after his enthronement Blomfield arrived in the House of Lords one afternoon to hear Lord Wharncliffe delivering a tirade against the clergy of the Established Church for opposing Roman Catholic claims. As soon as the noble peer sat down the Bishop was on his feet severely rebuking him because an inroad upon the constitution was intended by the Emancipation Bill and clergy had a duty to speak out. Later in the debate, when Earl Somers noted the lack of charity amongst the clergy, Blomfield was heard to say that he 'does not understand what he is saying'. Defending tithes was more difficult but, in reply to Lord King, he suggested they were part of clergy property and should be defended in the same way the noble Lord would defend his property in Ockham. He regretted he had to oppose the Duke of Wellington, 'to whom personally I owe a debt of gratitude for the favourable opinion which led him to recommend me to His Majesty for an important office in the Church'. Using the thin-end-of-the-wedge argument, he warned the country that, although small in numbers, the Roman Catholic Church might get great power in England. 'Success is far more likely to kindle than to extinguish the hope of future triumphs'. He asked what Roman Catholic members of Parliament might do, and he warned the House that the question of titles for Catholic bishops in England was not as marginal as their Lordships supposed, for once given a title it was evident that the temporal endowments then in the hands of the Established Church might be asked for by the newcomers. The Bishop realised he was on a losing wicket and finished by saying that he would have to acquiesce cheerfully to the result of the vote. The Bill received the King's reluctant assent on 13 April 1829. In his Charge of the following year the Bishop said, 'the Measure compels us for the future to depend more entirely upon our internal resources and will be a test of their sufficiency'. In the Lords the only bishops Wellington could rely on to vote for Emancipation were the brothers Sumner (of Winchester and Chester), Bathurst and Ryder. Evangelicals and High Churchmen were united in detesting the measure, but their Canute opposition had no effect. To calm down the clergy of the Established Church the Government announced that they would renew the Church Building Grant for one year only.

King's College London

Five months after his enthronement Blomfield attended a meeting in Freemasons Hall chaired by the Duke of Wellington to consider the matter of 'the godless institution in Gower Street' which had been founded in 1826 by the efforts of Jeremy Bentham and his secularist friends Henry Brougham, James Mill and Joseph Hume. University College London had been deliberately set up to exclude the provision of a chapel, as well as religious instruction and theological teaching of any kind. Clergy were scandalised and the Revd Hugh James Rose, rector of Hadleigh in Suffolk, drew attention to the enormity in a sermon at Great St Mary's, Cambridge in October 1825. Dr George D'Oyly, rector of Lambeth, sent a 39-page letter to Sir Robert Peel to enlist his support and Blomfield decided to attend the meeting to put matters right. The two archbishops and six other bishops contributed to the £2,000 raised and the ultra-Tory newspaper *John Bull* declared 'the finishing blow has been given to the style of the infidel building at the end of Gower Street'.[6] The inevitable committee was formed: it included Blomfield, who was asked to chair the Council set up on 14 August 1829. It worked hard, and two years later the Archbishop of Canterbury presided over the opening ceremony of King's College London on 8 October 1831. The Bishop of London preached on the duty of combining Religious Instruction with Intellectual Culture. Knowledge, he said, is not necessarily wisdom, which could only be achieved if 'the light of divine truth and energy of heavenly motives' were also present. After a five-minute break the newly-appointed Principal, the Revd William Otter, vicar of St Mark, Kennington, delivered a lecture. The two orations together occupied four hours. The Principal was 'a man excellently calculated to allay animosities, to close controversies, to soothe sensibilities and to promote peace', but he also had to build bridges between the colleges in Westminster and Bloomsbury, and ensure that King's from its outset would not be identified with one particular section of the Church. His reign only lasted five years as he was appointed Bishop of Chichester in 1836. Blomfield took his duties as chairman very seriously indeed and often held council meetings at his home. By the end of the first session there were more than 700 students on the books and the teaching staff, all of whom had to be Anglican, were of a very high standard. Blomfield was particularly pleased that ordinands began to emerge from the College and in 1845 he ordained the first of these, Samuel Slater, as deacon. Between June 1848 and June 1852 he ordained eight 'Theological Associates of King's College London' deacon and in 1852 five to the priesthood.

When in 1845 the Principal wanted to appoint an outstanding chemist, Justus von Liebig, Blomfield vetoed it, pointing out that the gentleman was a Lutheran. Instead William Miller, 'a sound rather than a brilliant chemist', was offered the chair.

Another controversy appeared in 1853 when the Revd F. D. Maurice, who had been a professor in the department of theology for seven years, published his *Theological Essays*. He had already caused the Principal, Dr Jelf, some embarrassment by his support for the new Christian Socialist Movement. On this occasion he dared to cast doubt on a dogma dear to the Victorian heart, the eternal punishment of the wicked. Dr Jelf consulted various Oxford divines who found the book muddled and confusing. Bishop Wilberforce of Oxford disliked it but thought Maurice was more orthodox than his essays. Jelf suggested resignation but Maurice said, 'I must bear what testimony I can for the right of English divines to preach the Gospel of God's love to all mankind'.[7] In October at a special council meeting Blomfield moved that Maurice's opinions expressed in the book were 'of a dangerous tendency and calculated to unsettle the minds of the theological students at King's College', and that 'the continuance of Professor Maurice's connection with the College as one of its professors would be seriously detrimental to its usefulness'. Professor Chadwick notes that it was not a full council meeting as Dean Milman of St Paul's was not present, the Dean of Westminster had gone mad, Lord Harrowby was in Ireland and Bishop Lonsdale of Lichfield received no notice to attend. Gladstone's amendment asking that competent theologians should examine the essays was defeated, and a fortnight later a smaller council meeting consisting of fifteen of the forty-two members agreed with Blomfield and dismissed Maurice. It was regarded by many, particularly lay people, as an act of gross injustice and Chadwick points out that Blomfield was inconsistent because in the same autumn he assisted at the consecration of a disciple of Maurice, John Colenso, as Bishop of Natal. At Archbishop Sumner's suggestion Colenso published an open letter affirming his belief in endless punishment, so the consecration went ahead. Blomfield died four years later but the other bishops 'lived to regret the day'.

Sunday observance

Late in 1829 a group of Dissenters approached the Bishop and asked him to use all his eloquence to draw attention to the present misuse of the Sabbath day. Whilst he agreed that country life fostered church-going, he had long been worried that the distractions of town life meant fewer people in the pews. This was, he thought, 'an evil of great and crying magnitude', so he decided not to trouble his clergy but to write direct to the laity of London which he did in his letter *On the Present Neglect of the Lord's Day* published in May 1830. It received a mixed reception – Dickens thought the Bishop's strictures were reserved only for the poor, not the rich, and *John Bull*, the High Tory journal which was published on a Sunday, accused him of Puritanism, maintaining no city in the world was as strict in Sabbath observance as London. The editor noted that Blomfield disliked the publication of twelve Sunday newspapers, – 'we ourselves should be better pleased if there were but one' – and thought the Protestant religion 'has nothing of austerity in its composition'. The *Morning Post* which was read by all aspiring members of fashionable society thought that the letter was an audacious forgery, as such an able and pious divine as the Bishop could not write such a piece.

In the *Letter* Blomfield wrongly noted that those who shout loudest for more recreation are not poor labourers or little tradesmen but 'the notaries of fashion, the wealthy and the gay'. The gentry should set an example by refraining from having Sunday dinner-parties, which could lead to intemperance and gambling, and certainly make more work for servants. As to card parties, 'those who give and those who frequent them are ... beyond the reach of ... admonitions'.

Fulham in the 1830s was a rural 'pretty village' and Blomfield's household there had a quiet and peaceful atmosphere on Sundays, rejecting all thoughts and talk of the world. He agreed that church attendance had increased, but so had the population. More pews would be filled were it not for Sunday trading. By an Act of Charles II the sale of everything on Sundays except milk and mackerel was illegal, but the law was ignored in the markets throughout the capital, and many shops did more business on Sundays because workers with a six-day week only had Sunday to do their shopping. In the *Letter* he singled out the New Cut and Smithfield for particular condemnation, and thought the 'populous suburbs' to the east and north-west of London offered 'frightful scenes of depravity and ungodliness'. In Green Park boys played ball games during the hours of Divine Service and in one month 6,000 people travelled aboard steam packets on the Thames passing his palace, bound for Richmond. In May 1833, having warmed to his subject, he presented in the House of Lords a petition from 110 master newsvendors who claimed they had no rest on Sundays, and Baptist Noel, supporting the Bishop, inveighed against Sunday newspapers which were bought 'by shopboys and milliners' apprentices.'

The low price of alcohol meant that the poorer classes as well as the rich could indulge in a tipple, and a shocked Blomfield reported there were eighty liquor shops in one street between his old parish of Bishopsgate and Shoreditch. The *Letter* ran through seven editions, causing much interest, and it provoked Dickens to write a pamphlet *Sunday Under Three Heads*, which he dedicated to the Bishop. The editor of *The Times* felt that he should aim his criticism at the upper classes, but as he had 'crouched for preferment to them' this was unlikely.[8] The Bishop had in fact declined an invitation from William IV to dine on a Sunday.[9] All this made Blomfield popular particularly with the Evangelicals who approved of a strict sabbatarianism. Most of the Victorian middle classes wanted tighter controls and a Sabbath Observance Bill received a second reading in the Lords in 1834. Melbourne disagreed, telling the Archbishop of York that he thought going to church twice on a Sunday was puritanical,[10] and no one at Holland House went to church at all – which is probably why Sydney Smith enjoyed dining there so much. Gladstone always refused invitations to dinner on Sundays even when they were issued by Peel, and Queen Adelaide was strongly criticised for holding Sunday supperparties even though she had earlier endured a service of two and a half hours in St George's Chapel, Windsor. Pressure on politicians increased, and in 1856 Palmerston was forced against his better judgement to close the British Museum and National Gallery and ban band concerts in Kensington Gardens on the only day when most poorer people had free time to visit such places.

On 3 August 1831 the Bishop presented a petition in the Lords from fifty clergy who were concerned at the evils of alcohol. He asked for beer-houses to be closed on Sundays and when the London Temperance Society was formed he agreed to be its president. The Beer Act of 1830 attempted to move people away from drinking spirits, but people now drank both. In London it was estimated there were 4,073 public houses and gin shops, and a further 1,182 beer shops. Blomfield, together with the bishops of Chester, Worcester and Gloucester, attended a huge temperance meeting in 1833 and six years later a Sunday Closing Act for London was passed. Not everyone agreed: in 1840 Melbourne said he considered 'temperance as a greater heresy than excess', but, as Mitchell has remarked, the Lamb family were reputed to find the ten commandments rather taxing so subsumed them into one: 'Thou shalt not bother'.[11]

The leaders of politics and fashion drank copious amounts of alcohol at this time, so were not a good example to the middle or lower classes. The Prince Regent himself led the field. In his youth there had been many drunken and debauched evenings in the company of Charles Wyndham and Anthony St Leger and on one occasion he was arrested in Mount Street and confined in the watch house until someone recognised him.[12] On 15 March 1812 the *Examiner* had printed an anonymous poem which turned out to be written by Charles Lamb:

> Not a fatter fish than he
> Flounders round the polar sea.
> See his blubbers – at his gills,
> What a world of drink he swills.

Pitt and Sheridan drank six bottles a day (their bottles contained the equivalent of two-thirds of today's bottle). Ale or claret were drunk at breakfast, hock and soda for a hangover, madeira or sherry with biscuits mid-morning, and champagne or wine at dinner, followed by port or brandy. More champagne was consumed at supper. Gin was cheap – 'drunk for a penny, dead drunk for tuppence'. Very few were worried about drunkenness at this time and Lord Byron in *Don Juan* remarks

> Few things surpass old wine; and they may preach
> Who please – the more because they preach in vain.
> Let us have wine and women, mirth and laughter,
> Sermons and soda water the day after.

The 1839 Sunday Closing Act for London greatly reduced drunkenness and this was followed nine years later by a Bill which made Sunday morning closing compulsory throughout England. Blomfield, ever practical, realised total abstinence was beyond most people and worked to restrict the availability of alcohol. Beer houses could be haunts of thieves and prostitutes, but they could also be places where men might meet, buy bread and cheese, and enjoy their time off. This was particularly so in villages. The Bishop thought that the Church should provide rival attractions such as men's clubs, and his Ealing allotments laid out in 1832 were an attempt to substitute his beloved gardening for drinking as a pastime.

The Bishop and the Sovereign

In 1830 George IV fell ill and the question of the succession became pressing. William, his brother and heir, had been persuaded to leave his mistress, Mrs Jordan, by whom he had had ten children, and to wed Princess Adelaide of Saxe-Meiningen. It was unclear whether the newly-weds would have children, so Princess Victoria, aged eleven and daughter of the Duchess of Kent and her deceased husband, the third son of George III, now became aware of 'the probable station she would eventually fill'.[13] The young princess reading a book of English history which listed the line of succession, observed, 'I see that I am nearer to the throne than I thought'.

On 16 June Blomfield met the two archbishops to draw up a form of prayer for George IV's recovery 'in a business-like manner' but sadly the Almighty had other plans, and the King died ten days later. At his funeral his successor, William IV, talked constantly and walked out early. 'We never saw so motley, so rude, so ill-managed a body of persons', reported *The Times*.[14] William loathed ceremonial and tried to dispense with his Coronation altogether. Eventually he agreed to allow it to proceed, but its limited liturgy meant it was mockingly known as the 'Half-Crownation'. It cost £42,298 (£1,600,000) compared to George IV's £238,238 (£7m) ten years earlier. Blomfield preached the sermon, and the King thanked him for giving him 'good advice instead of fulsome flattery'.[15] It was, however, a somewhat disappointing sermon urging the Royals to realise that they were 'ministers of God for good'. Perhaps the Bishop was overawed by the solemnity of the occasion, because Bishop Wilberforce thought him a very effective preacher indeed despite flinging his head about too much. 'I think he is the best preacher in his diocese'. David Cannadine has noted that the clergy at this time were indifferent or hostile to ritual, and were little concerned with the performance of services. At Westminster Abbey most of the minor canons and lay clerks were old and incompetent and there was much absenteeism, indiscipline and irreverent behaviour in the choir, so it is not surprising that the Coronation on 8 September 1831 was so slovenly.[16]

Earlier in the year the Duchess of Kent had asked Blomfield and

Bishop Kaye of Lincoln to assess whether Victoria's education was appropriate to her station. The Duke of Kent, her father, had died when she was only eight months old, so the Duchess was anxious to hear the prelates' views about the education she had provided for her daughter. The Duchess sent them reports from the tutors, who were all men except for two women who taught Victoria 'carriage and dancing'. George IV, said the Duchess with evident relief, had not interfered in the arrangements but 'now I feel what has been done should be put to some test', and 'the plan for the future should be open to consideration and revision'. The bishops were asked if 'the course of education pursued had been best ... if the Princess has made all the progress she should have done ... and if the course I am to follow you would recommend'. She felt that her daughter had 'Religion at her heart' and was pleased that she regularly went to Divine Service. Somewhat surprisingly the Duchess said she herself attended 'almost always myself every lesson or part'. The Revd George Davys, Principal Master, and other tutors sent the bishops their reports. From these we read that Victoria had learned about 1,500 words 'of common occurrence in German', and that her pronunciation was 'particularly remarkable for its softness and distinctness'. She had read and translated a series of moral tales for young persons. In geography and history she was better informed than most young persons of the same age but her Latin was 'not far advanced'. In Religion she was reading part of the two Testaments, could repeat the church catechism and 'appears to comprehend the doctrines which were taught in it'. The list of books studied is formidable with several works by a Mrs Trimmer – moral stories, introduction to nature, history of England and Rome, and an abridged version of the Bible. Jehoshaphat Aspin contributed 'a picture of the manners, customs, sports and pastimes of the inhabitants of England' and a Mr Gay some poetic fables. Each year five or six French books were read. It all sounds very worthy, and even the young Victoria's 'absence of mind' which had been earlier so much lamented by the Duchess had been corrected. She worked six days a week, beginning at 9.30 am for two hours. Then came 'walking or playing' before and after dinner at 1 pm. Lessons continued from 3 to 6 pm, then more playing.

The bishops were greatly impressed by all this, and after three weeks spoke of their 'entire approval' of the four years' programme. In a letter to the Duchess, they said they had examined Victoria and 'in answering a great variety of questions ... the Princess displayed an accurate knowledge of the most important features of Scripture, History and of the leading truths and precepts of the Christian

Religion as taught by the Church of England'. All subjects were satisfactory and the pencil drawings 'are executed with the freedom and correctness of an older child'. The Duchess was very pleased with their report and signed her thank-you letter, 'your very sincere friend, Victoria'.

Mr Davys, the Principal Master for fifteen years, was later rewarded with first the deanery of Chester, then the see of Peterborough. A simple, safe parson, his writings, which presumably the Princess read, included a moral tale of prosperous Will Wise who tells his friend, the perpetually poor Ralph Ragged, that after abandoning the pub seven years before he was able to save four shillings a week until he had accumulated £90. Having courted for several years Mary Manage who by similar prudence had saved £60 they were able to be married and live happily ever after.[17] The Princess must have been deeply moved. Victoria was later to write that in her youth she had 'a great horrror of bishops' with their strange wigs and incongruous aprons, the exception being her father's old preceptor, John Fisher, Bishop of Salisbury, who used to kneel down beside her, letting her play with the badge he wore as Chancellor of the Order of the Garter.[18] There was a slight possibility that Queen Adelaide might have had children, but this was not to happen, and on 20 June 1837 the succession passed to Victoria, who at Kensington Palace was woken at 6 am by Archbishop Howley and the Lord Chamberlain, Lord Conyngham, to be told the momentous news.

Archbishop Howley presided over Victoria's coronation in Westminster Abbey and Blomfield preached. Unlike 1953, when the Earl Marshal was heard to say a week before the event, 'If necessary we shall stay up all night until the bishops walk in step', there was no rehearsal, which meant that several hitches occurred in the elaborate ceremonial. The Archbishop forced the ruby ring on to the young Queen's fourth instead of her fifth finger, causing considerable pain, and Victoria was only able to remove it later by dousing it in cold water. He asked for the orb, only to find she already had it. The Bishop of Bath and Wells turned over two pages of the Order of Service and conducted the Queen too early to St Edward's Chapel where the altar was covered with sandwiches and bottles of wine. The Prime Minister, Lord Melbourne, wearied by the five-hour ceremony, managed to drink a glass before the Queen was ushered back for the Hallelujah Chorus. (Later, at her marriage to Albert, the Archbishop put the ring on the right instead of the left hand.) The choir was pitifully inadequate. It was claimed that Sir George Smart, organist of the Chapels Royal to whom the musical arrangements were entrusted, would play the organ and give the beat to the orchestra simultaneously – a prediction which the *Musical World* regarded with scorn on the grounds that he was unable to do either singly. Coronations in the early nineteenth century were not, as today, a jamboree to delight the masses but 'a group rite in which the aristocracy, the church and royal family corporately reaffirmed their solidarity (or animosity) behind closed doors'.[19] There were no media to pick up the mistakes. Blomfield appears in the splendid painting by C. R. Leslie, *Queen Victoria receiving the Sacrament at her Coronation*. The Queen, wearing the dalmatic but divested of crown and jewels, receives Holy Communion from Howley. There is a very good likeness of Blomfield, who as Dean of the Chapels Royal, stands close to her. Melbourne thought Leslie's picture would 'knock all the others down' but Sir George Hayter's *Coronation of Queen Victoria* is the official painting. Blomfield had two sittings in 1839 with Hayter, which is surprising as he is hardly seen amongst a group of bishops.[20]

Blomfield had preached at William IV's coronation, so began by listing his gifts which included 'an honest desire to do impartial justice to all; a prompt and enlarged benevolence, a willing condescension and kindness, and a careful observance of all the ordinances of religion'. He conveniently forgot that before his accession the King had lived for many years with Mrs Dora Jordan and had ten children by her. Blomfield's text from 2 Chronicles recalled another young monarch, Josiah, king of Judah, and he reminded Victoria that sovereigns are 'ministers to us for good' who 'should diffuse from their dazzling but fearful eminence a salutary and purifying light over the whole range of society to check the progress of evil and to promote the growth of all that is good'. In his lengthy and ponderous sermon the Bishop insisted on the duty of national religion as the only source of true and lasting prosperity. Lord Melbourne as always had another view. Shortly afterwards he told the young Victoria, 'Nobody is gay now; they are so religious. I think you will live to see this country become very religious, too much so. I think there will be a good deal of persecution in the country before long and that people will be interfering with one another, about going to church and such things.'

Blomfield remained as close to the Queen as any subject could be, and she asked him to remain as Dean of the Chapels Royal after his retirement. Relations remained friendly with the royal family and many visits to Osborne were made. On 11 August 1845 Queen Adelaide, the Queen Dowager, visited Fulham Palace for lunch with the Bishop and Mrs Blomfield.

Life in the Lords – State reforms

In the 1820s parliamentary reform was in the air, much to the horror of the bishops and clergy, most of whom were Tory, but the case for change was overwhelming. Leeds, Birmingham and Manchester had no representatives in the Commons, whereas Dunwich, half under the sea and possessing only fourteen voters, had two members as did Old Sarum with seven voters. Cornwall had forty-two members and of the 658 MPs, 424 were nominated by landowners or agents of the Government. Many churchmen felt that the Tory Governments which had been in power since 1812 had betrayed them by passing the Test and Corporation Acts and by the success of Catholic emancipation. Fears of what a Whig administration might do to make the situation worse were realised when the Whigs came to power in 1830. Alarmed by another outbreak of revolution in France, and by rioting in several country areas in England, many people thought that talk of parliamentary reform would shake the constitution's foundations even more. Van Mildert, Bishop of Durham, felt that no further concessions should be made to the innovators. After all, if reform succeeded in Parliament it would soon arrive at the gates of the Established Church.

The first attempt at a Reform Bill passed its second reading in the Commons on 23 March 1831 but was defeated in committee. A general election was called and the new Parliament containing more reformers met in an electric atmosphere; the Commons were for reform, the King and the Lords against it. Church leaders knew that much of the criticism directed at the Church came from large towns where church attendance was the weakest; these were the very areas which would be enfranchised by the Reform Bill and their elected members might well be Dissenters or Papists. Twenty-one bishops, including the Archbishop of Canterbury, voted against the second Reform Bill in October, thus defeating it in the Lords by forty votes, but most of them realised that constitutional reform was inevitable particularly as the Commons had voted for it. Bishop Copleston of Llandaff thought the Bill would turn all power over to the Commons; 'the only thing that has kept us from pure democracy has been the influence of the Crown and the nobility or the great proprietors in the representative body'.[21] Henry Phillpotts, the new Bishop of Exeter, furious that the Government had delayed his consecration until he surrendered his rich living of Stanhope, Durham, felt that the Whigs, Lord Frey and Lord Brougham were slaves to the newspapers. Their plans for reform 'have all the air of coarsest flattery of the lowest and most ignorant of the revolutionary talkers of the day'. Sydney Smith remarked that he had to believe in the Apostolic

Succession to explain Phillpotts' descent from Judas Iscariot.

If the bishops had supported the Bill it would have been passed in the Lords, but their opposition had defeated it; much fury was consequently heaped upon them, and there were several calls for disestablishment and the exclusion of bishops from the Lords. The Archbishop was mobbed at Canterbury, and Bishop Gray of Bristol saw his palace set alight. The Archbishop of Dublin whilst passing through Birmingham found his coach surrounded by 'a dense mass of squalid and lowering faces'. Thomas Arnold reckoned that no human power could now save the Church of England, and *The Times* noted 'that huge, hideous, and lubberly leviathan, the law – church, is almost at its last gasp, the events of the last few years have armed a million hands against its fetid existence'.[22] The Dean of St Paul's was in his diocese of Llandaff and noted in his diary, 31 October 1831,

> Heard of the dreadful riots at Bristol yesterday, the destruction of the mansion house, the custom house, the excise, the bishop's palace, the gaols and fifty private houses. My own servants seem to think it unlikely that this house may be attacked. A mob of half a dozen would be enough to demolish it and all within it. The only precaution I have taken is to have a round hat and a brown great-coat in readiness, should it be expedient to escape at the back of the house over the fields.

Blomfield was not present for the debate and so did not vote. His father had died and the funeral was on 5 October, so he used this as an excuse to stay away. His critics noted that he had preached at the opening of King's College London, which was the same day as the vote in Parliament. Dr Biber defends him by saying there is a difference between a 'solemn and tranquil discharge of an ecclesiastical function and participation in an excited debate on a hotly-contested political question'.[23] Obviously the Bishop was glad of an excuse to absent himself, particularly as he did not want to oppose the wishes of the Archbishop and the majority of the bench. Only the Whig bishops, Maltby and Bathurst, supported the Bill. *The Times* screamed at Blomfield, 'The nation will not be served by half measures'.[24] The parishioners of St Anne, Soho, who had invited him to preach wrote to tell him they would walk out of the church when he walked in. The sermon was cancelled.

The Government realised that they must win the bishops round and Blomfield was the man to do it , so Lord Grey, the Prime Minister, and others went to Fulham Palace to see what could be done. *The Times* warned Grey not to condescend to 'such miserable trifling' but

Blomfield agreed to back a new Reform Bill and by February 1832 he had ten supporters among the bishops. When this third version of the Bill came before the Lords on 26 March the Bishop of London was the only bishop to speak. In the second reading he said, 'It would be as vain to expect the sun should trace back its degrees on the dial as that the people of England would ever return to the same channel and thought of opinion as before this measure'.[25] The King was pleased with the speech and thought it would help to convert waverers. The Lords read the Bill a second time, 184 votes to 175, twelve bishops voting in favour, fifteen including the Archbishop of Canterbury voting against it. Blomfield stood by the Whig Government, but their plans were defeated in Committee, and they urged the King to create more peers to push the Bill though Parliament. In May an amendment was passed postponing the disfranchising of pocket boroughs, three archbishops and thirteen bishops voting for it. The Archbishop of York later said he had not understood what he was voting for. Once again the crowd showed its anti-episcopal fury. Dr Ryder of Lichfield had his charity sermon at St Bride's, Fleet Street, drowned by yells, hisses, groans and coughs, there was a fight between sidemen and hecklers and his departing carriage galloped down Fleet Street with the mob in pursuit.[26]

Eventually on 4 June 1832 the Lords gave the unamended Bill its third reading, Blomfield supporting the Government in all divisions. Only twenty-two peers registered dissent and not a bishop amongst them. Despite all the fuss only 217,000 voters were added to the electorate of 435,000. Greville after the final debate asked Lord Holland if he was satisfied. 'Yes, very well', came the reply, 'but the Bishop's the man'. The Tories never forgave Blomfield, and the Whigs never forgot how much they owed him and in future consulted him on a number of major issues. It was the Whigs, in office for nearly all the 1830s, who were to pass the Church Reform Bills.

A few months later, in December 1832, the Tories suffered as great an electoral reverse as that of May 1997. Only 175 Tories survived in a house of 658 members. The Whigs, who had dominated eighteenth-century England, were now firmly in control, and there should have been a fundamental transformation in British politics as Parliament had at last begun to be the voice of the people. However, not a lot changed, for as L. G. Mitchell says in his biography of Melbourne, 'Whiggism was as much a social organisation as it was a political party', and one of the Whig cousin-hood, Melbourne, became Prime Minister, which showed a 'remarkable confusion and inertia in British politics'. His appointment was 'greeted with rudeness and incredulity from friend and foe alike'.[27]

Chapter Four

A social conscience

Hell is a city like London –
A populous and a smoky city.
　　　　Percy Bysshe Shelley, *Peter Bell the Third.*

London was now spawning pauperism, misery, crime and disease on
a scale hitherto unknown. Piecemeal attempts had been made to
combat such horrors, mainly by private benevolence, but these had
little effect. During his incumbency at Bishopsgate, Blomfield had
been made aware of this, and particularly of the plight of the needy
Spitalfields weavers. That area, close to the City, was depressed with
unhealthy, poor inhabitants whose stature was small owing to under-
nourishment. In 1826 he was appointed chairman of the committee to
relieve these unemployed weavers, but no one knew what to do, and
Greville a few years later drew a sombre picture of a population of
62,000 most of whom were unemployed, 6,000 receiving parochial
relief and 1,000 living in a crowded workhouse. The administration
of all charity was wasteful and ineffective at this time, and the situation was common throughout the diocese. What could be done? The
conditions in which the poor lived were indescribable. They were
usually herded together in filthy cellar tenements and, as sanitation
was a new science, they were surrounded by dirt and germ-ridden
filth. Roadways were often composed of earth, soft rubbish and
brick-dust saturated with foul water. Society, and particularly the
Church, made half-hearted attempts to help by founding agencies like
the Blanket Society, the Lying-In Hospital, the City of London Truss
Society, the Spitalfields Association for the Distribution of Coals,
Bread and Potatoes and the London Mendicant Society. These hardly
scratched the surface of the problem and it became evident that only
Government could relieve the suffering.

　　At the end of 1831 a serious cholera epidemic broke out in
England. It soon spread from the seaports, and by the following

spring it had reached London, where the first case was reported in Bermondsey. Blomfield was convinced that this was a sign of Divine Wrath and reminded his fellow countrymen that he had forecast such a calamity unless they mended their ways. Churchmen were particularly shocked when Parliament in drawing up the Cholera Prevention Bill made no reference to divine punishment, but the Bishop soon put this right by moving a resolution in the House of Lords which was carried unanimously, asking the Almighty for mercy. Parliament declared a General Day of Fasting and Humiliation and Blomfield ordered his clergy to keep it with 'contrite and penitent hearts'. On that day he preached before the young Princess Victoria whose schooling he was helping to supervise. He listed the evils which had incurred the divine wrath, characteristically stressing the neglect of the Lord's Day. He deplored the fact that 'the cup of our prosperity' after the Napoleonic wars had been poisoned in the hour of triumph. Few bothered 'to increase the comforts and improve the moral character of the poorer classes'. No one had made an effort to change things and bring them into line with God's will.[1]

At the same time the gentle Howley of Canterbury was spurred into action by the 'cruelty and oppression' that kept children in factories all day. He felt it was a disgrace to a Christian civilised nation to allow such exploitation 'merely for putting money in the pockets of master manufacturers'.[2] Legislation was necessary, and it came in the Factory Act of 1833 which allowed children under thirteen to work a 9-hour day or 48-hour week, with no children under the age of nine to work unless they were in a silk mill. A child between thirteen and eighteen could work 12 hours a day, 69 hours a week. Blomfield, who until now had taken a *laissez-faire* attitude, agreed to become a member of the Manufacturers' Relief Committee to help the unemployed in industrial districts, and in the following twenty years he was able to devote much time to helping in the alleviation of social ills.

Poor Law

in 1832 the Bishop was asked by the Chancellor of the Exchequer to chair the Poor Law Commission, and he agreed to invest the considerable time needed because he thought that most parish clergy would agree that the present laws were ineffective and new ones were needed. He and another member, Bishop John Bird Sumner, who had followed him at Chester and would later become Archbishop of Canterbury, felt that the laws should be abolished but soon realised this was not possible. The existing poor laws, some dating from the time of Elizabeth I, were a fearsome tangle of ineffective devices and regulations. The 'Speenhamland system' paid out money to supplement wages with the result that farmers paid low wages knowing that ratepayers would have to add money to make a reasonable income for the person. In 1818 £8m had been spent on poor relief and in 1832 the figure was £7m, a fifth of the national budget; it was administered in many different ways, usually locally by farmers or publicans. The drive to overhaul the system was led by Edwin Chadwick, a disciple of Jeremy Bentham. Born in 1800, he had been called to the Bar in 1830 but never practised. He became a journalist and it was his articles on social issues which brought him to the attention of Bentham, who invited him to stay at his house. Appointed as Secretary to the Commission,

> he was tactless, impetuous and cocksure ... yet if the road behind him was strewn with his enemies it was strewn also with his ideas. His harsh, domineering mind was lit up by a passion for administrative efficiency and the reform of public health. He was endlessly inventive; he worked at high pressure ... representing the official mind in its most ruthless and impersonal form.[3]

He shared many of Blomfield's qualities, and their paths crossed and recrossed. In 1848 they were to work together on the Board of Health, where Chadwick's incessant attacks on vested interests made himself and the Board unpopular.

The Commission concentrated on the able-bodied poor, and for the first time distinguished between them and the sick, orphan or lunatic. Richard Whately, Archbishop of Dublin and a former professor of economics at Oxford, stressed that productivity must be increased to create new jobs, and he urged Chadwick not to support the lazy or indigent, suggesting that all paupers be tattooed on the foot so that if they were caught begging they could be punished. He also suggested that female paupers could be shorn of their hair as this might fetch five shillings. Whately, like Blomfield, gave large donations to the poor, but obviously had little idea of human dignity. Sumner, a gentle pious prelate, made the distinction between poverty and indigence:

> These conditions it must be remembered are essentially distinct and separate; poverty is often honourable and comfortable, but indigence can only be pitiable and is usually contemptible. Poverty is not only the natural lot of many in a well-constituted society but is necessary so that a society may be well constituted. Indigence on the contrary is seldom the natural lot of many, but is commonly the

state into which intemperance and want of prudent foresight push poverty; the punishment which the moral government of God inflicts in this world upon thoughtlessness and guilty extravagance.'[4]

The Bishop thought that so long as the poor married too soon and produced too many children indigence would plague English society.

Blomfield attended every meeting of the Commission, and their report, written probably by Chadwick, was issued in February 1834. It recommended that poor relief be taken out of the hands of local authorities and churches and given to a central Board of three Commissioners who would administer the laws and build new workhouses, dividing the country into new administrative areas. At local level ratepayers should elect a Board of Guardians who would appoint a local Poor Law Officer. Relief should only be for temporary distress, and anyone receiving it should not have a more pleasant life than the poorest worker.

Some suggested that the relief paid should be a loan, but this was not incorporated into the Bill brought to the House of Commons in April 1834, which received little opposition. A nasty feature of the legislation was that illegitimate children would be the responsibility of the mother who could only obtain relief for her child by entering a workhouse. This profoundly shocked Bishop Phillpotts of Exeter, who welcomed 'another opportunity to club the loathsome Whig Government and throw a few sharp jabs at the compromising and influential Bishop of London'.[5] He queried the logic and Christian spirit behind sending a single mother to a poorhouse. Would it make her more chaste and help her or the child? What of the father? He might be difficult to trace, but both parties were responsible and it was unfair to treat the woman so badly. Blomfield attempted to defend what seems an inhumane and unchristian measure, saying he could find no scriptural authority to make him or the Commission change their minds and that he believed immorality would be checked. Natural law suggested a mother should suffer more, and English law had always been directed against the woman, not the man. Fathers were required to do no more than pay something to support the child, said the Bishop, and this was to assist the parish rather than the mother. Soloway feels that these bastardy laws were a direct result of 'a growing obsession about domestic morality as a fundamental pillar of social stability which had been intensifying since the French Revolution'.[6] Blomfield was one of a new breed of prelates who wanted to correct the wanton behaviour of the lower orders, so he thought that a single mother must not be rewarded for her folly and thereby be encouraged to repeat it. He even told his clergy not to church women after an illegitimate birth.[7] There should be no blessing, no easy forgiveness, no practical help from working-class friendly or benefit societies; she should go to the workhouse. This would soon reduce the number of illegitimate children, said the Bishop, and the House of Lords agreed with him, passing the laws by a majority of 93–82. Ten prelates including Phillpotts voted against.

Dr Welch feels that the report of the Commission was 'a curiously inhuman document which breathes an active hatred of the poor'. No training was given for those administering the local provision, with the result that there were several reports of the petty tyranny of officials, corruption among the Guardians and brutality in the workhouses, but David Thomson writes 'at the price of considerable human hardship in the short run the reforms did succeed in checking the demoralisation and pauperisation of the working classes'.[8] Parishes were grouped into Unions and by 1846 most of 643 Unions had their own workhouses.

During the debates in the Lords, Blomfield explained that the Commission's aim was to return the labouring class to an independence they had enjoyed fifty years before. The poor should be sent back to the parish of their birth, and if necessary forced into the workhouse there. The real hope lay in the next generation, and the Bishop strongly argued for separating pauper children from their parents and educating them away from their disruptive influence. Evidence showed these children made the best servants, so there would be no difficulty in finding employment.

The presence of two bishops on the Commission was meant to be a guarantee that the interests of the poor would be humanely represented. Instead, as Soloway points out 'their spiritual guardians clearly sided with the propertied classes and presented the Church's many enemies with yet another sensational example of its hostility towards the labouring masses'.[9] William Cobbett suggested that the Poor Law only existed because the Church had abandoned its obligations to the poor after the monasteries were suppressed in the sixteenth century.[10] In reply Blomfield's chaplain William Hale pointed out that there had never been a legal division of church revenue or property to provide specifically for the lower classes. Whatever legal rights there were had been dissolved along with the monasteries; 'If the poor have been at all defrauded, the guilt lies not at the door of churchmen but at that of the laity whose families have been enriched by the plunder or purchase of Church lands'. Clergy were particularly sensitive on these matters, realising that some people wanted to abolish tithes and use the money to relieve suffering, and if their critics succeeded in disestablishing the Church then ecclesiastical monies might be used to improve the conditions of the labouring classes.

Three good harvests after 1834 helped the new Poor Law to be implemented, but the Tory press hammered away at its shortcomings, describing the evils of the workhouses and the abuses of centralisation. Bishop Phillpotts was the only bishop to continue in opposition to the proposals, and he directed his clergy to have special collections to alleviate the suffering of the poor.

It soon became apparent that it was not physically possible to restrict relief by herding all the paupers into workhouses, and in 1842 well over a million people, mostly in the north of England, were receiving cash grants. In the same year Blomfield changed his mind and supported an appeal for London's unemployed. Two years later the unpopular bastardy laws which the Bishop had pushed through the Lords were revoked, and three years after that the Commission was replaced by a new Poor Law Board. Everyone realised that private benevolence led by the Church was still necessary and Edward Denison, Bishop of Salisbury, felt that clergy should take no part in administering the Poor Law because workhouses were such an abomination. It seems certain that the diagnosis of the problem of poverty by the Commissioners was faulty, because it did not look at the situation in relation to the economic life of the country as a whole, and it failed to realise that there are different sorts of unemployment. In rural areas it can become chronic but in urban areas it might be temporary. Nor did they realise the differences between the north and south of England. The Commissioners were in a hurry, and it showed.

Blomfield honoured his promise to give time to the Commission, and attended all its meetings. Mr N. W. Senior, a member of the Commission, later wrote to the Bishop's son, 'During the two years that the Commission was at work he was present at all our meetings, never fewer than once a week, often more numerous. I do not believe that we could have agreed on our report if the courage and authority of your father and of the late Bishop Sumner had not supported us.'[11] Blomfield was an effective chairman because he had a good business sense, possessed great powers of concentration and a knowledge of the workings of the old Poor Law. He dismissed attacks on the Commission as 'gross and malignant', and he had sufficient debating skill to demolish opponents in Parliament. He was the only bishop to speak at the Bill's first reading in the Lords on 2 July 1834, and he was always in the Chamber for all the debates.

Edwin Chadwick, not himself an MP but the archetypal new civil servant and thus a 'statesman in disguise', was largely responsible for the Poor Law Amendment Act. He realised that the infirm, sick and dying formed a high percentage of the inmates in the workhouse, and arranged for them to have special isolation wards. Diseases like smallpox, measles, whooping cough and scarlet fever threatened a social collapse, so he wanted able-bodied paupers kept out of the workhouses. He believed disease was caused by miasmata, gases given off by putrifying organic matter – smell and filth were to blame, so the next step was to take sanitation seriously. The Thames was heavily polluted at this time. 'He who drinks a tumbler of London's water', Sydney Smith told Lady Grey in 1834, 'has literally in his stomach more animated beings than there are men, women and children on the face of the globe'. Private water companies piped their water from Chelsea to London, but few people could afford their charges, and had to drink the foul river water.

Sanitation and sewage

The Commission's second report in 1838 described the desperate situation in different parts of the metropolis. In Lambs Fields about 300 feet of ground was 'constantly covered by stagnant water in winter and summer. An open filthy ditch encircles this place and into the ditch the privies of the houses in North Street emptied their contents.' From Virginia Row to Shoreditch, a mile in length, 'all the lanes, courts and alleys pour their contents into the centre of the street where they stagnate and putrefy. Families live in the cellars and kitchens of these undrained houses, dark and extremely damp.' The tasks were obvious – organic filth and refuse had to be removed, roads paved, sewers and drains built and a fresh-water supply installed. Only the Government could do this.

A year later, in the fifth annual budget of the Commission, three physicians pointed out that improvements had been carried out only in the wealthier parts of London. In 1842 Chadwick's *Report on the Sanitary Conditions of the Labouring Population* called for a national public health authority to direct local boards of health to provide clean water, drainage, paving and cleansing the streets, together with a new sewage system. Blomfield and Sumner supported Chadwick but many opposed them, thinking that centralisation would take away local responsibility. Chadwick's single-minded advocacy of administrative reform with central control and enforcement by an inspectorate made him the focus of fierce opposition, *The Times* describing him and his supporters as 'heated with all the zeal of propagandists and all the intolerance of inquisitors'. He must have been glad of the Bishop's support. In September 1847 another Royal Commission was set up to look at the health of the metropolis, and a year later a Central Board of Health was established with each town council becoming responsible for sanitation, drainage, and water supplies. Local medical officers of health were not appointed in London for another eight years, and even then their relationship with local bodies was strained. The vestry of St James, Piccadilly, reduced its medical officer's salary from £200 p. a. to £150 p. a. to check his enthusiasm.[12]

In 1855 the Thames was described by Michael Faraday as a river of soft brown liquid. People drank it and died, because the excrement of two million citizens flowed between its banks. A comprehensive sewage system had to wait until 1858, when panic broke out in the House of Commons because of 'the great stink arising from the Thames'. Windows were hung with sheets soaked in chloride of lime, and tons of lime were emptied into the Thames. The House adjourned, but within months Sir Joseph Bazalgette had been commissioned to create a grand new sewage system which still serves the inhabitants of London. Some eighty-two miles of sewers were constructed in an undertaking which entirely changed the nature of London. Bazalgette's biographer, Stephen Halliday, considers that the biggest adversary was the humble water-closet. For years the 'night soil', as excrement was quaintly described, had gathered in cesspools. Now the water-closets marketed by Thomas Crapper were discharging it into an antiquated sewage system which led straight to the Thames. Thomas Cubitt remarked that 'the Thames is now made a great cesspool instead of each person having one of his own'.[13] The ingenious intercepting sewers of Bazalgette's designs changed all that.

Working Conditions

In 1843 the Bishop again turned his attention to unemployment. He spoke in the Lords and voted for legislation to improve the lot of chimney sweeps, and with Mr Gladstone founded the Metropolitan Visiting and Relief Association. He was particularly shocked by the employment of women and children in the mines, and was not persuaded by colliery-owner Lord Londonderry's argument that they were as healthy as their counterparts above ground. He felt that the evil of this system 'was eating into the very vitals of the country'.[14] No more reports were needed, he said; it was time for action.

Another Factory Act reducing a child's working day from eight to six and a half hours in textile factories was delayed because the proposal to educate factory children in Church of England schools was opposed by Dissenters. Masterminded by Sir James Graham, who took great care to 'communicate with the Bishop of London', it received much opposition. He told Kay-Shuttleworth to press ahead but to 'keep open the door of friendly communication with the Bishop of London' to meet his demands as far as he could. In the event, it was the views of Wesleyans and other Dissenters which prevailed, and the education clauses were removed before the Bill was passed. Women were now given a maximum working day of twelve hours, and in 1847 a proposal to reduce this to ten hours was supported by Blomfield along with new bishops like Samuel Wilberforce of Oxford. Gone were the days of *laissez-faire* as the new bishops now condemned the idea that a government which governed least, governed best. Interference was needed to prevent exploitation. For too long children had been seen as instruments for making money, and if their parents would not defend them, then the law must. Factories and mills, said the Bishop, were prisons where endless work injured health and brought early death. Statistics showed that factory workers had twice as high a death rate as other urban employees. Mechanisation would mean that profits would not be lost by these measures and owners would soon have the satisfaction of seeing children educated in church schools. Blomfield's paternalistic approach to the problem could be put alongside that of those who felt that the ten-hour bill was common sense.

Housing

As people poured into London, housing became even more of a problem. Half a million men in the metropolis had to live near the docks and markets where they worked, and near the houses which their wives cleaned – the census of 1841 counted 168,721 domestic servants. In 1837 the Bishop launched a private appeal to improve conditions in the slums but he soon found that property-owners were opposed to improving their houses even at someone else's expense. The money collected had to be returned. Two years later he supported members of the Government who wanted to clear the slums, but little was done, thanks to the Victorian view that private property is sacred. The same census revealed that 27 properties in a turning off Tottenham Court Road housed 485 people: 125 families and 64 single women and men; and 27 dwellings averaging 5 rooms each in Church Lane, Westminster, housed 655 people, which increased to 1,095 six years later. This was not untypical of all poorer parts of London. Demolition of properties to widen the streets or build railways made matters worse. New Oxford Street, built in 1847, cleared the St Giles' slums, but this only meant that people migrated to other areas. 'In beautifying some parts of the Metropolis the authorities had brutified others' said the Bishop.[15]

Lodging houses known as 'rookeries' were often owned by the Church, property magnates or City livery companies. Renting a whole house cost 7s 6d, a room 2s. In St Giles the costermongers, street sweepers and herring hawkers often lived 17 to a room which only had one bed.[16] Blomfield in an important speech supported the Public Health Act of 1848, and in that year he opposed Lord Ashley's proposal for building another infirmary, saying it was much more important to use these funds to encourage model housing. In fact, four years earlier Ashley's Society for Improving the Condition of the Labouring Classes had erected several houses in King's Cross Road, accommodating 23 families and 30 single women. In 1847 Metropolitan Dwellings were erected off Pancras Road and the following year 54 flats, which still stand, were built in Streatham Street off New Oxford Street. Blomfield must have agreed with a correspondent in the 1855 *Builder* who said, 'It is of no use preaching religion or making education cheap while the present state of things exists. Give to the poor man a clean and cheerful home at a price his means will bear and then order and sobriety will ensue.' Many disagreed, believing that poverty came from the sovereign laws of supply and demand, so there could be no solution.

Next to godliness

In 1846 the Bishop strongly backed the Bath and Wash Houses Act which permitted local boroughs to establish them on the rates. He said cleanliness would raise the poor man from destitution and help to relieve 'the urgent pressure of misery', and anyway, it made people more accessible to moral teaching if they were housed, fed and clean. At one time he had thought that enlightened self-interest would make property owners rehabilitate their overcrowded and filthy dwellings, but now he realised that Parliament must force them to do it. Bathhouses, he thought, should not be free; there should be a charge of 2d to discourage idle use. In Westminster the baths could be divided by class: 1s for the middle classes and 3d for mechanics. Middle-class water was constantly replenished and then fed through a filter bed to the lower-class baths.[17] Blomfield calculated that this investment would bring a return of 10% and there would be 'beneficial effects of bathing and washing on the poor which were most striking to all those who came into contact with them'.[18]

On 8 June the Bishop presented petitions to the Government urging them to provide public baths for the poor; one of these petitions was signed by 121 parochial clergymen. He pointed out that often two families, each with five or six children, were living in one room. Dry clothes were an impossibility. In the recently-established bathhouse in Glasshouse Yard, 87,000 people were served, so more should now be opened. It was a scandal that between 70,000 and 80,000 houses in London had no water supply. Dukinfield, the rector of St Martin-in-the-Fields, was one of the clergy fired by Blomfield's enthusiasm, and he persuaded his Vestry to open a bath- and washhouse. In 1848 he and Charles Dickens spoke at a meeting chaired by the Bishop, which proposed that the metropolis should be included in the Public Health Act, and a deputation waited on the Prime Minister. There was no response.

Progress had been made, but London remained a place of degradation. In 1847 cholera struck again, the first time since 1832. Churchmen, because of the efforts of Chadwick and Blomfield, were now better educated in questions of sanitation, so prayers were once again asked for, but this time Blomfield pointed out to his clergy that disease hits the poor hardest because of 'a want of cleanliness' and, in an inferior degree, intemperance, and an insufficiency of wholesome food. There was something they could do. Action was needed; committees should be formed in slum areas to improve sanitation and provide nourishment for the needy. In a Pastoral Letter to his clergy he pointed out that 'people will be filthy and prone to disease if they live packed together in miserable tenements or apartments at rents the excessive amount of which cripples their means of comfort and cleanliness'. Fresh water, ventilation, good washing facilities and improved sewerage are all essential. The rich must provide a decent life for those who labour for them, and the clergy should show that it is not the fault of the poor that they live in such appalling conditions. Many of his clergy responded to the Bishop's letter, including William Bennett of St Paul, Knightsbridge, who set up a board of wealthy members of his congregation who provided a soup kitchen, a dispensary and a lay worker who investigated the complaints of the poor and made charitable gifts. Bitter conflicts surrounded the Bishop's plans as local officials quarrelled with the Board of Health, whilst in London alone 14,000 people died. Thanks to Blomfield, a new awareness of social ills was now apparent amongst the clergy, from those sitting in the Lords to those working in Bethnal Green. Samuel Wilberforce, the new Bishop of Oxford, was startled by Blomfield's enthusiasm. On arrival at London House in St James's Square he was bundled into a carriage by the Bishop, who was on his way to attend a meeting which discussed what sort of soap should be used in the new bathhouses. Wilberforce noted in his diary that he had enlisted the Bishop's help for one of his schemes 'in return for my supporting him in the soap suds'.

Death and burial

Blomfield was one of the few people who liked and respected Edwin Chadwick, whose *Report on the Sanitary Conditions of the Labouring Population* in 1842 showed that 570 out of every 1000 children died before the age of five in Manchester and Leeds. Almost certainly the same was true for London, as little had changed since the eighteenth century. Death knocked at all doors. Blomfield's successor at London, A. C. Tait, lost five daughters from scarlet fever in 1856. Other killer epidemics included TB, typhus, diphtheria, and especially cholera, which claimed 18,000 lives in London in 1832. Charles Kingsley's anger was vented on clergy who called for National Fast Days, telling them they would do much better working for sanitary reform. Hospitals at this time were feared almost as much as workhouses, for there was a good chance that a patient might die whilst within their walls. University College Hospital had a death rate of 25% in 1874 and Edinburgh Infirmary 43%.[19] Few of the doctors or nurses understood what was going on, or how diseases should be treated. Chadwick himself thought that cholera could be cured by removing all noxious smells – open sewers, corpses etc. Local vestries opposed his plans for clean water and decent burial grounds because they could see their interests threatened.

The condition of parish graveyards in London caused great concern and Dickens complained that 'rot and mildew and dead citizens form the uppermost scent in the Capital'. The City churchyards were filled to overflowing. 'There', says Jo in *Bleak House*, looking through a cemetery gate,

> 'over yinder, among them pile of bones, and close to that there kitchin winder! They put him very high, the top. They were obliged to stamp upon him to get him in. I could unkiver it for you with my broom if the gate was open. It's always locked. Look at the rat. There he goes! Ho! Into the ground!'

One magazine, noting that 50,000 corpses were stacked every year in 150 churchyards, asked if this really could be Christian burial. Clergy were very suspicious of any change, realising that the closing of their overcrowded churchyards would mean the loss of substantial fees. In 1838 the vicar of St Giles-in-the-Fields received £764 (£30,500) in funeral fees, and the rector of St George's, Hanover Square, £597 (£24,000). The vicar of Paddington reckoned that the new Kensal Green cemetery reduced his income by £200 pa (£8,000). Compensation for the clergy was mentioned but never paid by the government.

The newly-founded private burial grounds and chapels, which numbered around fourteen in 1835, operated in a shady fashion with non-clerical officiants who undercut church fees. Bodies were burnt and mutilated, quicklime was used to hasten decomposition, bone-stealing to provide manure was common, and a local tradesman in a surplice usually took the service. In 1839 George Walker, a surgeon who obviously had a strong stomach, visited fifty London graveyards and then published a book which described drunken gravediggers, second-hand coffins and illegal exhumation. 'In making a grave a body partly decomposed was dug up and placed on the surface at the side, slightly covered with earth; a mourner stepped upon it, the loosened skin peeled off, he slipped forward, and nearly fell into the grave.'[20] In February 1830 George Carden, a barrister, began a campaign for public burial grounds and the London Cemetery Company was formed. Two years later the garden cemetery in Kensal Green was opened and became an instant success, and very quickly other companies opened seven cemeteries which would provide 336 burials a year. Chadwick was certain that burials in the centre of towns should be 'entirely prohibited' and, aware that the cheapest grave at Kensal Green cost thirty shillings (£67), called for special cemeteries for the poor.

Clergy led the resistance to these non-churchyard burials but nothing could stop the new movement. Highgate Cemetery opened in 1839 and attracted an interesting clientele because of its terraced layout, paths and paintings. Brompton opened its thirty-nine-acre cemetery a year later; it was laid out in park-like avenues, culminating in the catacombs and chapel at the far end. Blomfield disliked these newly-opened cemeteries, saying that they often had an unseemly queue of cabs outside their gates waiting to be admitted. He attempted to keep them under parish control, but this was no longer possible. The Metropolis Interments Bill became law in 1850, giving local Boards of Health supervisory powers, but because it was so imperfectly drafted it soon became ineffective. The Board had no money to buy burial sites, and after eight months of vexation no old graveyard had been closed. However, a new fashion for funerals had begun. According to wealth or class, the dead were now taken either to local council graveyards on a wheeled bier, or more likely to a

faraway burial ground in a horse-drawn, glass-sided hearse with
attendant carriages. One enterprising private cemetery, the London
Necropolis Company at Brookwood, Surrey, had an arrangement
with the London and South Western Railway to use their track from
Waterloo to transport coffins and mourners in specially-designed
first- or third-class carriages, and this lasted until 1941. The clergy
of St Alban, Holborn, availed themselves of this facility and still do,
although the journey to Brookwood now has to be made by road. The
1850 Act was repealed two years later, and London vestries were
empowered to form Burial Boards and provide new local cemeteries
of their own. Cremation was at this time unknown, but the 1850
edition of the *Builder* reported: 'An association has been formed at
the City of London Mechanics Institution to promote the practice of
decomposing the dead by the agency of fire. The members propose to
burn with becoming solemnity such of their dead as shall have left
their remains at the dispersal of the Association'.[21] The Cremation
Society, however, was not formed for another twenty-four years, and
when the Bishop of Rochester refused permission for a crematorium
on consecrated ground in his diocese, one was opened at Woking in
1885.

The Victorians were particularly talented at providing new buildings for their various institutions – railway stations, prisons,
bathhouses and water boards – so it is not surprising that their architects came up with several ideas for cemeteries. One particularly
splendid plan was devised in 1830 by Francis Goodwin, who wanted
to purchase 150 acres of Primrose Hill to erect a temple built on the
same scale as the Parthenon. On the same spot Mr Thomas Wilson
suggested that a brick and granite-faced pyramid with a base area the
size of Russell Square and a height 'considerably above Saint Pauls'
should be built. This would provide 215,296 catacombs on 94 levels,
and an observatory would be placed on the top floor. St Pancras
Vestry studied both plans, but no more was heard of them. However,
the new garden cemeteries were a great success and soon became
popular places to visit and enjoy walking amongst the trees, plants
and headstones. Today many remain havens of peace in busy urban
surroundings.

Present and future

As the Bishop walked in the nearby Fulham churchyard where he
himself was to be buried, perhaps he realised that many who had died
during his episcopate could have been saved. Few in the nineteenth
century had done more to create better social conditions for

Londoners than he, and one wonders how he found time and energy to suggest and support so many successful initiatives. He realised that many men and women need not have died

> had timely and effectual measures been taken for cleansing and ventilating dwellings, preventing overcrowding and draining the courts and alleyways in which they were situated. We will be guilty of great sin if we neglect to profit by the dearly-bought experience of the past and fail to take prompt and energetic measures for improving the condition of the labouring classes.

The legislature had to interfere; the problems were too huge for voluntary effort alone, said the Bishop. He told the Lords that unless the Government provided 'Convenient and commodious dwellings with all the appliances of health and comfort such as an adequate supply of water and pure air ... they would do but little to prompt moral and religious elevation'.[22]

The medical founder of the *Journal of Public Health*, Benjamin Ward Richardson, has left us a picture of Blomfield's activity:

> There was in his own nature a love of research and an administrative zeal, which made him a ruler of men altogether, rather than of any section of men, however respected and eminent. The Bishop was nothing unless he was strong, and all that he wished to be connected with must be of the magnificent order. He was a great layman as well as a bishop and had he by fate, entered the House of Commons instead of the Church he would perchance have given England such a Prime Minister as she had never seen before. Into Mr Chadwick's grand sanitary design, the Bishop of London threw himself with all his heart and strength; and I am but repeating what Mr Chadwick has confided to me many times, that Bishop Blomfield made comparatively easy a task which, but for him, might have been delayed until the friction brought against it had been all but impossible to overcome.[23]

During his lifetime Charles James had changed his mind, realising that the 'rich man in his castle, the poor man at his gate' theology was far removed from the teaching of Jesus. Things need not remain as they are, and an Established Church should lead, not follow, in matters of social improvement. Blomfield used his position in the House of Lords to draw attention to the evils which caused so much suffering, and he willingly gave time to the many committees which formulated policies and plans for change. Later in the century Canon

Henry Scott Holland commented that if one believes in the Incarnation one is interested in drains. Blomfield would have added 'and bathhouses, unemployment, working conditions, housing, and cemeteries'.

Chapter Five

Church reform

*It is the Church of England which makes us what
we are – a nation of honest men.*
Arthur, Duke of Wellington.

*At the end of the Season coaches leave Brighton as full as
a vicar's belly and return as empty as a curate's kitchen.*
Anon.

Facing the problem

Once the storms surrounding parliamentary reform had passed,
people began to take a closer look at the Established Church, which
everyone agreed was in need of attention. Whereas the liturgical and
doctrinal reforms of the Church had been undertaken in the sixteenth
century, no administrative or financial reforms had been put forward,
so by 1830 the organisation of the Church from top to bottom was
cloaked in chaos. No one except Parliament could give the necessary
sanction for change as Convocation had not been an effective body
since 1717, so there was no central ecclesiastical body able to legislate, except possibly the bench of bishops. The finances of the
Church were shaky; tithes and church rates were unpopular and the
capital sums inherited from the past were being misused. The
inequality of clergy stipends was glaring: the Bishop of Durham
earned approximately £19,000 (£722,000) per annum whereas the
average curate's stipend was £86 (£3,268). Such poverty meant that
clergy were often forced by circumstances to hold more than one
living and the *Extraordinary Black Book*, published in 1831, claimed
that one-third of the clergy were pluralists and three-fifths did not
live in their parishes.

The dioceses covered a vast area – the size of them had not
changed since the time of Henry VIII, who had considered founding

twenty-six new bishoprics but only created five. Thirteen suffragan bishops were appointed and Elizabeth added three more. No new sees or suffragan bishoprics were created from then until the nineteenth century. Reforms were made to church structure and finance during the Commonwealth period, but these were reversed at the Restoration.

Everyone had their own plan for church reform. Radicals such as John Stuart Mill (whom Gladstone called the saint of Rationalism) and J. A. Roebuck wanted disestablishment, but Thomas Arnold despaired even of that, suggesting that the Established Church should open its doors to all Christians in England and thus make itself a truly national Church. Radicals and Dissenters were united in concentrating their attack on church property. Years before, Jeremy Bentham had used this argument against the Church in a splendidly-titled pamphlet *Mother Church Relieved by Bleeding* saying, 'The life of this Excellent Being is in her gold – take away her gold and you take away her life'. Mill agreed and urged that all money be taken away from the Church even if it had been donated by generous benefactors of previous centuries, arguing that the Church of England could not oppose this as she herself had received much property from the Roman Catholic Church at the time of the Reformation. This was held in trust for 'the spiritual culture' of the people of England, so he suggested that the State should withdraw these endowments from its present possessors if it felt they were not fulfilling their obligations. The Church was now, in fact, failing in its duties, so the trust money should be made public money. These criticisms explain why so many clergy, including Blomfield, were anxious to show that the Church was still a useful institution. 'It is difficult to resist the conclusion', writes Dr Best, 'that by far the greater part of the clergy ... were primarily concerned with the political, educational (in the widest sense) and social functions of the Establishment.'[1] Later the Tractarians and Evangelicals were to recall the clergy to their real duty of leading souls to salvation, but in 1830 the bulk of the clergy still thought their main job was to diffuse good morals and a respect for the law of the Lord in every class of society, so the Church was often looked upon as a department of State, a Ministry of Morality.

The nature of the Church's Establishment had now to be restudied. At the time of Elizabeth only one society existed; Church and State were considered to be one. In Hooker's time the whole body of the realm was the Church, so Convocation was the synod of the clergy, and Parliament was the synod of the laity. The legislation of 1828–32, giving freedom to Roman Catholics and Dissenters, had changed all this. Parliament had been unlike a lay synod of the

Church of England ever since the dark ages of the eighteenth century, and now the Church of England began to feel unsure of herself, uncertain and self-conscious. Blomfield thought that Church and State should freely enter into an alliance for the mutual advantage of both, so the State must support the religious body which represented the majority of its members. Within this framework the Bishop saw the State acknowledging the Church's function and the Church realising what that function is. He wanted no political privileges as bulwarks, and made this clear at the time of the repeal of the Test and Corporation Acts. Needless to say, Blomfield himself did not look upon the Church only as a legal institution; he saw it as the Body of Christ.[2] Melbourne told his mother that Dissenters were more zealous and thus more intolerant than the Church of England, so if the country was to have a pervading religion he thought it ought to be 'cool and indifferent'.

Parliament had not been financially generous to its Established Church over the centuries. It had founded Queen Anne's Bounty in 1704, enabling it to augment poor livings by over £3 million in the following 140 years, but it granted no extra money to the Church for the rest of the eighteenth century. In 1809, £100,000 (nearly £3m) was given to the Bounty and this was renewed with one exception every year till 1820. £1m (approx £30m) was granted for church building in 1818 and a further half million in 1824, the last of the State grants.

In the countryside, where most parishes were to be found, people looked to the Church to provide baptisms, weddings, funerals and Sunday services, but there was a cost, because every householder had to pay a church rate to keep the church fabric in good order. Tithes had to be paid on St Luke's Day, and the Revd John Lettice, vicar of Peasmarsh in Sussex 1785–1832, said it was good on that day to hear 'the music of the sovereigns and crown pieces, not to mention the pleasing whispers of their five-pound notes'.[3] Tithes were extremely unpopular; 75% of them were owned by incumbents, 20% by lay people and 5% by institutions. The Act of 1836 brought commutation, when cash compensation or an acreage of land was negotiated, and this ended the unfortunate haggling by church officials over dues, or the embarrassment of entering a farm to demand poultry, cattle or corn. Clergy preferred to receive land as this gave them social standing and a good rent.

Fees comprised a large part of a cleric's income in the towns, and in Blomfield's diocese the larger the parish the more would be received. In 1841 Marylebone had a population of 135,000, St Pancras 125,000 and St George's, Hanover Square, 65,000. The Parliamentary Return of 1833 shows that the fees for that year were £1,068 (£40,584) at Marylebone, £1,147 (£43,586) at St Pancras, and £969 (£36,822) at St George's. If there was no population there were no fees, so St Bartholomew the Less and All Hallows Bread Street in the City of London received £3 (£114) and £5 (£190) respectively. Pew rents were also charged, and these continued for many years.

In his *Plan of Church Reform* Lord Henley, an Evangelical, suggested that incumbents should be paid between £800 and £1,200 p. a. (£30,400–£45,600) where the population exceeded 1,500 or 2,000, and the minimum stipend should be £400 p. a. (£15,000 p. a.). In fact the 1835 Commission Report showed only one-third of incumbents exceeded £400 p. a. and a third did not even earn £200 p. a. (£7,600) which put them on a level with teachers, shopkeepers and other lower middle class professionals. This was not to the liking of the clergy, who thought themselves gentlemen, and nearly all of them had at least one servant. James Woodforde, the famous Norfolk cleric, had seven servants.[4] Several clergy (including Blomfield when a curate) supplemented their income with teaching, and at Dunton the future Bishop, one of the country's leading classicists, charged £300 to £400 p. a. (£11,400–£15,200) to teach each student. 'At this time', says his son, he probably regarded ordination 'as affording means and leisure for literary pursuits rather than as offering in its own peculiar duties that wide field of usefulness which ere long opened upon him'.[5]

Because of Establishment the Bishop knew that any changes in the Church would have to be brought about by the ordinary processes of politics. Only Parliament could help the Church reform itself, but fortunately there was in Parliament a man who was sympathetic to the Church's needs – Sir Robert Peel. In 1828 he described Establishment as that Church to which the King must conform, whose bishops sit in the Lords and which has an 'inalienable claim to its property'. Peel, a cold shy man whose smile was likened to the silver fittings of a coffin, and his fellow Tories, had to arbitrate between the Whigs and the Radicals – some of whom wanted all church property to be taken over by the State. Peel, the statesman who was to lead the parliamentary negotiations, has often been likened to his ecclesiastical counterpart, Blomfield. Disraeli once called him, 'The greatest member of Parliament that ever lived', and said he was 'Like his great compeer, Bishop Blomfield, to whose character his own bore a strong similarity, and with whom he co-operated cordially in his Church reform measures.' Thanks to these two men the Church of England faced its crisis and came through it triumphantly. Dr Brose has written, 'The Establishment met the challenges to its property, privilege and utility after 1832 through a specific kind of defence, which had for its negative side the defence of Church property, and for its positive side the entire programme of administrative reform and social adaptation.'[6]

Ireland – the first step

The Church in Ireland was in greater need of reform than the English Church as many of its clergy had received no income for three years, and because Ireland was 'England writ large' it would be a test case if reforms were carried out there. Blomfield, while Bishop of Chester, had agreed that tampering with the Irish Church would be permissible if it would make the Church here more able to do its job.

Catholic emancipation had hardly affected the people of Ireland, as most of them were not eligible for high offices of state, and the peasantry were destitute, living in hovels with little to eat or wear. The Established Church in Ireland, as Professor Chadwick has pointed out, 'was not minded to missionary endeavour. Rich in proportion to its population, it was quiet, reasonable, instructed and expected that in time the Roman Catholics would be converted by reason, and by education'.[7] Some 30% of its incumbents were non-resident, pluralities were common and there were far too many bishops for such small numbers. Tithes were fiercely unpopular and violence often accompanied their collection. The Lord Lieutenant of Ireland, the Marquess of Anglesey who had lost a leg at Waterloo, believed disestablishment was the only cure for disorder, but Earl Grey and the Whigs, although wanting reforms, thought this too radical. In 1831, Grey appointed his brother-in-law to the bishopric of Derry and then filled the Archbishopric of Dublin with Dr Richard Whately, who compared himself to a helmsmen called to the rudder of a crazy ship in a storm. Grey believed that Roman Catholic priests should be employed by the State and their stipends should be paid by the Established Church.[8] By 1833 it was clear that the Whig Government planned to reduce in number the four archbishoprics and eighteen bishoprics which ministered to tiny congregations, and a plan was put forward to use the funds realised to repair churches, augment stipends and build schools. The plan's controversial Clause 147 left the door open for Parliament to use the surplus in whatever way it wished, perhaps to pay Roman Catholic priests. This clause was removed. John Henry Newman, infuriated by the whole concept of the Bill, wrote to Grey, 'Well done, my blind premier, confiscate and rob, till like Samson you pull down the political structure on your own head'.

Many, including Blomfield, supported the Bill, thinking the reforms were for the better health of the Irish Church, and the Bill was passed in June. The Irish members were incensed at the removal of Clause 147 and were not satisfied with the other provisions, which included abolishing ten bishoprics, merging them with their neighbours, reducing the income of two wealthy sees and abolishing the church tax paid by parishioners to keep the building in repair. In England Blomfield received abuse because he supported this 'sacrilegious spoliation', and the Duke of Newcastle told him he had lately 'collated himself to the office of high priest in the temple of expediency'. In reply the Bishop said he agreed with Paley that there are cases in which expediency might be a guide, and with reference to the office conferred on him he had no objection to receiving it even at hands so little qualified to bestow it as those of His Grace.

The following year Blomfield objected most strongly to the all-lay commission appointed to inquire into the revenues of the Irish Church, and also to the proposal to take its dues away and use them for secular purposes. His speech in the Lords was full of 'manly courage'.[9] In 1835 the Government tried again, suggesting that all parishes with less than fifty worshippers be suppressed, the income of all livings be reduced to £300 p. a. (£11,400) and surplus funds be devoted to educational purposes. In the Lords, Blomfield spoke forcefully, appealing to their Lordships' Protestant feelings: 'I implore your lordships by all that you hold sacred, by the gratitude that you owe to that Church from which you have imbibed your Christian principles and knowledge, in whose consolations I trust you delight – and may you all experience their efficacy at the closing hour of your existence – not to give your consent to this measure'. The Bill was dropped by the Whigs, and Blomfield was hailed as one of the saviours of the Church of Ireland.

'The Church no human power can save'

The newly-reformed Parliament now turned its attention nearer home. Those who wanted the Church to be disestablished were not a united force, so members tended to agree with Blomfield that a new form of establishment was needed and many abuses needed to be corrected.

Early in 1831 the Archbishop of Canterbury had introduced three Bills into Parliament, dealing with pluralism, tithes and clerical stipends, but these were shelved as minds were too occupied with parliamentary reform and, anyway, Parliament was dissolved. In his 1830 Charge Blomfield had asked for pluralities to be limited, not abolished, but he opposed Howley's attempt to curb them. The proposed legislation suggested that an incumbent could not have a second living if his first was worth more than £400 (£15,200). He himself had held more than one living and he said he felt that the upper classes would be deterred from entering the ministry if stipends were smaller. In the Charge he reminded his clergy of the immensity of his task, 'Lord, who is sufficient for these things?' and tells them that recent legislation has repealed Acts which were thought necessary for the safety of the Established Church. 'We must now depend entirely upon our internal resources', and face the fact that there is 'a greater number of people who take no interest in the consolations of religion and its ordinances.' He forbids non-residence, except in the City of London, and says there is no reason not to reside in the vicarage as pure water can now be laid on and houses can be made comfortable. Even in the City, if a parsonage house has been rented out as a counting house it must be brought back to church use. Clerical agencies should not be approached to provide deputies who will take services. Blomfield, however, prepared the way for reform by telling the Lords that 'An active enquiry into the state of the revenues of the Church of England' would be propitious as its enemies were wildly exaggerating the amount of church wealth and property. Such an enquiry would 'form the ground-work of a more equal distribution of the ecclesiastical revenues'.[10] Members took his advice and an ecclesiastical inquiry commission was appointed shortly afterwards. In another debate he said 'I am aware that one of the greatest blessings to the Church would be to increase the comforts and respectability of the poorer members of the clergy; but that must be done without the risk of weakening the efficiency of the Establishment as a whole.' The Duke of Newcastle inquired whether this reform had begun, and the Bishop replied that it had been going on 'for many years: but it has been accelerated by recent events, and I trust it will be still further accelerated'.

Obviously much needed to be done, so in 1831 Blomfield's close friend, Joshua Watson, drew up a scheme for an Ecclesiastical Commission consisting entirely of clergy.[11] Grey rejected this. On 23 June 1832 a Royal Commission was appointed 'to make a full and correct inquiry respecting the revenues and patronage belonging to the several Archiepiscopal and Episcopal Sees, to all cathedral and collegiate churches and to all ecclesiastical benefices ... with or without cure of souls in England and Wales.' The two archbishops and Blomfield were joined by three bishops, five clergy and eleven laity. Blomfield approved of this step, and in the following December he wrote to Howley, 'I have long been convinced of the necessity of a mixed commission of clergymen and laymen to consider what measures should be adopted in the way of church reform.' He also said he was uncertain whether the Commission should be a permanent one or not, and whether it should initiate all legislative measures affecting the Church.

In his 1834 Charge, Blomfield again spoke of the need for reform, and he regretted that Dissenters, with the possible exception of the Wesleyans, would never be satisfied as they desired the destruction of the Church, exhibiting in their churches a 'secular and political strain'. Mr C. Lushington was stung by this to reply in a pamphlet which said that the 365 Dissenting chapels in London were supplementing the Church of England's work, and suggested that the Bishop adopt a more conciliatory approach. Perhaps he had forgotten that a huge gathering of Dissenters had in May 1834 called for a separation of Church and State. Several of those present, particularly the Baptists and Congregationalists, had called for the estates of the Church to be nationalised and for an end to State Churches. J. B. Sumner, Blomfield's successor at Chester, told his clergy he had concluded that the attacks on the Church had been a blessing in disguise and had led the clergy to examine their role, stirring them up to 'unwonted exertions'. Dr Welch felt that the opponents of the Church were badly organised and that many began to look kindly on the Established Church even if its clergy were 'a little forbidding but dignified and decorous, with a profound belief in good works and preaching'. Blomfield told his clergy to use this waiting period before the Commission reported to 'go round the bulwarks, and mark the defects thereof with a view to their restoration'. The Church must continue to plead for its 'temporal possessions and immunities'.[12] He himself had made a start by raising the value of all the smaller livings in his gift to an annual value of £200 (£7,600). Bishops, he said, were not wealthy; it was the cathedral chapters who should be helping with sizeable grants.

Pluralism and non-residence were the two evils to be eradicated, but they did have their defenders, such as Bishop Phillpotts who considered a rich pluralist could serve the poor better; others thought they enabled a clergyman to gain a wide professional experience, and some felt that curates might lose their jobs if reforms were made. Howley said pluralism meant 'a more liberal maintenance of the Church's ministers, the encouragement of sacred learning and the remuneration of professional merit' (Charge, 1832). It is difficult to assess how many livings were held in plurality, but it is thought that in 1830 one-third of all incumbents held a second living: a few had a third or fourth. In his Charge of 1834 Blomfield said he had come to realise that pluralities were 'wrong in principle', but that he was uncertain how to stop them without impoverishing the clergy. Financial help from the Government was out of the question, as the Bishop realised.

Non-residence disgraced the Church: in the 1820s only four out of every ten parishes had resident incumbents; 2,878 livings had no rectory or parsonage house and in 1833 1,700 parsonages were declared unfit for habitation, so non-residence was to be expected. If the incumbent was ill or infirm he would probably live elsewhere, and if a living was tiny the small, insufficient stipend would have to be supplemented by another benefice income. A curate could be installed by the incumbent at a very modest cost, or he could ask neighbouring clergy to take services. Virgin reckons that approximately half of the 10,550 parishes had no resident incumbent in the early 1830s.[13]

The 1838 parliamentary return lists 3,088 curates looking after parishes with no resident incumbent. Their lot had been improved by the Stipendiary Curates Act of 1813 which had ordered non-resident incumbents to pay their assistants a minimum of £80 p. a. (£2,560), and as curates were allowed to hold three titles they had a chance of earning a living wage. Lord Harrowby in the debate in the Lords said he disliked seeing clerics 'galloping about from church to church', but the Act was passed. By 1850, thanks to the legislation of the 1830s, the number of resident incumbents rose to 70% and by 1879 it was 90%.[14]

Creating more resident incumbents slightly lessened the number of curates seeking jobs. Between 1834 and 1843 the number of ordinands averaged 535 each year – double that of a hundred years before – but these could be condemned to a life of refined poverty or 'genteel beggary' unless they were known to patrons of livings or were able to teach. After the 1840s new urban livings were created, but some men preferred to remain in the country. No pension schemes meant no retirement, so a young man had to wait until a clerical funeral before he could move into an incumbency. A survey in 1830 showed that half the incumbents were over 50, but surprisingly only 10% were over 70.[15] Peter Virgin reckons that one in five clergy would not become an incumbent.

The 1832 Commission of Inquiry worked slowly, mostly because the clergy characteristically delayed sending in their reports, some of which were written in an 'aggrieved and apprehensive spirit'. Ten per cent of the returns had to be estimated, and the tenure of the Commission had to be renewed twice because of these delays. Towards the end of 1834 the King with relief parted company with his Whig ministers, and after a few months of Wellington's premiership Peel took over and told Bishop Phillpotts that his main object was 'the interests of the Church of England' and that he was in favour of an improved distribution of church revenues. On 4 February 1835 Sir Robert Peel and his new government appointed the Ecclesiastical Duties and Revenues Commission which became the Ecclesiastical Commission proper a year later. Strictly speaking the two bodies were separate, but their membership was identical so the present Church Commissioners can date their birth from 1835 rather than 1836. Sir Robert was their founding father at Westminster, as was noted by an irate cleric who later wrote, 'Sir Robert Peel in his short administration of 135 days did more mischief to the Church than 135 years will be able to repair'.[16] The new Commission, which met for the first time in Peel's house, was told not only to make enquiries but also to suggest new ways of handling church money and properties. The two archbishops, Blomfield, and two other diocesan bishops were among the Commissioners. One wonders why Bishop Phillpotts of Exeter was not on the Commission from the beginning, because he sent in some excellent suggestions including that of paring down the income of cathedral canonries: a stall in St Paul's was worth £2,000 p. a. – (£76,000). He did not wish them to be abolished completely as cathedrals could become educational institutions or seminaries for young clergy.

The numerous stalls at Westminster Abbey could, he said, be used to relieve the poverty of Chester Cathedral. The canonries of Canterbury could be annexed to the rectories of St George, Hanover Square; St James, Piccadilly and St Martin-in-the-Fields. (One wonders why he chose these wealthy churches instead of three East End livings such as Stepney, Hackney and Whitechapel). Phillpotts suggested that as the Bishop and chapter of Durham were 'offensively opulent', they ought to help fund churches in the new manufacturing districts of Yorkshire and Lancashire.

Peel asked Howley if it would be useful to have three or four clergy below the rank of bishop on the Commission. The Archbishop agreed, suggesting some archdeacons might be chosen, but Blomfield was opposed to the idea. Jealousy, he said, would be caused and no two cathedral chapters were alike. Anyway, bishops had once been ordinary clergymen and they still had the interests of the Church at heart. The suggested plan would create a large, unwieldy committee and he would have none of it.[17] This was a blunder, because the cathedral chapters and the 'inferior clergy' were to feel unrepresented and powerless in the years ahead.

The Commission, which had its counterparts in other spheres – the

Poor Law Commission, Board of Health, and the Committee of Education – was told to consider the revenues of the English and Welsh dioceses, episcopal duties, livings held in commendam, the residence of the clergy, plans to make the cathedral and collegiate churches more efficient and the best means of providing care of souls in thickly-populated areas. 'The future of our Church is in your hands', Peel told the Commissioners. He attended every general meeting and several of the commitee meetings until the first Report was issued. Considering he had a country to run and a shaky administration to hold together, this is a remarkable tribute to his committment to reform. Fortunately, he was able to rely on the support of his Chancellor of the Exchequer, Henry Goulburn, who was a member of the Commission.

After two months Peel was replaced as Prime Minister by Melbourne, whose only change to the Commission was to replace its Tory laymen with Whigs. Blomfield was always the leader of the Commission and, once, an influential London clergyman who had some important business with the Commissioners tried to hurry it through, but Archbishop Vernon Harcourt told him, 'It is no use for you, Mr. L., to come to *us* to finish your business; we never do anything more than nib our pens till the Bishop of London comes'. Sydney Smith called him 'The Church of England here on earth', because he possessed more power than any prelate since Laud. 'The Bishop of London is passionately fond of labour, has certainly no aversion to power, is of a quick temper, great ability, thoroughly versant in ecclesiastical law and always in London. He will become the Commission.'[18] With Peel at the prow and Blomfield at the helm the work had begun, and Melbourne and Russell did not change course when they took office.

The reports

Three reports were issued by the Commission: they all showed how urgent the need for reform was. The first report took only forty-one days to prepare and was issued on 17 March 1835. It gave details of the size of dioceses, numbers of incumbents in them, and their financial position. Discrepancies were glaring – Lincoln had 1,200 incumbents, Rochester 94. Ely with a population of 126,000 was very rich, Chester with two million was poor. The total net income of the English and Welsh bishoprics amounted to £157,737 p. a. (£6m) and that of the cathedral chapters £284,141 p. a. (£11m). The clergy, including 178 who had made no return, were paid a total of £3,005,451 p. a. (£120m). This was an average annual income of

£278 (£10,564) for each living. There were, however, 4,883 out of 10,718 benefices which had an income below £200 p. a. (£7,600) and nearly 300 parishes in England and Wales were worth less than £50 p. a. (£1,900). In the diocese of London's 608 benefices the average benefice income was £399 p. a. (£15,162) and the 355 London curates each received an average of £98 p. a. (£3,724). Two new sees – Manchester and Ripon – were recommended, and it was suggested that Llandaff and Bristol become one diocese, and likewise Bangor and St Asaph. The number of bishops would thus remain the same, which was just as well because Parliament had no intention of increasing the number of seats in the Lords held by the Established Church. Blomfield said there must not be two classes of bishops; it was 'manifestly injurous to episcopacy'. Phillpotts disagreed, saying that those bishops not in the Lords could spend more time in their dioceses. Newman wanted to create suffragan bishoprics, but Blomfield felt this had great disadvantages, and opposed it.

The Commission's work was enormously helped by the appointment of its first Secretary, Charles Knight Murray, a capable young barrister who had been one of the London stipendary magistrates and the Judicial Commissioner for Lunatics. This was a good preparation for his appointment in 1830 as Secretary to the Ecclesiastical Courts Commission, where he soon became known to several bishops including Blomfield. On his appointment he kept his magistracy, which made Lord Melbourne wonder if he did all he should. The Commissioners told the Prime Minister that he was indispensable, and Dr Best notes that 'whatever hot water he got into his employers always protected him and protested his excellence. Either he really was a first rate administrator or else (as some later evidence suggests) he had a mesmeric power of making his employers believe he was so.'[19] Blomfield, who had appointed Murray's brother Thomas to a London incumbency, had the very highest regard for him; they worked well together over the next few years until scandal struck in October 1849, when Murray speculated in railway shares, and it was alleged he used church monies for his own use. He confessed his misdeeds and, before a prosecution could be brought, fled to Australia to become a high-ranking official in the New South Wales Government.

The second report suggested suppressing 360 prebends. Sydney Smith, seeing prebendal stalls in St Paul's tottering, was furious. Usually he crackled away 'like a genial bonfire of jokes and good sense and uproarious laughter',[20] but on this occasion his humour deserted him, saying that on the tombs of the Commissioner bishops would be written, 'Under their auspices and by their counsels the destruction of the English Church began'. However, he grudgingly agreed that most chapters were a' miserable lot' who would run a mile 'if a bishop was to come in his pontificals and charge them'. The report ended with Blomfield's summary of a Bill for the Regulation of Pluralities, Residence and the Employment of Stipendary Curates. The next report proposed a third union of Sees – Carlisle with Sodor and Man.

The most important recommendations were made in the fourth report which was never signed by the Commissioners; in it they suggested that a permanent Commission be founded to administer church monies and property. They wanted it to legislate on church affairs under the sanction, not of Parliament, but of the Sovereign in Council – using Orders in Council to bypass Parliament.

Action

Three Bills, based on the Commission's reports, were passed by Parliament between 1836 and 1840. The first of these was the Established Church Bill (1836) which created a permanent Commission as in Ireland. Its recommendations were able to bypass Parliament because they were made Orders in Council, passed by the Sovereign sitting in Council. This permanent Commission, which at first consisted only of the two archbishops, the bishops of London, Lincoln and Gloucester and eight prominent laymen, was increased in 1840. It was able to hold real estate and to receive episcopal and capitular incomes. All episcopal incomes were now to be controlled by the Commission, and the glaring inequality of these incomes was changed by a fairer distribution of money. Opposition was loud but not large in size. Archdeacon Thorp of Durham predicted that all clergy would be reduced 'to the condition of stipendaries under the control of the executive government'.[21] Bishop Bagot of Oxford declared that the reforming State was imposing upon a reluctant Church a power 'as irresponsible as ... gigantic'.[22] Other criticisms were more telling. Radicals who had hoped to use Parliament to clip ecclesiastical wings were horrified to see their opportunity slip away. The speed at which the Bill was pushed through Parliament enraged some people, including Charles Buller MP, who saw the responsibility for ecclesiastical legislation being handed to 'another body'. He thought that members of both Houses of Parliament were 'being asked to sign a blank cheque, the encashment of which could benefit only the Church'. Whigs were being asked to support a Tory venture. Conservative clerics like Phillpotts pointed out that only three commissioners were independent, *ex officio*; the rest were members of government or appointed by the Crown. Charles Sumner, Bishop of Winchester, agreed and pointed out the despotic potentialities of delegated legislation. He was sure that there would be no public discussion. The changes of 1840 were to address these criticisms.

The second Bill (the Plurality Bill) made new enemies for the Commission because it forbade an incumbent to engage in trade, restricted the amount of land he could farm, made it illegal to hold two benefices which were more than ten miles apart and whose population was over 3,000, forbade anyone to hold preferment in more than one cathedral, and renewed the old system of licences for non-residence which had to be renewed after six months with the permission of the archbishops. If two livings were held the maximum aggregate value of the two should not exceed £1,000 p. a. (£38,000). In 1850 the permitted distance between the parishes was reduced to three miles.

The Commissioners met regularly (daily in the autumn of 1836), and early in 1837 they crossed swords with Lord Melbourne and his government over church rates. Melbourne wanted to abolish them but the Commissioners pointed out that this was a matter for them to discuss, not Parliament. At one time Blomfield thought the Commission might break up, and spoke eloquently in the Lords telling 'The noble viscount' that his church rate bill was impractical and inexpedient; its recommendations were nothing but 'sacrilegious spoliation'. In the face of such opposition Lord Melbourne dropped the Bill.

Churchmen like Newman and Keble were suspicious of the new Commission because it was a Commission. 'They could not bear to think of clergymen cringing in the chambers of ministers or bowing before parliamentary committees.'[23] As Peel told J. W. Croker, many were not sure of Howley and considered Blomfield 'an enemy'.[24] Cathedral chapters had vested interests at stake so, led by Sydney Smith, they naturally opposed the Commission and its recommendations. The hurried legislation meant 'You are cashiered and confiscated before you can look about you'. Blomfield said he found Smith's Letter to Archdeacon Singleton 'Less funny than I expected ... I don't think the Chapters will be very proud of their advocate.' Perhaps he was smarting from Sydney's comment, on hearing that the Bishop could not come to dine because he had been bitten by a dog: 'I should like to hear the dog's version of the story'.[25]

Radicals were also loud in their opposition to the Commission (for not going far enough) as were the Tories (for going too far). The Bishop was well used to criticism and stood his ground. In a speech of 1840 he gave his reasons for supporting the Commissioners' proposals.

I traverse the streets of this crowded city [he said] with deep and solemn thoughts of the spiritual condition of its inhabitants. I pass the magnificent church which crowns the Metropolis and is consecrated to the noblest of objects, the glory of God, and I ask of myself in what degree it answers that object. I see there a Dean and three residentaries with incomes amounting in the aggregate to between £10,000 and £12,000 p. a. I see, too, connected with the Cathedral twenty-nine clergymen whose offices are all sinecures with an annual income of about £12,000 ... I proceed a mile or two to the east and north-east and I find myself in the midst of an immense population in the most wretched state of destitution and neglect ... to the number of at least 300,000. I find there upon an average about one church and one clergyman for every 8,000 to 10,000 souls. I naturally look back to the vast endowments of St Paul's, a part of them drawn from these very districts, and consider whether some portion of them may not be applied to remedy or alleviate these enormous evils. No, I am told, you may not touch St Paul's ... The duties performed there are too important to admit of any diminution. One sermon is preached by a residentiary and another by a clergyman appointed by the Bishop and paid by the Corporation of London; while the non-residentiaries either preach an occasional sermon or pay a minor canon for preaching it ... Yet my opponents assert that not a farthing must be taken from these splendid endowments.

The Bill which changed this state of affairs was the Dean and Chapter Bill of 1840. Lord Henley, Peel's brother-in-law and a friend of Blomfield, had already eight years earlier published a detailed plan to reform the Church which paid special attention to cathedrals which, he suggested, should be staffed only by a dean and two chaplains. All prebends should disappear, except in Oxford where they would be annexed to parishes in the city.[26] The 1840 Bill caused more trouble than all the rest put together. 317 prebendaries were abolished and approximately £200,000 (£6m) passed to the Commissioners for other uses. Only 20 non-residentiary prebendaries remained. It was a step in the right direction, but many thought it did not go far enough. All cathedral chapters except three protested, and Gladstone bitterly opposed the Bill, saying the cathedral chapters were, or should be, necessary councils of the bishop. Sydney Smith, not exactly a disinterested cleric, felt the plans were too revolutionary, pointing out that the proposed pillage of the cathedrals would only result in each incumbent receiving an extra £5 12s 6½d. He singled out Blomfield and blamed him for this 'change, fusion, and confusion ... such a scene of revolution and commutation as has not been seen since the days of Ireton and Cromwell, all the cathedrals are subject to the irreconcilable energy of one man'.[27] He is responsible for the creation of a ptochogony, a generation of beggars. A Christian bishop, said Sydney, in cold blood will use cathedral monies to found a thousand livings of £130 p. a. (£5,000). In Edmonton, Blomfield had already divided a living into three, thus making three beggars, in charge of chapels at Winchmore Hill and Southgate, and the church at Edmonton itself. Sydney thought that when men entered the Church they hoped to avoid small stipends in the same way a barrister hopes to survive his briefless days. Thanks to Blomfield there would now be no valuable prizes to attract men to become ministers – they would instead remain 'consecrated beggars'. It should be remembered that cathedrals were places of worship; no lectures on chemistry or lessons on dancing were given although he did agree that chapters should be responsible for the care of diocesan clergy and for education.[28] Melbourne disagreed. 'The study of theology may be a very good thing in its way, but it is not a thing we want in these days.'

'We knew from the first', said the Bishop, 'that we were undertaking an invidious and unpopular task.' He never shrank from unpopularity and Dr Best suggests that he was 'one of those men who doubt whether they are doing their duty unless they make themselves unpopular'. Goulburn, Peel's second in commmand in ecclesiastical affairs, reported that in Cambridge there was 'great jealousy lest the Bishop of London should lead the Government', but both men trusted Blomfield and supported him even after they left power. All three of them were taken aback by the violence and vehemence of the opposition to the legislation but, having looked at all possible alternatives, they refused to change their minds.[29] 'We have acted conscientously in the performance of an ungracious duty, according to our own convictions of what was best for the real interests of the Church and the Country', Blomfield told the Lords in July 1840.

All of Blomfield's ability and eloquence were needed to push the Bill through. He said he would prefer his council to consist of the archdeacons and rural deans for they were more in touch with the contemporary situation than cathedral canons. When the final vote was taken in the House of Lords the bishops were 11–9 against, but they were outvoted by the other peers. The money did not immediately go to the Commissioners, who had to wait until the leases of cathedral lands ran out. This meant there was little cash for the Commissioners to use at first and it was not until 1870 that most of church land came under their control. Dr Welch says this Bill was not adventurous enough:

'Real reform, capable of stirring men's hearts would have meant that Church and State should unite to make dramatic and heroic sacrifices required by the common good. It seems very safe and pedestrian merely to redistribute church property.'[30]

The Dean and Chapter Bill also provided for a change in the membership of the Commission: all the English and Welsh bishops were now invited to become *ex officio* Commissioners together with three senior deans. Eight permanent lay Commissioners were also appointed, six by the Crown and two by the Archbishop of Canterbury. Before this the proportion of lay to clerical was 8-5, now it was 19-30. Two of the deans were already bishops, so the non-episcopal clergy were still not represented. At the first meeting of the new body only Blomfield and eight others attended, with five apologies. Christopher Bethell, Bishop of Bangor, wrote to say that the secretary might as well save himself the trouble of summoning him as he would not be coming till further notice.

The Commission

In the years ahead the Commission continued to grow in power and in 1847 it was subjected to an Inquiry by a Select Committee which found that 49 members was too large a number and recommended a division of duties, separating the ecclesiastical business from the management of property. The larger body might be retained to consider the former, and three men could be paid to manage the Commission's property. The Archbishop of Canterbury would appoint one and the Commission two. Joseph Hume, the radical who opposed the Commission, said that bishops should not be allowed to sit on the Commission as it would give them too much influence and they would be tempted to build palaces for themselves instead of alleviating spiritual destitution. He received little support, and in 1850 the Ecclesiastical Commission Bill was passed by Parliament, who incorporated the Inquiry's suggestion so that three Estates Commissioners were appointed. Many feared that it would carry the process of centralisation in the Church even further, but time has shown that this has not happened. The new Estates committee which had absolute charge of all the Commissioners' property, its sale, purchase, exchange, letting, managment etc. was a powerful body. It consisted of the Earl of Chichester, who remained First Estates Commissoner till 1878, Shaw Lefevre and Henry Goulburn. Sir James Graham and Bishop Blomfield were appointed to the commitee by the Commissioners.

There is no doubt that Blomfield was the Commission's leader, but some thought that his decisiveness ought to be tempered by kindness or tenderness, and *Fraser's Magazine* admitted that the Bishop moved 'along with something of the air of an autocrat' although it insisted that this was 'an inevitable accompaniment of great mental superiority'. Certainly Blomfield had an eighteenth-century haughtiness and masterful bearing and he could administer crushing rebukes, such as his reply to a young priest who had ventured to quote St Augustine at him; 'St Augustine was Bishop of Hippo but you will be good enough to remember that I am Bishop of London'.[31] Many thought that the Bishop was amassing too much power, and H. Merivale, Drummond Professor of Political Economy, rejoiced when Connop Thirlwall was appointed Bishop of St David's, because he would stand up to Blomfield 'whose strides towards the Popedom of England are quite fearful'.

> Busy meddling treacherous priest [screamed the *Spectator*], look around after a few years and you will behold the desolation you have created ... choirs will soon cease to be, and Purcell and Tallis will be driven to take refuge elsewhere. Our Whig contemporaries are dumb because Lord Melbourne and John Russell are wet nurses to the Bishop of London's bantling. Mute are also the Tory oracles in deference to his Lordship's will.

Blomfield was accustomed to such abuse and defended the Dean and Chapter Bill on the grounds of expediency, necessity and urgency. 'It is', he said, 'unfair to speak of the Commission as governing the Church, it is merely trying to stop spiritual destitution.' Many of the clergy never forgave Blomfield for supporting the Bill and the *Guardian* considered it the greatest blot on his career. Even one of his biographers expressed his grave disapproval: looking back over the Commission's work Dr Biber thought that the lot of the parochial clergy was certainly not improved, the cathedrals' usefulness in teaching and training had ceased, and dioceses were bigger than ever.[32] However, the Bishop remarked, 'they now blame me for these measures but they will hereafter confess that those very measures have been the saving of the Church.' History has proved him right.[33]

A powerful friendship – Peel and Blomfield

In a speech to his constituents which became known as the Tamworth Manifesto (1834) Sir Robert Peel declared his committment to church reform:

I cannot give my consent to the alienating of church property ...
from strictly ecclesiastical purposes. But I repeat now the opinions
that I have already expressed in Parliament in regard to the Church
Establishment in Ireland – that if, by an improved distribution of
the revenues of the Church, its just influence can be extended, and
the true interests of the Established religion promoted, all other
considerations should be made subordinate to the advancement of
objects of such paramount importance.

In December 1834 Peel was holidaying at the Hotel de l'Europe in
Rome with his wife and eldest daughter when he was suddenly
summoned back to England to be Prime Minister. The Whig administration had collapsed and Wellington refused to go to Downing Street
again, saying its occupant should now be a member of the House of
Commons. He strongly recommended Peel. Sir Robert was a shy
solitary man, son of a rich Lancashire cotton-spinner, educated at
Harrow and Christ Church Oxford. Somewhat surprisingly this had
given him no confidence and ease when moving in aristocratic
circles; he lacked polish, and was, said Melbourne, 'too religious,
too uxorious, too prim. He was all prudence and calculation.'[34] The
Queen felt Peel's extreme shyness made her shy, and she disliked his
habit of pointing his toes and thrusting out his hands to shake down
his cuffs like a dancing master.[35] Wellington agreed with Victoria,
saying he himself had 'no small talk and Peel no manners'. Charles
Greville, the diarist, reports 'the vulgarity of Peel. In all his ways,
his dress, his manner, he looks more like a dapper shopkeeper than a
prime minister. He eats voraciously, and cuts cream and jellies with
his knife. Yet he has genius and taste and his thoughts are not vulgar
though his manners are to such a degree'.[36] Despite this Peel was
immensely popular and his work, particularly for the Church and for
the police force, had far-reaching results.

As early as 1827 Blomfield had singled out Peel as the one man on
whom the Church could ultimately rely. He supported Peel's
economic policies and when increased taxes were announced wrote to
him, 'I shall have to pay rather more than four times as much in the
way of taxes as I pay at present, but I cordially approve of the
measure proposed'.[37] The two men became firm friends: the Bishop's
letters changed from 'Sir – your obedient and faithful servant' (1825)
to 'yours very sincerely' (1835), and in 1843 Peel writes 'My dear
Bishop of London'.

On 4 January 1835 Peel had a long interview with Howley and
Blomfield, and the next day wrote to the King proposing that a
Commission should review the pastoral duties of the Church. The

bishops, he said, must be an integral part of the process, so he would leave the archbishop to nominate the clergy members and he himself would appoint the lay members. He ignored a letter from the Tory journalist, J. W. Croker, who said that the clergy had little confidence in the archbishop, 'and worse than none in the Bishop of London'. Peel pushed the Commission hard, but was not in office long enough to achieve legislation. Dr Chadwick notes that he 'changed the history of the Church. He showed that even Tories wanted reform and so made reform inevitable ... above all he created in the Commission an instrument for church reform.'[38]

In the early 1840s Peel leaned heavily on Blomfield's advice to make appointments to the bishoprics of Ely and Lichfield, the deaneries of Westminster and Peterborough, and the masterships of various Oxbridge Colleges. One of the London archdeacons, Lonsdale of Middlesex, was elevated to the see of Lichfield. In 1843 Peel paid Blomfield the greatest possible compliment when he wrote from Scotland offering him the archbishopric of Canterbury, which was somewhat premature, as Howley recovered from his illness.

In his own diocese Blomfield found Peel very accommodating concerning the division of large parishes. When Archdeacon Jones retired from the living of West Ham, Peel said he would accept any plan proposed by the Bishop, and agreed that 'the rich and overgrown parish' of St George's, Hanover Square, should be divided into six or seven districts and the same should apply to the parish of Barnet. These would need an Act of Parliament.[39] Sometimes Peel declined to help the Bishop in his plans. When Blomfield asked if it would be possible to take over three London sites to build churches, Peel was not enthusiastic and after a long delay said he thought the necessary legislation would not get through Parliament. Despite further requests Peel refused to help. The Bishop also had to concede defeat on the Dissenters' Chapels Bill which allowed Unitarians to keep property acquired before 1813. He told Gladstone he felt he had been thrown overboard by Peel.

Blomfield and Peel kept in close touch until Peel's death following a riding accident in July 1850. They had much in common: both were considerable classical scholars, both were practical, businesslike and earnest, and both worked hard. The Bishop was once called 'an ecclesiastical Peel'. Blomfield liked to be at Fulham with his 'attached and united family' and Peel liked to be at Drayton Manor, but it is difficult to imagine him following the Bishop's example and singing in a glee anthem at a private soirée. Both men were suspicious of the Tractarians, Peel telling the Bishop that they brought division into the Church, so that he would not make them bishops or

give them positions at Oxford. He thus ensured Dr Pusey had no
preferment, and thought the elevation of Samuel Wilberforce 'a
hazardous measure.'

Revival of Convocation

Bishop Blomfield was one of those responsible for the recall of an
active Convocation after a lapse of 130 years. In his early life he had
often said this would be a foolish step as there was nothing it could
do, and secretly most of the bishops agreed, because the House of
Lords already provided a place for them to air their views. They
needed no other assembly. Many thought Convocation's revival
would lead to greater party strife in the Church, others said its decisions would probably be reversed by the ecclesiastical courts. Now
he changed his mind, although he realised Convocation's constitution
and membership would have to be changed. In 1843, 12,000 parishes
sent 42 members whereas there were 104 *ex officio* members and
proctors of cathedral chapters. Scotland and America already
possessed legislative bodies for their Churches: why not England?

For well over a hundred years the Convocation of Canterbury had
been summoned to transact business but was prorogued before it
could do anything useful apart from sending a loyal address to the
sovereign. Blomfield felt the laity should be included but one of his
staff, John Sinclair, vicar of Kensington and archdeacon of
Middlesex since 1843, was not so sure. Contention, he said, was
certain to arise. It was 'easy to conceive the general turmoil, the
strife, the jealousy, the exasperation' which would be engendered.
Members of today's General Synod know what he means. 'The irri-
tability and impatience' would balance any advantage to be gained,
but he did concede that Convocation might do much important if
modest work – revising rubrics, authorising hymns, changing canon
law and protesting against the encroachments of 'the Roman
System'.[40]

Blomfield disagreed with his archdeacon and in his Charge of 1850
once again paved the way for reform. 'In theory ... the Church ...
possesses the right of deliberating in her collective capacity upon
questions of doctrine or discipline, but in practice she is restrained
from exercising it'. This is 'a fit subject for complaint' and all legitimate methods must be used to change the situation. With such
support from the highest ecclesiastical level the members of the
Society for the Revival of Convocation called a meeting at
Freemasons Hall on 14 January 1851. Many speeches suggested that
the crippled state of the Church of England was a direct consequence

of the long-continued suppression of her synodical functions. Was it surprising that Roman Catholics were gaining ground? The meeting requested Blomfield to present petitions to the Convocations and to the Queen. He agreed, but due to illness had to ask the Bishop of Chichester to deputise for him.

On 11 July Lord Redesdale initiated a debate in the Lords on the revival of Convocation and Blomfield in a strong, effective speech laid down three important principles: the House of Bishops should decide matters of doctrine; the laity should have a share in the deliberations of the new synod, and the parochial clergy should be better represented. Forty men representing 16,000 clergy was not enough.

Bishop Wilberforce and Lord Lyttelton joined forces with Blomfield in his campaign, but in February 1852 everyone was outraged when Archbishop Sumner, following the example of his brother at York who liked to keep the northern Convocation in a state of 'enforced coma', prorogued Convocation when it started to discuss business. Samuel Wilberforce, in despair at the 'miserable and humiliating position of the Church', asked Gladstone what could be done with 'a Primate so mischievously good'. Blomfield made the most of his influence at Court by having a discussion over breakfast with Prince Albert who seemed less than sympathetic and, anyway, was always suspicious of clerical lobbying. It was the Archbishop who needed to be influenced – his Evangelical friends were asserting that it was 'a delusion and a suicidal act' for clergy to ask for more responsibility. Someone had 'to reduce the Archbishop to reason'.[41] The Whig government was clearly anti-Convocation, but in January 1854 the Archbishop and Blomfield went to see the new Prime Minister, Lord Aberdeen, who agreed to let Convocation appoint committees to discuss the way ahead. Blomfield presided over these, and in July 1854 presented their reports. These suggested that each archdeaconry should elect a proctor in convocation who would be voted for by beneficed and licensed clergy; a permanent diaconate should be established; and cathedrals should possess a chapter of clergy specialising in various fields such as education. Blomfield described the 'harmonious atmosphere' of the two committees and felt that this was a happy augury. The acrimony which many expected and feared was not visible, nor need it be.

The Archbishop was gradually brought to see that an active Convocation was needed, and soon afterwards Lord Aberdeen agreed. He required a commendatory letter from Sumner which was obtained quickly by Blomfield to strengthen his hand in Parliament. The battle was over. Convocation met 6–9 February 1855 and did a great deal of useful work. The Archbishop told the Prime Minister that there were many demands the clergy would accept from Convocation which they would not accept from an individual bishop and agreed that the lower house might sit for as long as business required. There were many frustrations ahead, especially as Lord Aberdeen went out of office soon afterwards, which meant that further petitions for more freedom were coldly received. Blomfield persuaded both houses to petition the Queen on 28 June 1855 that the constitution of Convocation be modified, but the royal reply was disappointing: 'Her Majesty has not been advised to comply with its prayer'. But now at least the Church had a central body, a sacred synod, to discuss its business and legislate if necessary. Wilberforce and Blomfield had begun the democratisation of the Church of England.

In every sphere in the nineteenth century men were putting new wine into old bottles. In the Established Church there were so many legal, ecclesiastical and political problems that it was impossible to make tidy plans full of logic. Despite this, Church and State between them hewed out a breathing space in their relationship which has lasted until today. The continuation of an Established Church was made possible by the formation of the Ecclesiastical Commission, and the Church today is still the one to which the sovereign must conform, the one whose bishops sit in Parliament, and which still has an inalienable claim to ecclesiastical property.

During the reforms of the 1830s Blomfield led the way, and his great capacity for business and his immense practicality fitted him for such a role. Sydney Smith thought he possessed the greatest power in the Church since Laud, (whose description by Trevor-Roper also fits Blomfield: 'that little active wheel that set all the rest to work by his active motion'.) Many thought the Bishop inconsistent, which was probably true because he was always ready to change his opinions if he was proved wrong. Some considered his ideas were second-hand, but he had the courage to put them into practice and to do what others could not or would not do. This brought him much unpopularity. One thing is certain – whereas in the liturgical and doctrinal reform of the Church of England several names come to mind, in the administrative reforms which came three hundred years later, only one man stands out: Blomfield.

Chapter Six

In the diocese

*If upon some occasions my opinion may appear to you too decided
or the expression of my wishes too earnest you will, I trust, ascribe
it to the sincerity of my convictions and not suspect me of being
deficient in feelings of sincere respect and affection for my brethren.
I am accessible to reason and thankful for advice.*
Bishop of London's *Charge*, 1830.

Blomfield was appalled at the godlessness of London people, blaming
it on the scarcity of ministers and church buildings, and he lost no
time in hitting out at abuses, beginning in May 1830 with *A Letter on
the Present Neglect of The Lord's Day* addressed to the inhabitants of
London and Westminster. He denounced Sunday trading, steam
packets on the Thames 'crowded with gaily dressed sabbath break-
ers', Sunday newspapers, race outings, dinner parties, card games,
and he reserved his fiercest venom for the upper classes who, he
said, ought to know better. Several papers poured abuse on the
Bishop's letter, including *The Times* which branded him a puritan.

Charles Dickens leaped to the defence of Londoners, writing his
Sunday under Three Heads as a reply, and Harriet Martineau poked
fun at the 'Prelate in his purple, sitting in his palace at Fulham counting the people who came for fresh air on their only day off in seven'.
Despite opposition the *Letter* won much support from the middle
classes and it speedily went through seven editions.

London and all the big towns presented a particular problem to the
Church because 'the quiet customary alliance of church and gentry
working more by attractive influence and unostentatious pressure than
by bluster or bayonet could not operate there'. The church found it
hard to fit into the slums and dingy urban housing estates. One-class
parishes, usually working-class, were a new phenomenon far
removed from rural parishes with their mixture of gentry, middle
class and labourers. Blomfield realised that the higher classes had no

legitimate influence in towns, so they could not work hand in hand with the clergy, and he tried hard to alert people to the spiritual needs of London and other large towns, but few saw the urgency. Even Sir Robert Peel was surprised in 1835 to learn that a lay impropriator who owned the parish tithes and church property could receive £2,000 p. a. and only pay the incumbent £50 p. a. and that some incumbents relied solely on pew rents and Easter offering for their income. Peel, because his brother-in-law had a cathedral stall worth £1500 p. a. and four livings together worth £3000 p. a., was shocked at the existence of the Society for Clothing Indigent Establishment Clergy, and Howley had to assure him that such an organisation existed.

In his diocese the Bishop liked to think of himself as a disciplinarian, but in fact he was not good at putting ideas into practice. He often made the mistake of trying to please everyone with the usual result of pleasing nobody. Because his ideas were uncertain and vague they were often difficult to understand and impossible to put into practice. He belonged to no particular church party, which was an advantage in that he could see clearly the different factions, but a disadvantage because his remarks were often so ambiguous that each party interpreted them as support for its cause. Evangelicals were barred in Exeter, Tractarians in Winchester, but London was big enough for all to live side by side.

The gross income of the Bishop of London in 1829 amounted to £22,139 p. a. (£841,283) but fell to an average of £15,000 (£570,000) over the next seven years and remained at this level until the Bishop's retirement. The account books, now kept at the Guildhall Library, make interesting reading and reveal that the expenses of Blomfield's translation from Chester amounted to £755 17s 4d (£29,000), and that each year the Bishop sent 10 guineas to the doorkeeper and 10 guineas to the coach callers at the House of Lords and 10s (£19) to his Minute Carrier. The vergers at St Paul's Cathedral received only one gift, in 1846, of £5 (£225).

The new Bishop's patronage was considerable. He alone appointed his five archdeacons (London, Middlesex, Essex, Colchester and St Albans), and in his cathedral he appointed the chancellor, precentor and treasurer as well as thirty prebendaries who all received a stipend. In the diocese he held patronage of 12 City churches (5 alternating with another patron) and 65 other incumbencies. In his gift he also held 7 livings in other dioceses.

To many Blomfield appeared doctrinally uncertain; his convictions never seemed to shape themselves into a definite and coherent theology or philosophy. P. G. Welch says, 'His doctrinal pronouncements seemed either confusing or opportunist ... His debating powers, generally so considerable, seemed in doctrinal matters to desert him. Often no one really knew where he stood'.[1] However, as Welch says, the Bishop did 'originate a tradition of impartiality and comprehensiveness which the London diocese has never quite lost sight of'. Arthur Foley Winnington-Ingram continued this tradition when he presided over the diocese 1901–39 and it continues today.

Blomfield commanded nothing except an obedience to the rubrics and canons of the Church. His 1830 Charge tightened up discipline regarding plurality, non-residence, and the training of ordinands, he forbade baptisms and churchings in private houses, and insisted that he license all preachers. In this Charge he said that he preferred confirmation candidates to be aged sixteen at least, and he showed great foresight by appealing for 'one or more theological seminaries' so that ordinands could be trained properly. He also supported weekday prayers in church even if numbers were low, and suggested that parochial visiting associations be founded. These would enable the laity to keep an eye on their non-church neighbours. Coleridge called this scheme 'a scotch eldership in disguise'.

Blomfield was one of the first bishops to revive the ancient office of rural dean, the eyes and ears of the bishop, and in 1833 appointed 47 men each to preside over 10 or so parishes. The Bishop also showed remarkable gifts of foresight on church affairs. On 18 September 1841, whilst on holiday in North Devon, he writes to Dr Pusey about the question of training colleges for the clergy. He says these are urgently needed particularly for men wishing to work abroad and those who have come over to the church from 'various dissentory bodies', three of whom were in touch with him at the time. He tells Pusey that the National Society and SPG have asked him to help found some training colleges and to expound his thinking about the whole question. He also explains his ideas about ordination and points out that he has never ordained men from Dublin, on the principle that they should not desert their own church, and that curacies in this country should go to men from English universities.[2]

Blomfield's foresight can also be seen in his letter to the Archbishop of Canterbury, 11 January 1847. On the subject of employing more clergymen in the service of the Church, he says that both he and several other bishops would like to see more men admitted to the permanent diaconate, and suggests that Scripture readers be officially recognised because of the invaluable work they do amongst people the clergy cannot reach. He also asks that the Church recognise 'an order or class of laymen as Readers or Catechists'.[3]

In various letters during 1842 the Bishop said he was pleased that the clergy were now saying the daily Offices in church and suggested that country clergy follow suit. He said that he did not want to find any church in his diocese where Communion was only celebrated quarterly but seems to be in some doubt about weekly communions; he points out, however, that the Prayer Book implies that Communion should be held more than three times a year. Amongst other suggestions he asks that the Prayer for the Church Militant be said, and he ruled that a surplice should be worn at the Eucharist.

The Bishop realised that the lot of a town incumbent was not a happy or lucrative one. Anthony Trollope says this is in fact the least honoured if not the least honourable task in the clerical profession;

> he is subjecting himself to the heaviest clerical work but with a small prospect of large clerical loaves or fine clerical fishes; and he is prepared to live in a much lower social rank than that which is enjoyed by his more fortunate brothers in the country. The country parson is all but the Squire's equal ... but the town incumbent is not equal to the town Mayor, and in the estimation of many of his fellow townsmen is hardly superior to the town beadle.

People come to his church because it is the nearest, or because the pews are cheap or because they like his preaching. He does not know all the families in his parish as does his rural counterpart.

> Those who want him will come to him and pay him as they do the baker or the dentist. If they don't think he suits them then they will leave him ... if he can fill his church he will live well and become sleek. Among town incumbents the rusty greatly exceed the sleek in numbers.

The Tractarians

The Evangelical and the Tractarian parties in the Church had tried to help the urban clergy face up to their tasks. Trollope was suspicious of Evangelicals because he said they were not gentlemen, but he thought that Puseyites stirred up throughout the country so strong a feeling of religion that it made 'episcopal idleness impossible and clerical idleness rare'.[4]

The Tractarians caused Blomfield much trouble, and his dealings with them are not impressive. Unlike many other bishops, he did not actively oppose them until after 1842. He had always been suspicious of them and in 1839 he thought they were 'corrupting the simplicity of the gospel of Jesus Christ and the scriptural character of our own

Church', but he did admit that 'they have placed many points concerning the Church's authority and office in a striking point of view and have done much to counteract the evil effects of that low church spirit which has of late years weakened the Church and encouraged the Dissenters'.[5]

It seems odd that the bishops paid little heed to the Tractarian Movement during its early years. Considering that men like Newman had a high view of the episcopal office, it is not surprising that he should ask 'What might not the movement have been if the bishops had understood us?'. Silence is a weapon which members of the bench still use daily, particularly with difficult correspondents whose letters are ignored, but their reticence in the 1830s may have been due to the uncertainty surrounding the ideas put forward concerning doctrine, ceremonial and discipline by the Tractarians. Lord Melbourne, who had a passing interest in matters theological, if not ecclesiastical, was very confused. Writing to Lord Holland he complained, 'I hardly make out what Puseyism is. Either I am dull or its apostles are very obscure. I have got one of their chief Newman's publications with an appendix of four hundred and forty-four pages. I have read fifty-seven and cannot say I understand a sentence or any idea whatever.'[6] The writing of tracts was usually an Evangelical pastime, but men like Newman, Keble and Pusey questioned why the Evangelicals were obsessed with biblical writings and ignored those of later centuries.

The Tractarians failed to fit into any political party pattern. They did not support the Tories, whose taste for tradition should have appealed to them, but neither were they supporters of the Whigs, who had blotted their copybook by attacking the Irish Church. Keble and Newman toyed with disestablishment and disendowment, so it is not surprising that in the 1830s the bishops, including Blomfield, found it hard to understand what the Oxford Movement stood for. It was obvious that its members wanted to recall the Church of England to its catholic heritage, but did this mean a return to Rome? In 1835 Bishop Sumner of Chester declared his opposition, and Wilson of Calcutta denounced Tractarian teaching as a corrupt and cancerous mass. Phillpotts of Exeter and Sumner of Winchester spoke appreciatively at first, but later changed their minds, Sumner refusing to admit Keble's curate to priest's orders. Bagot of Oxford kept silence until 1838 saying he admired their 'devotional spirit' but when *Tract XC* was published he commanded that no more should be issued.

The early Tractarians had little interest in ceremonial; their discussions centred on doctrine, which was of no concern to the majority of church people. Later, when their teaching began to influence the apparel of the minister and the conduct of services, everyone from the Prime Minister downward felt involved. A wish to express continuity with the past and a desire to introduce dignity and beauty into liturgy inspired changes in ceremonial, bringing colour and music into the Communion service. The first centre for this was the Margaret Chapel where from 1839 Frederick Oakeley's devotion and industry attracted large numbers. Gladstone told Blomfield that he felt the congregation there was the most absorbed in devotion he had ever seen in any country or communion.

Two years earlier, after consulting Pusey, Blomfield had appointed Oakeley the preacher for the University of Oxford at the Chapel Royal, Whitehall, an appointment which greatly pleased Newman. 'You will have very elegant and interesting sermons from him'. This was not quite as easy as it sounds, because the acoustics of the chapel were so poor that many found it hard to hear anything, and Sir Robert Peel, a regular worshipper, asked for printed copies of the sermons because, although present, he had not heard a word of any of them.[7] On 5 July 1839 Blomfield appointed Oakeley to the Margaret Chapel – a somewhat surprising move as a few months earlier he had agreed that Oakeley's printed sermons could be dedicated to him, but had withdrawn his consent when he read the fifty-seven-page preface. Dr Galloway, Oakeley's biographer, considers that Pusey once again influenced Blomfield, who was either being very forgiving or was finding it hard to find a suitable candidate for the job.[8]

The Margaret Chapel was an eighteenth-century building which Oakeley described as 'a complete paragon of ugliness ... low, dark and stuffy; it bore no other resemblance to the Christian fold than that of being choked with sheep pens under the name of pews ... it was begirt by a hideous gallery filled on Sundays with uneasy school-children'.[9] The sanctuary was filled by a three-decker pulpit reaching almost to the ceiling, and there was no central aisle. An holy table was just visible behind the pulpit. Oakeley, a gentle, lame academic, had no wish to leave his fellowship at Balliol College, Oxford, but had been inspired by Newman, Pusey and Keble, so agreed to take charge of this odd building and turn it into a showcase of Tractarian worship. The pulpit and pews were removed, the altar adorned with a crimson frontal, cross, candlesticks and triptych placed above it, daily Offices were said and regular Communions celebrated.

> I can honestly say that the motive which actuated me in trying to improve upon the ceremonial practice ... was to give worship as much reverential beauty as was consistent with the strict obser-

vance of such rubrics as were plain and incontrovertible, and free interpretation of others which seemed to me to admit without undue straining of a more catholic sense than that which they commonly received ... I must maintain that the ritual at Margaret Chapel whatever may be said for or against it, was simplicity itself ... no Catholic however uneducated, could possible have mistaken the communion service at Margaret Chapel for High Mass.

For the next six years Oakeley was a frequent visitor to London House, having to explain to his diocesan why he had candles and flowers on the altar and why he wore a surplice. Were they decorative, or symbolic of sinister practices? Blomfield agreed that the candles could stay only if they were unlit and the flowers could be arranged provided they were of mixed colours and not red on festivals of martyrs or white on virgins' days. In 1842 he wanted to know if the Roman Breviary or any other Roman Catholic book of devotion was in use at Margaret Street. Are crucifixes used 'in this institution as stimulants to private devotion?' Oakeley usually did as the Bishop commanded, and in later life he wrote that these situations were probably 'as painful to his Lordship as they were to me. I am sure that in all his dealings with me he was activated by a conscious sense of duty while I am not so sure that on my side I was as careful as I ought to have been to make due allowance for the difficulty of his position'.[10]

In February 1845 following an open letter to the Vice-Chancellor of Oxford University, Oakeley wrote another open letter to Blomfield claiming the right to hold but not to teach all Roman Catholic doctrine. The Bishop once again sent for him, but what appeared a pleasant interview resulted in Blomfield later demanding Oakeley's resignation, no reason being given. Several letters were exchanged and Gladstone wrote to the Bishop describing Oakeley as 'a restorer of the inward life and spirit of divine worship among us'. On 26 February Oakeley was informed that his diocesan was not now minded to revoke his licence, but needed to consider what action should be taken, so permission was given to stay at Margaret Street temporarily on the condition that no Roman Catholic doctrines were taught or preached. In a private interview the Bishop was kindly, and it seemed that no proceedings would be taken, but at London House Blomfield was saying he would proceed 'cautiously and regularly'. Diocesan lawyers were consulted, and in June Oakeley was prosecuted under the provisions of the Church Disciplne Act of 1840. Preliminary hearings were held, but many supporters including Gladstone feared the worst and the affair filled several columns in the newspapers. On 3 June, realising he could not win, Oakeley resigned, but Blomfield said he intended to persevere with the case and declined to accept the resignation. Oakeley refused to appear or to be represented at the Hearing in the Court of Arches which began on 9 June. Three weeks later Sir Herbert Jenner Fust delivered his verdict, saying he felt that he must 'for the sake of the public, inflict such a punishment as may have the effect of preventing others from falling into the same errors'. Oakeley's licence was revoked, and he was forbidden to discharge any priestly duties until he 'shall appear or retract his errors'. When he decided to become a Roman Catholic four months later he tried to persuade his congregation to follow him, but they were determined to keep the Chapel as a centre of Tractarian life and liturgy. All this could have given Blomfield an opportunity to close the place down, particularly as the lease from the Crown estate expired in 1848, but instead he promoted William Upton Richards, the assistant minister, to take Oakeley's place. He was made incumbent four years later, then vicar in 1868. This act of kindness meant that All Saints', Margaret Street, continued and continues to be an important centre of Anglo-Catholic spirituality. Blomfield remained friendly to All Saints' and somewhat ill-advisedly wrote in 1851 to Charles Baring, the rector of nearby All Souls', Langham Place, forbidding him or his curate to visit any parishioner of All Saints'. The *Record* got to hear of it and reported that a dying woman had refused the ministrations of Richards, 'a Puseyite', and had asked Baring to visit. *Punch* in a cartoon showed Blomfield taking up a red-hot poker marked Puseyism and burning himself with it.[11]

Newman's *Tract XC*, published early in 1841, shook the Church. Blomfield reserved judgement, but wrote a private letter to a clergyman in Oxford saying that he hoped many tutors and 'men of weight' in the university would protest against it. 'It is really hardly possible to believe that the writer of such a Tract can be of the Reformed Church'. After reading it he said to a dinner table of young clergy, 'No power on earth should induce me to ordain any person who held systematically the opinions of that Tract'.[12] On 2 March he said he hoped no more tracts would be published, and by the end of 1841 many people in the diocese and beyond were asking him to state his views in public. 'The eyes of all are upon you', said Dr Hook, the vicar of Leeds; 'We are prepared to follow as you shall lead'. In his reply the Bishop observed that the Tractarians only seemed to obey one bishop (of Rome), and said his views on the matter would please nobody because he was unable to agree with any particular party.

The Charge of 1842 caused a greater reaction than all the other Charges put together. In it the Bishop referred to the 'learned and pious men who are calling attention to a branch of duty too long imperfectly performed', observing the commands of the rubrics of the Church. He warned his clergy not to try to make the Articles of Religion mean something they were not intended to mean. He attacked the Roman Catholic Church which, he said, was very sly in trying to blur the edges between herself and the reformed churches. 'It is us who have to go all the way to meet her, their rulers will not advance to meet us'. 'What real good is to be effected by any attempts to make our reformed church appear to sympathize with that from which she has been separated in some of the very points which formed the ground of that separation, I am at a loss to imagine.' He commended some of the Tractarian practices – daily prayers in church, observance of fasts and feasts, baptism at public services and more frequent celebrations of Holy Communion, monthly if not weekly. These are not novelties, he observed, but a return to what the rubrics direct. Discretion will be needed when reintroducing them.

His ruling on church ornaments was that attention should be paid not to the usage of the early church but to the rubrics and canons. Flowers should not be placed on the Communion Table – 'this is worse than frivolous', the candles on the Table must only be lit at Evening Prayer, and the correct wear for preaching at morning service is a surplice although a gown is permissible. He said he heartily disapproved of the books of devotion recently published which contained many superstitions, Roman and unscriptural practices such as prayers to saints ('a practice which began in poetry and ended in idolatry'), intercessions for the dead, auricular confession (a practice 'utterly unknown to the primitive Church' and a source of unspeakable abominations), and mixing water with wine at Holy Communion.

The Charge was well received at first – only the *Record* voiced its opposition, because it said the Bishop was propounding the doctrine of baptismal regeneration. The *Christian Examiner* published a series of articles refuting the Bishop's views. P. J. Welch says, 'Blomfield deeply offended those who believed that the character of renunciation, of repentance, of obedience to Christ Jesus was the true, the genuine spiritual regeneration and that baptism brought pardon and salvation only when repentance and faith accompanied it'.[13]

The Times and the *Church and State Gazette* gave favourable accounts of the Charge, and Evangelicals like J. W. Cunningham, vicar of Harrow for fifty years and the editor of the *Christian Observer* welcomed it because it seemed to condemn Roman Catholic teaching. Many, however, thought it too lenient towards the

Puseyites, and *Punch*, as usual, cruelly suggested the Bishop might give a lecture to a Mechanics' Institute on 'Church Candles: Showing how you may with the same breath blow them out and blow them in again'.

The quietness was shattered when Blomfield began to make concessions. Archdeacon Hale had already alienated the Islington clergy by his Charge of May, 1843. Now they told their Bishop that it was not possible for them to comply with some of his instructions. The Bishop gave in to them on one or two minor points (wearing a gown for preaching, and omitting the prayer for the Church Militant after Morning Prayer). Immediately other parishes began to seek concessions. The Bishop was placed in an awkward position, because in some parishes the incumbent had supported him in face of his people's opposition. Whom was the Bishop to support now? He did not know what to do.

At the beginning of 1845 Howley intervened, asking for hostilities to cease, and the *status quo* to be maintained until an authoritive statement could be made. The Bishop realised that a return to the rubrics' commands was good in theory but hard in practice owing to centuries of neglect. He tried to consider each parish and its needs separately, and wrote many letters of direction to individual clergy. 'Most motley will be the state of the diocese in a few more Sundays', screamed the *Record*. In several of his letters[14] he shows that his views regarding rubrical obedience remain unchanged, but enforcing them must be left to the parish clergy to do in their own time.

The whole affair was very damaging to the Bishop's reputation in his diocese. His health was not good, which might partly explain his weakness, but as Dean Church wrote later, 'He was singularly unsure of himself' in this particular matter. His compromises seem strange and his views on ceremonial odd, but such matters were taken very seriously indeed at this time. Victorian religion without doctrine was unthinkable, and, as ceremonial expressed doctrine, it was accorded much importance.

Blomfield was, in fact, very patient with the Tractarians who quite incorrectly interpreted his Charge as giving unqualified approval to their conduct. Many of them were hard working parish priests, but complaints about their teaching and ritual poured in to the Bishop. In his next Charge, of 1846, he denounced the Oxford Movement in no uncertain terms, saying it had undermined the very foundations of the Christian faith. The Tractarians in consequence felt let down because their so called supporter was now attacking them.

Saint Paul's, Knightsbridge

The Bishop now began several campaigns against the Tractarians, the most famous of which was the long-drawn-out quarrel with W. J. E. Bennett, vicar of St Paul's, Knightsbridge. Bennett had been appointed to this, his first living, in 1842, so was a member of the congregation in St Paul's when Blomfield delivered his controversial 1842 Charge. Bennett later wrote that he had already agreed with much of what the Oxford divines taught, but had doubted whether he should openly follow it. The Bishop's Charge dispelled all doubts. 'It seemed to say, "Follow these men in their practices and doctrines, allowing for some few exceptions. Do not go into certain extremes; yet, in the main, follow them and you will be consenting to my wishes as your Bishop".'[15]

St Paul's was a very lively church. It had the care of 14,000 people, and Sunday services were well attended. Matins was sung at 11 am followed by the Eucharist with usually 120 communicants, ending about 2.30pm. Baptisms and Churchings followed, and then two well-attended Evensongs, one sung and one plain. Each day there were Morning and Evening Prayers and a Eucharist and Lord John Russell, a communicant member of St Barnabas, said he had learned more about the Church from Bennett than from anyone else. He was to change his mind. The drawback of St Paul's was that all sittings cost £15 p. a. which meant that the poor of the parish from the Pimlico area had nowhere to worship. Bennett decided to build a church with all its sittings free, and within six years of his induction the church of St Barnabas, Pimlico, with its school and clergy house, had been built. No one thought Blomfield would consecrate it, so great was the terrible list of enormities! – although he did consecrate other splendidly-decorated churches such as St Stephen Rochester Row. On 2 May 1848 he came to inspect the church. He said he disliked the screen as a matter of private taste but made no objection as long as there was no crucifix on it. Much to Bennett's surprise, the Bishop only objected to three things: the oak eagle lectern (some suggested he feared an idolatrous worship of the bird), flowers on the altar, and the cross on the altar. 'If it costs me my See I will have that cross removed'. One churchwarden removed it: the other put it back, nailing it to the table. There it remained.

The church was consecrated by Blomfield on 11 June 1850, and in his sermon he drew attention to the marks of the Catholic Church, saying that a lack of discipline is no reason to desert the fellowship of believers. Similarly there is no reason to leave if a doctrine is rejected by a few people: this does not invalidate the doctrine. The defects of the Church of England lie in its discipline, not its doctrine. At the supper afterwards the Bishop spoke warmly of Bennett's pastoral zeal and his vision in building the new church. The services at St Barnabas attracted large crowds and Bennett, 'a man of the poor', was a good preacher although during the Octave of St Barnabas he invited Keble, Pusey, Manning and Samuel Wilberforce to occupy the pulpit. On the day Pusey preached, the church was full an hour before the service began, the altar ablaze with '20 or 30 little tapers exactly like those at the oratory'.[16]

Soon afterwards the Bishop began to complain to Bennett of 'further deviations from the ordinary forms of our Church'. After a fortnight to consider the Bishop's letter, Bennett replied on 15 July 1850 saying that he disliked being continually watched, pried into, hunted down, complained of and accused unjustly, and he offered his resignation. The practices that the Bishop objected to included making the sign of the cross, beginning the sermon with the invocation of the Trinity, prayers for the dead, too much prominence being given to the surpliced choir, bowing at the Gloria Patri, altar lights and the eastward position at the consecration. Bennett said that he wanted help and guidance from his Bishop; it is to Blomfield's discredit that he did not reply for three months, but in his letter of 18 October the Bishop again ordered Bennett to give up these practices. Two weeks later Bennett replied, saying that he had given up some of the practices, but he referred the Bishop back to an earlier letter in which he had said that he would not give up the ancient practices of the Catholic Church if there was no definite prohibition of them in the Anglican formularies. He said he would continue to use the crucifixes and vestments, but again offered his resignation. A few days later Blomfield refused to ordain a curate on Bennett's nomination, and on 2 November he delivered a scathing attack on the Tractarians in his 1850 Charge. He denounced Romish practices which make church services 'almost histrionic'. 'I really cannot characterise by any gentler term the continual changes of postures, the frequent genuflections, the crossings, the peculiarities of dress ...'

The situation had been sorely aggravated by what became known as the 'Papal Aggression' which took place two months before the Bishop's Charge. In September the Pope had issued a Bull restoring the Catholic hierarchy in England and Wales, dividing up the country into dioceses. Territorial titles were obviously more convenient than the arrangement that had given Cardinal Wiseman the absurd title of Bishop of Melipotamus in Partibus Infidelium. Now he was to be the Archbishop of Westminster. The uproar caused meant that sheriffs of every county called meetings, and there were numerous Addresses and petitions. *Punch* in a cartoon depicted the Pope consecrating bishops of Clapham, Pimlico, Mile End and Margate. Lord John Russell speaking for the majority told the Queen that Pope and Puseyite constituted a threat to the Established Church. She was a willing listener and later told Lord Derby that Puseyites were unsuitable for preferment.

Blomfield's November Charge noted that innovations in ceremonial were now more frequent but it was difficult, he said, to stop them unless the law expressly forbade them. Five practices were particularly condemned: using books of devotion which gave all but divine honour to the Virgin Mary, making the mediation of the Saints a probable doctrine, prayers for the dead, using the sign of the cross and attributing a propitiatory value to the Holy Communion. 'A layman' pointed out that many observances now being adopted had nothing to do with Rome but were an inheritance of the Holy Catholic Church, but 264 London diocesan clergy joined Archdeacon Sinclair in presenting their Bishop with an Address congratulating him on exposing the 'character of the aggression made by the Bishop of Rome'. In reply Blomfield said the clergy must abstain from doing or saying anything which might bear the semblance of the doctrines of an erring, corrupt church. Certain practices had been laid aside by the Reformers and should not be reintroduced.

Riots began in St Barnabas and several other London churches on Sunday 10 November. Services were continually interrupted and several ugly scenes ensued outside. On 17 November a rabble led by Goss, a butler from Bryanston Square, tried to force their way into the church, but plain-clothes police kept them out. Goss was arrested and charged but Broderip, the magistrate, dismissing the charges used the occasion to deliver a discourse on the evils of Puseyism.

Matters were not helped by the intervention of the Prime Minister, whom Blomfield liked and respected. He had recently visited him to inquire about the mental health of the Duke of Wellington. The incident that worried the Bishop was trivial but amusing. A tiresome, troublesome horticulturalist, Mrs London who wrote books and pamphlets on trees, had written to the Duke for permission to measure his beeches. The Duke looked at the signature, C. J. London, and said 'What the devil can the Bishop of London want with my breeches?' He wrote to the Bishop to ask if the breeches he wore at Waterloo would be the ones the Bishop wanted to measure. Blomfield, thinking the Duke had gone mad, went to consult the Prime Minister. At length the matter was cleared and everyone enjoyed the joke.[17]

Lord John Russell now angered the Bishop by writing an open letter to the Bishop of Durham saying that the danger to the Church was not from the Papal Aggression but from the ministers of the Established Church who were 'step by step leading their flocks to the verge of the precipice'. He called upon the people of England to uphold the glorious principles of the Reformation. Several took the Prime Minister's advice too seriously and the riots continued. At one time they were so severe that men from Knightsbridge Barracks had to link arms to stop people pushing their way into the sanctuary of St Barnabas' Church. Much abuse was hurled at Bennett. At a public meeting Lord Shaftesbury announced that he would rather worship with Lydia by the banks of the riverside than worship at Mr Bennett's church. Someone else suggested that the church had the wrong patron saint: it should not be the Apostle Barnabas but the robber Barabbas.

On 16 November the Bishop again asked Bennett to give up the disputed ritual. In his reply of the 23rd Bennett said he was under pressure from the mob, and had no intention of changing anything. Four days later the Bishop asked him to give up the ritual in question or resign. On 4 December Bennett again sent his resignation and on 11 December he received a reply dated 9 December accepting it. Unfortunately the last page was missing. This was never sent to Bennett and his biographer firmly believed that all the Bennett–Blomfield correspondence, including this letter, was sent to the editor of *The Times* who forwarded this particular letter to Bennett after he read it. There is no proof of this, but Bennett gave his permission for publication after the presses had been set up![18] Next morning, *The Times* published the Bishop's version of the whole correspondence in *ex parte* extracts, and one of the main leaders of the paper vigorously condemned Bennett. The *Guardian*, whilst deploring the resignation, said that Bennett ought to have obeyed his bishop. The *Morning Chronicle* condemned the Bishop, asking him which principles of Mr Bennett he had objected to. Blomfield refused to say and also declined to receive a deputation from the parishioners. For the Bishop this very unsavoury affair had now closed. He remained silent on the subject but did remark to a friend, 'If I have erred in Mr Bennett's case it has been from too great forbearance'.

The Bishop never solved doctrinal matters from a legal or canonical standpoint, preferring to enforce his own arbitrary wishes. It is doubtful whether Bennett, despite his high doctrine of episcopacy, would have obeyed his diocesan, but Blomfield was also at fault in not going to see Bennett to talk the whole affair over with him.

Correspondence was a cold and unsympathetic way of dealing with a problem which was only a few miles away. However, it is to the Bishop's credit that four years later, after a domestic crisis in Bennett's family, on 6 November 1854 he wrote to him

> My dear Sir –
> Although unfortunately estranged from you by the events which took place while you were under my jurisdiction, I have not ceased to feel an interest in your welfare; and I hope you will not take it amiss, if I assure you of my sincere sympathy, under the heavy affliction with which it has pleased God to visit you; and of my prayers that it may please Him ... to give you strength to bear it ... I am, my dear sir, your faithful servant, C. J. London.[19]

The new vicar of St Paul's, Knightsbridge, was Robert Liddell, the younger brother of Lord Ravensworth and incumbent of Barking. He soon incurred the wrath of Westerton, one of his churchwardens, but the Bishop pointed out to Westerton that the rubrics and canons were being observed, and the services held by Liddell and his assistants, who included Charles Lowder, were popular and well attended. The Evangelicals supported Westerton, and on 18 July 1854 Admiral Harcourt presided over a well-supported meeting which protested at the 'Jack-pudding antics' of Liddell and his liking for 'millinery and bijouterie'. A lawsuit followed which reached the Privy Council, but the judgment there was indecisive. Charles Lowder, then aged thirty-three, went on to be one of the great slum priests of the century, but had caused consternation at St Barnabas by giving sixpence to a cousin of his who was a schoolboy at Christ's Hospital, to pelt with rotten eggs a sandwich man who was urging parishioners to vote for Westerton as churchwarden. The man complained to his employer, who called the police. Charles was hauled before the magistrate and admitted his offence, apologised, and the case was dismissed. The newspapers took the story up and on 3 May 1854 a note arrived at the clergy house: 'The Bishop of London requests the Revd C. F. Lowder to call at London House tomorrow at half-past ten o'clock'. Three days later Blomfield wrote severely:

> I consider it to be my imperative duty to mark my sense of the scandal occasioned to the church by your late indiscreet conduct. I had at first thought it would be necessary to revoke your licence but in consideration of your having made, though somewhat tardily, a public acknowledgement of your fault, I shall content myself with suspending you from the exercise of your functions as

a curate of Saint Barnabas for the space of six weeks ... In the way of punishment, I am sure that your own feelings will have been enough. I trust that you may be able to regain for yourself and for the Church the ground which you have lost.

Later the Bishop said the incident had not altered his opinion of Lowder as a 'zealous and conscientious clergyman' and was heard in conversation to refer to the eggs thrown as Mr Lowder's 'ovation'.[20]

Sisterhoods

One of the direct results of the Oxford movement was the flowering of the religious life in the Church of England after a gap of some three hundred years. Dr Pusey had long had this in mind and hoped his daughter Lucy would take vows as a nun, but sadly she died young. In 1845 he became the founder or 'spiritual superintendent' of a small house, 17 Park Village West, near Christ Church, Albany Street, in London, and eight residents arrived in the first few weeks. The inevitable committee was formed to oversee the project and Mr Gladstone, Lord Lyttelton and Lord Camden sat on it, as did Lord John Manners who wrote to Bishop Blomfield to enlist his support. He, however, said the proposal was dangerous at the present time.[21] But after consulting Archbishop Howley he wrote them a guarded letter which the committee took as permission to proceed, although Pusey always felt that religious orders need not be under the control of the diocesan bishop. The sisters were seen as nurses and visitors of the poor and few people cared about their vows or spiritual life. The idea soon caught on and several clergy considered setting up sisterhoods in their parishes, until Pusey pointed out that they were not just another parochial organisation. Their selfless devotion and piety began to wear down Protestant opposition but Blomfield was always cautious, particularly when a Mrs Welland testified that her sister aged thirty-five 'who was a bright healthy creature' had been driven to an early grave in 1854 by the bodily austerities she had endured at the Park Village Community.[22]

In his Charge of 1850 Blomfield said, 'I strongly deprecate the establishment of any religious or charitable society of females which shall have almost every peculiarity of a nunnery but the name. I fear that this is the case with some which have been already formed.' The sisters' work continued without his support – teaching in a school for poor children, running an orphanage and visiting the hovels of labourers near the Euston Road. Because of the lack of official episcopal support, many of the first sisters of the various new communities joined the Roman Catholic Church, including the first superior of Park Village West.

In a letter to Pusey of 3 December 1850 Blomfield explains his attitude further. He objects to the sisters of Park Village using Pusey's books of devotion and dislikes their being under the spiritual guidance of a clergyman who has no connection with the London diocese. The sisterhood's 'general tone and tendency appeared to me to be towards Rome ... Add to this that two instances at least were reported to me of young ladies who were admitted into the Institution against the earnest wishes of their nearest relations.' Pusey had another try to reassure him in 1855, but received a reply from Fulham, dated 4 June 1855.

My dear Dr Pusey,
I have ascertained the feelings of the clergy of that part of the Metropolis where Miss Sellon's Sisterhood is working and I am confirmed in my resolution not to sanction its introduction into my diocese. I write to decline all further discussion of the question. I am, my dear Dr Pusey, Yours faithfully, C. J. London.

In 1848 the Bishop did help found a sisterhood of nurses at 36 Fitzroy Square, but he assured everyone there would be no vows of poverty, chastity and obedience. He probably gave this venture his support because it was the brainchild of Robert Bentley Todd, a professor of medicine in the newly-founded King's College London of which the Bishop was chairman of governors. In 1840 Todd had helped to found King's College Hospital, and came to the conclusion that nurses needed a religious discipline to assist them in their work. He was an Irish Protestant which must have reassured Blomfield who told him that he knew of a Lutheran order of deaconesses in Kaiserswerth in the Rhineland where the women were not bound by vows. With the help of the new Principal of King's College, Richard Jelf, an inaugural meeting was held at Hanover Square Rooms on 13 July 1848 with the Duke of Cambridge in the chair. Four bishops attended including Blomfield, who as always stated his views in no uncertain terms: there must be no vows, no cloistered seclusion, 'no tyranny exercised over the will or conscience; but a full, free and willing devotion to the cause of Christian charity'. He agreed to chair the Council which would employ a Master and a Lady Superintendent. Sisters were received on six months' probation, then on a two-year contract. They were expected to subscribe fifty pounds p. a. and their duties included training the nurses and giving them religious instruction. Nurses were engaged for five years and paid £1 a month. Each of them had to be baptised and bring a certificate from her parish incumbent saying that she was of good moral character. In 1851 there were nineteen nurses in the house.[23] As the local church was St John, Pancras, the sisters were and still are known as the Community of Saint John the Divine, their only house now being in Birmingham which in 1999 had eleven sisters and two novices in residence.

In the autumn of 1853 London was struck by an epidemic of cholera which lasted six months, so the sisters, now in 3/4 Queen Square, Westminster, helped at the local hospital. After this the number of sisters declined, and had it not been for the Crimean War all would have ended. The Master, the Revd C. P. Shepherd, asked permission to take some nurses to Scutari. Blomfield went to see Sidney Herbert, the Minister of War, but was told that the proposed expedition would be led by Miss Florence Nightingale. She and Mr Herbert attended a council meeting chaired by the Bishop to discuss plans, and later six nurses were accepted by Miss Nightingale. On 21 October 1854 the party left Victoria Station *en route* for Paris and the Crimea, the 'ladies' refusing to share the same railway carriage as the 'hired nurses'. Shortly afterwards Dr Todd announced that he had asked St John's Community to take charge of the nursing at King's College Hospital, then in a derelict workhouse to the south of Lincoln's Inn Fields, and from 1857 onwards St John's House maintained a training school for probationer nurses.

The Bishop's dealings with the Tractarians do not do him credit. Doctrine was not his strong point and his efforts to interpret it through ceremonial practice were unconvincing. The wrangles over ceremonial came at a time when he was past his prime. The cares of the Church in his diocese, in the country and overseas were pressing so hard on him that he was unable to see clearly the issues at stake. His judgements were arbitrary and he often changed or modified them. *Punch* lampooned him unmercifully in 1854:

You object to the perpetual Bowing, [he is made to say] I quite agree with you and think that no persons should bow in church, except when they see an acquaintance, when of course, common politeness dictates smiling recognition, whatever part of the ceremony may be going on. But this practice is too universal among the orthodox to need my sanction. There is a very good paper in Addison's 'Spectator' on the subject, but, as its argument goes the other way, you need not read it unless you like.

Blomfield did occasionally try to exert his authority but found it difficult to be firm, and both his first biographer, Dr Biber, and Dean Church of St Paul's agree that particularly in ceremonial matters he was uncertain in purpose and vague in direction. Could he have been otherwise?

Chapter Seven

New churches

In the course of his long tenure at London Blomfield consecrated
nearly 200 new churches.
He was the dean of church-building bishops.
R. A. Soloway, *Prelates and People.*[1]

Shergold Boone, the formidable vicar of St John, Hyde Park, was
not a happy man in 1847 and he made sure Blomfield knew it.
Three thousand of his wealthy parishioners had been siphoned off
to create the new benefice of All Saints, Norfolk Square,
Paddington. To no avail he complained bitterly that pew rents worth
£877 (£40,000) had been lost to him. Disputes of this kind were
common, because Blomfield wanted to cut the size of London
parishes and build more churches. He promised Steventon, the first
incumbent of All Saints, that he would be given a vicarage, but the
Commissioners refused to help as they thought the parish was too
wealthy to receive a grant. Pew rents have rightly been condemned,
but they brought in a considerable income and meant that those who
could afford to pay them felt they had a stake in what went on in
their local parish. Incumbents like Augustin Edouart of St Michael,
Burleigh Street, Holborn saw the damage they did to poorer parishioners and called them 'an un-church-like tax' and 'a serious
obstacle'. Blomfield had two minds on the matter, seeming to
approve of the system because of the revenue they realised, telling
one dissatisfied correspondent that the demand for pews exceeded
their supply in wealthy areas. Even in the poor parish of St Luke,
Berwick Street, Soho where rents were low, the 608 pews brought
in an annual income of £467 (£18,680) almost all of which went to
the incumbent. The patron of the living, the rector of St James,
Piccadilly, said he would not be able to find the stipend in any other
way. Robert Brett, vicar of St Matthew, Stoke Newington, had to
dispense with a second curate when he gave the system up.

Blomfield, when rector of St Botolph, Bishopsgate, had realised that pew rents emphasised social distinctions in church so minutes before the service he opened all unoccupied pews, and later advised his clergy to do the same. He never resolved the dilemma and sent an episcopal scolding to the new incumbent of St James the Less, Bethnal Green, who was charging pew rents in this newly-built church, pointing out that an endowment had been given on the condition that all sittings were free. A correspondent in the *Record*, 22 July 1857, summed the situation up, suggesting that the poor will always stay away from church because 'they are not made to feel welcome there ... Almost invariably unless they dress like ladies and gentlemen, they are thrust into some out-of-the-way uncomfortable seat, behind a pillar or near the door.'

The Church of England in the early nineteenth century had made very little impact on the new urban areas and manufacturing districts, regarding them as larger versions of villages and country towns where a settled population was centred around a mediaeval church. To many the Church seemed fit 'only for the rich and for the refined, the repose of villages and the quiet dignity of arts and letters'. Blomfield knew this must change if the population of London were to receive the ministrations of the Established Church. A strategy must be put in place which would include building yet more places of worship. Since the Reformation there had been three eras of major church building – at the end of the seventeenth century after the Great Fire of London; then in 1711 when the Fifty New Churches scheme was presided over by architects such as Hawksmoor and Gibbs and in the early nineteenth century when Parliament gave two grants totalling £1.5m (£57m). Leading laity, like Joshua Watson who had earlier helped to found the National Society, worked to establish what came to be known as the Church Building Commission to oversee the spending of this money. Blomfield was appointed to the Commission in 1825, while still at Chester, and found that the Commission was instructed to help only parishes which could raise funds themselves or provide a site. Part of the seating was to be rented and part free. Some London congregations responded magnificently. Daniel Wilson, vicar of Islington, persuaded his people to vote £12,000 (£454,000) in 1825 to build St John, Upper Holloway which still stands, and St Paul, Balls Pond Road and Holy Trinity, Cloudesley Square which are used by others. The Commission gave £27,843 (£1,058,000) for the three churches. £20,000 (£750,000) was the maximum grant given by the Commission and 612 churches in England and Wales benefited including over ninety churches in the present London diocese.[2] However, by the mid 1830s Blomfield realised that all the money had been spent, although when loans were repaid further small grants could be made.

In his Charge of 1834 the Bishop gave some facts and figures: there were 608 benefices in his diocese with an average income of £399 p. a. (£16,000); the stipend of the 355 curates averaged £98 p. a. (£4,000) which meant, said the Bishop, that clergy were using their private income to subsidise the Church. In the east and north-east of the Diocese ten parishes containing 353,460 persons had 18 churches served by 24 clergy, so on average each church had to serve 19,000 and each minister care for 14,000 people. Blomfield felt that every 3,000 people should have a church with 2 ministers so in these 10 parishes there was a deficiency of 99 churches and 210 clergy. Today we would think this provision wildly generous, but many would also agree now that one priest cannot care for more than 6,000 people. In the Charge the Bishop reported that 64 new churches and chapels had been built in the Diocese since 1814 so now was the time to open more. He considered that if a church was built and a minister appointed then a hall, school, vicarage and even gymnasium would follow.

Money had to be raised and in 1835 many people, including Baptist Noel, petitioned Blomfield to open a Metropolitan Building Fund. According to Hugh James Rose the Evangelicals offered to raise £150,000 (£6m) for such a fund.[3] Blomfield had been in the Diocese six years and felt that he could now plan this building programme, so in April 1836 he published his *Proposals for the creation of a Fund to be applied to the Building and Endowment of additional churches in the Metropolis*. An earnest appeal was made by the Bishop 'to all the inhabitants of London and its suburbs who possess the means of doing good but especially to the owners of large property in the Metropolis; to great companies and commercial establishments; to the merchants, bankers and opulent tradesmen'. Appealing also to the clergy he told them he had already had promises of £40,000 (£1.5 million) and had himself given £2,000 (£76,000). Dr Biber suggests that during his episcopate Blomfield gave approximately £30,000 (£1,140,000) for church building, which included the erection and endowment of St Stephen, Hammersmith, at his sole expense. In later years he gave his reasons for starting this fund;

> I built churches as a means to an end. I considered that to build a new church in a district where the means of public worship were wanting was a sure way of increasing the number of clergymen in the district and that it would be a centre from which would radiate

all around the light of the Gospel truth and the warmth of Christian charity in the various benevolent institutes etc.[4]

Blomfield felt the spiritual destitution of London keenly. It was impossible, he said, to walk through the capital 'without seeing enough to make the heart faint'. There were districts like Whitechapel, a hotbed of crime, which only had one dingy church for 36,000 people and the nearby St Dunstan, Stepney, had to serve around 60,000 people. Even in Chiswick the vicar reported an increase in population from 3,000 to 5,000 in 1841 so Christ Church, Turnham Green, was opened to help relieve the situation.

Blomfield's first aim was to build fifty churches in the more thickly populated areas of London. Endowments would be made and patronage would rest with the bishop. He hoped for government help but anti-Church feeling had increased since 1818 so this was no longer possible. In June 1835 Blomfield presided over a distinguished company of people at London House and from them a committee was elected consisting of all shades of political and Anglican belief. Men such as Dr Pusey, Joshua Watson, Mr Gladstone and William Cotton agreed to serve on the committee, the King agreed to be Patron and Howley Vice-Patron. The Bishop did not mince his words, saying he had a right to call on everyone to sacrifice a few luxuries in order that men might be saved from irreligion and vice. Many thought the building programme too ambitious and Dr Chalmers, who was organising a similar appeal in Scotland, suggested that the target be much lower than fifty new churches. Dr Pusey who had been sent the proposals two months earlier by Blomfield, 'for the purpose of ascertaining whether it would meet your views', sent an anonymous gift of £5,000 (£190,000) which meant that he had to give up his carriage and reduce the number of his servants. The *Guardian*, founded by Tractarians, later commented that Pusey and his friends stopped the Fund degenerating into a 'mechanical distribution of certain Bethesda-like accumulations of bricks and mortar in ugliest but not by any means the cheapest forms throughout certain of the poorest parts of the Metropolis'.[5]

Londoners did not have to wait long for results, for within two months of the fund's being opened £74,000 (£2,812,000) was received and by the end of the year £106,000 (£4m) had been raised. The first new church, Christ Church, St Pancras, was consecrated in the following summer, 1837. The *British Critic* was full of praise for the Bishop: 'he has done what no other person could have done half so well'. In six years following the Fund's foundation several churches were consecrated, most of which have now disappeared although Christ Church, Chelsea, St James, Muswell Hill, and St John, Hyde Park, still stand and Holy Trinity, Stepney, is awaiting another use.[6] Every new project received the Bishop's careful attention. All Souls College, Oxford gave a site in Kensal Green for a new church and schools; £400 (£16,000) had been raised but £1,300 (£52,000) was still needed and this was beyond the means of the 3,000 inhabitants, most of whom were farmers and landworkers. Blomfield arranged to divert some of the income of the prebends of St Paul's who had land in Willesden, and the church of St John, Kensal Green, was thus built and opened in 1844. It still stands.

The clergy of London viewed the Bishop's plans with mixed feelings. Men like Dale, vicar of St Pancras where in 1847 at least 140,000 people lived, shared the Bishop's enthusiasm. When he became vicar in 1846 he found that although there were several daughter churches in the parish the Acts of 1816 and 1821, despite giving them definite districts to work, had not enabled their ministers to take baptisms, weddings and churchings there. These were limited to the parish church. The clergy working at the daughter churches had no security of tenure and were curates of the parish church. The vestry meeting tried to stop the vicar appealing to Parliament to have this changed, but after a great deal of negotiation the ten districts were given more independence and after 1851 their ministers could not be removed at will by the Bishop or the incumbent. Blomfield and Dale worked together to initiate this scheme, but they were continually harried by the necessity of parliamentary legislation at every step.

Blomfield did not find all his clergy so co-operative. He had to tell Shergold Boone that his personal feelings must not be allowed to stand in the way of progress in pastoral work, pointing out that 10,000 people was too big a population for one man to look after and that there should be a church and two clergymen for every 3,000 people. Where the population of a parish exceeded 4,000 another church should be built. Attempting to reassure Mr Boone, the Bishop told him that his fears were groundless because his 'talents and eloquence as a preacher' were well known. The incumbent of Eaton Chapel, now St Peter, Eaton Square, objected to the proposed new church in Chester Square which he said was almost on his threshold and was bound to interfere with his schools, and anyway only seven inhabitants of Chester Square were on the list of donors. Blomfield took no notice, probably because the Marquis of Westminster had given the site and £5,000 (£190,000) on the condition that he and his heirs had the patronage of the new living, and three pews in the gallery free from rent. It was not only clergy who were difficult. The church workers at St Jude, Bethnal Green, insisted on altering the church without the Bishop's permission, so he refused to give them a grant from the Bethnal Green Churches Fund. The wardens at St John, Bethnal Green, refused to light the church!

The Bethnal Green Fund

After the first enthusiasm had died down donations began to arrive more slowly, averaging £5,000 (£190,000) a year. In 1839 it was decided to open localised funds in order to stimulate fresh interest. The Bethnal Green Fund was the most successful of these – 10 new churches were built in the area, 19 more clergy were able to work there and 8 schools were opened. In 1840 the population of Bethnal Green, was about 70,000, served by St Matthew's, opened in 1746 and St John's (1828). The Fund built 10 churches so all twelve apostles were now represented. St James the Great (1844), nicknamed 'the Red Church', was given by the Bishop's sister and brother who also donated the school and vicarage. The church still stands and, like St Bartholomew, Buckhurst Street (1844), is now converted into apartments. The only other two buildings still standing are St Peter (1841) and St James the Less (1842) which are still in use as churches and St Matthias' School is still open. St Jude's School is now part of the Raine's Foundation School.

An interesting and amusing account of the clergy of these Bethnal Green churches is contained in a letter written by the Reverend J. Gibson, curate of St Matthew, Bethnal Green on 25 April 1859. Mr Gibson came to the East End in 1842 so knew the clergy well. He tells us that St Peter's, (whose present vicar, John Weir, now possesses the letter), 'retains Mr Packer as incumbent, a worthy man without much energy – the church about half filled on Sundays, the schools flourishing'. We are told St Andrew's had been most unfortunate with respect to the clergy:

> Mr Lawson, the first incumbent, though an excellent and learned man, was too much an ascetic in his habits and his sermons too erudite and recondite for Bethnal Green, so he was not the right sort of man. [Mr Woodard who succeeded him was] too Romanizing in his views and practices ... and he had been condemned by our late good and ever-to-be-lamented Bishop [Blomfield]. [Woodard] 'soon withdrew for Shoreham ... where his doings have been too notorious for you to be ignorant of them. He was followed by the Revd G. H. Parker from Plymouth whose sermons centred on the destinies of the French Empire ... His schools are shut up, his church almost empty ... he himself is now

very ill at Brighton ... and it is thought he can never recover – atrophy seems to be his disease.'

At St Philip's the Revd G. Alston annoyed Blomfield and 'tormented and defrauded the clergy by marrying for 2s 6d including all charges, thus he brought people from all parts of London ... and used frequently to join together fifty couples per diem'. Mr Trivitt, his successor, was an amiable man, also earning money from marriages, 'but a disciple of Kingsley and Maurice, very lax and liberal in his notions'.

St James the Less, Victoria Park, 'has proved a uniform failure until recently. The first incumbent, Mr Coghlan, was a most extravagant and worldly man and after being there some years to the injury and disgrace of the church left head and ears in debt for some chaplaincy at Berbice.' He was succeeded by the Revd H. P. Haughton, whose wife was sister to a lady of title, but he 'had an aversion to coming into contact with poor people ... he was a sort of perpetual blister to good Mr Cotton and to our late good Bishop'. An exchange was effected with a Mr Grundy,

> the present incumbent who has gone away for three months to recruit his health. I hear from several who know him well that he is far from being a hardworking man. His wife goes to bed last and gets up first, she superintends a Provident Club, schools, and meets the District Visitors and thus takes the greater part of the work out of his hands. He thinks of little else but preaching and it is said he has preached all his best sermons and is too idle to make more.

The Revd W. James, who succeeded the first vicar of St James the Great, proved in 1843

> a very inefficient and immoral man, his wife and children being in the country ... he went to bed with his servant maid ... the matter was so well known in the parish that his usefulness was at an end'. Therefore he exchanged livings with the present incumbent, Mr Coke who came from Plymstock, Devon. James there seduced a servant girl so ... threw up the living and has since without character or employment resided at Exmouth ... When at Plymstock Mr Coke out-Herods Herod and walked about the the village in a curiously-made cassock with a long girdle or sash hanging down at his right side and played rather odd pranks and vagaries and so disgusted the people that they caused the bells to ring when they knew he was to leave them.

In Bethnal Green he shut up his schools and bought a house for his family at Tottenham so 'he is seldom in residence'. Every winter he collected for the poor but no one knew what became of the money. 'About four weeks ago he knocked down a pauper in his hall who asked him for a receipt for some shillings he had been sent as payment for his copies of marriages ... he sprained the poor man's leg as well as nearly breaking his arm.' Mr Coke was summoned to appear before the magistrates: he had to pay £5 to the poor man and £5 for expenses. 'He told me a year ago he is a Roman Catholic at heart ... he seldom has 20 people in his church. St James the Great is indeed dead in the pot.'

Mr Vivien of St Bartholomew, Bethnal Green, received much praise in Mr Gibson's letter but at St Matthias, Hare Street, the Reverend Joseph Brown is condemned as 'the most scheming and contriving man I ever knew. He was very much patronised by Lord Shaftesbury and some of the others of that clique but certainly was and is the most gracious and successful clerical humbug I ever met with'. His successor, Mr Colebourne, 'is an exact facsimile of the illustrious Joseph Brown'.

St Jude had for its incumbent the Revd J. E. Keane, 'an eccentric Irishman, red hot evangelical who disgusted Blomfield by letting his pews'. St Simon Zelotes had a first incumbent dogged by ill health but his wife, Mrs Arsted, was 'a meddling and quarrelsome person ... The present incumbent, Mr Christie, is only a slug in the Lord's vineyard consequently there is scarcely any congregation ... St Thomas has an incumbent who fraternises too much with the Romanizing Party.' Even allowing for a certain bias in Mr Gibson's account, it appears that the clergy of Bethnal Green did not live up to the high standard set by Blomfield when he built their churches.

The Bishop's efforts had been greatly hindered by an Act of 1818 which insisted that a church building must exist before a new parish could be created, but the 1843 New Parishes Act changed this. Now districts of over 2,000 people could be made into parishes even if no church building existed, and until a building was erected the Bishop could allow services to be held in schools or other suitable places. The first such parish was St Andrew, Well Street, Hackney, and in 1844 St Matthew, Bethnal Green, became six separate districts. The Bishop did not forget his new East End parishes, realising they would have a struggle to survive. In 1845 he persuaded the Ecclesiastical Commissioners to divert part of the income from two City parishes, St Mary Undershaft and St Mary Axe, amounting to £1,538 (£61,500) to help eight of these parishes, and in February 1846 despite opposition got a £1,000 (£40,000) grant for St Jude, St

Thomas, St Simon and St Matthias, Bethnal Green, all of which served labourers and weavers. The following year he persuaded the Commissioners to give part of the income of St Catherine, Coleman Street, which had 666 inhabitants, to six Bethnal Green parishes, each getting £50 (£2,000).

In the 1846 Charge to his clergy the Bishop reported that £179,855 (£5,400,000) had been raised for his building fund which would provide 63 new churches in the Diocese, 44 of which were already completed. He thought that the target should be 400 buildings but gave no indication where the necessary money might come from. He proudly drew attention to Bethnal Green where church attendance had risen sharply. In the seven new churches worshippers on average totalled 1,500 on a Sunday morning and 2,000 in the evening. The number of communicants exceeded 460 and there were 3,254 children in the Sunday Schools. Furthermore, the congregation in the mother church had not decreased, and in the 10 parishes or districts carved out of it there were now 20 additional clergy, 15 schoolteachers, 100 Sunday school teachers, 8 Scripture readers and 10 district visitors. Ten years later in his 1854 Charge he noted that in Bethnal Green baptisms had increased from 786 in 1840 in two churches to 2,030 in ten churches, and Sunday school attendance had increased from 920 to 5,802. When the foundation stone of the tenth new church was laid in May, 1849, 4,000 children and 200 adults joined in a huge tea party in a large railway shed loaned by the Eastern Counties Railway. Blomfield, delighted by it all, thanked William Cotton who had masterminded many of the projects. The Bishop said he planned to open more schools in the parishes of St Jude and St Bartholomew. He was glad that there was no public disorder on this occasion as there had been when the first church was opened. After all the controversies surrounding his work for church reform and education, the Bishop needed some good news and this building programme which he had masterminded provided it.

Who should have patronage of these new churches? This was a delicate, complicated issue because, although the Crown was the largest patron, many advowsons were inherited, bought or sold by great landowners. There was some discussion of establishing diocesan boards of patronage but this met with no response, so the obvious place for patronage was in the hands of the diocesan bishop and there it remained. Many subscribers had given donations hoping this would be so. There was no viable alternative, and Blomfield showed little reluctance to an increase in his powers in London, although at the outset of the Appeal he had told Dr Pusey he would prefer more private patronage.

The Bishop also attempted to arrange church facilities for seamen. Whilst at Chester on 4 August 1827 he wrote to Mr J. H. Marten, 'I do justice to the liberality which has prompted you to speak as you have done of the Episcopal Floating Chapel Society... Anxious as I am to see the plan carried into execution in all our ports I am not without my doubts as to the expediency of a general Society for that purpose.' Having arrived in London he changed his mind and fitted up a ship, the *Brazen*, as a chapel and moored it in the docks with a chaplain on board. The experiment was not a success so he quickly built St Paul's Church, Dock Street, nearby which was well attended – possibly due to the fact it was close to the Sailors' Home and the Destitute Sailors' Asylum! To supplement this, a Thames Mission was inaugurated with a chaplain who travelled in a small vessel to visit the different shore stations and ships between the Port of London and Gravesend.

Church and poor

No matter how many new church buildings were erected, Blomfield knew he could not solve the problem of working-class absentees from church. One of the main deterrents to their attending was that they had no decent clothes to wear. Church congregations were mostly respectable and smart, so poorer people disliked being seen near their wealthier fellow-Christians. Blomfield was well aware of this but did not know how to solve the problem. Building churches for poorer people would only make matters worse for it would draw attention to class distinctions. In a letter to the Chaplain-General to the Forces he explains the difficulty of the situation;

> The poor ... will not attend our fine churches, even where there is room for them. Most of the incumbents of the great London parishes have extra services for the poor in their schoolrooms, which are well-attended; but more is needed in the way of personal intercourse and instruction. The Scripture Readers have worked very well in subordinate capacity; but we want some more persons, deacons or lay readers, who will hunt out the poor at their homes on Sundays, the only day which they are met with there.[7]

Some churches were centres of social service which attracted people to the building. When Henry Mayhew was interviewing in the East End for his book, *London Labour and the London Poor*, he met a crippled street seller who told him he was religious but would be more so if he had clothes to wear. Some clergy took up the challenge and the Revd T. Dale, vicar of St Pancras, claimed that 50,000 people a year came to his three dispensaries for medical help. Few of these attended services, and those who did often had to sit in distant parts of the church as pew rents meant the better seats were spoken for. In Chelsea the wealthy residents had contributed to build Holy Trinity in 1830 and St Saviour's in 1840 reserving £1,300 (£52,000) for a chapel of ease, St Jude's, in the poorer district. Most of its sittings were free, which meant that there were no funds to pay the perpetual curate, Mr Paterson, and there was no funding for repairs. As the rector of Chelsea, Mr Burgess, had a huge income from pew rents of £840 p. a. (£33,600) he agreed to give his fees to St Jude's. Eventually the Ecclesiastical Commission granted £40 p. a. (£1,600) which, added to the fees of £90 (£3,600) and pew rents at St Jude's of £100 (£4,000), gave Mr Paterson a meagre stipend.

The Bishop realised that pew rents emphasised social distinctions, but could see no other way of raising money. Churches in Holland, Scandinavia, northern Germany and France also raised funds in this way and often pews were auctioned. As long as the purchasers resided in the parish they had the freehold of the pews. One of Blomfield's archdeacons, Sinclair, wished to extend the practice with 'cheap sittings for the middle ranks and the superior class of artisans as well as more expensive accommodation for the wealthy'. In 1837 Blomfield told the Revd F. W. Rhodes, a future vicar of Walthamstow, that he did not approve of abolishing pew rents unless a more ample endowment could be provided. There were always seats available for the poor, and he could not imagine how any person above the lowest scale would prefer Popery to Protestantism for the sake of half a crown a year.[8] If at all possible he would try to provide an endowment to secure 'a due proportion of free sittings for the poor'. However, churchwardens could not resist letting as many pews as possible and at St James, Sussex Gardens, the income from them in 1843 amounted to £1,008 p. a. (£40,000) all of which except £20 went to the incumbent. At St John, Hyde Park, in 1832 the pew rent income was £619 (£23,500) and at Holy Trinity, Paddington £1,091 (£43,600) was received in 1845. Many churchmen including Gladstone hated the practice, realising that the consequences of it were disastrous. The poor felt excluded and the reverberations of this continued well into the twentieth century. As a teenager in the 1950s I remember avoiding pews with small brass plates containing the names of dowagers who usually arrived in their fur coats which smelled of mothballs.

The Square Mile

The City of London churches presented a grave problem to Blomfield. There were far too many of them and on Sundays some were deserted. He thought attendance was low but by today's standards the figures are very respectable indeed. St Olave, Hart Street, had 165 in the morning and 39 in the afternoon; St Mildred, Bread Street – now part of the parish of St Mary-le-Bow – 48 and 14. The Bishop knew that there would be an outcry if he closed any of them, and despite various estimates there were still hundreds of people living in the City. The rector of St Martin Ludgate said that the City parishes 'are small ones, badly attended owing to wealthy merchants and tradesmen living in houses westward. The houses in the City are divided into offices with no inhabitants'. At St Lawrence Jewry, now the Guildhall Church, the congregation seldom exceeded 30. Other figures for the census of 1851 are shown in table 1:

Table 1. *Attendance figures for some City churches in the 1851 census*

Church	Morning	Afternoon	Evening
St Andrew-by-the-Wardrobe	480 + 168S	50 + 70S	691 + 60S
St Martin Ludgate	137	–	85
St Stephen, Coleman Street now part of St Edmund Lothbury	332 + 153S	–	–
St Michael, Wood Street now part of St Vedast's	63 + 12S	–	51 + 12S
St Alban, Wood Street now part of St Vedast's	50 + 20S	30 + 20S	–
St Olave Jewry now part of St Edmund Lothbury	54 + 27S	42 + 27S	–
St Alphege now part of St Giles Cripplegate	76	6	–

Figures given are for congregations, with Sunday School attendance where applicable S = scholars

Blomfield thought that empty churches were caused by clerical negligence and suggested with remarkable foresight that the City churches should hold weekday services for business people. The City clergy should be an effective missionary body who would stir up the wealthy merchants so that England's capital city might be more Christian. A correspondent in the *Guardian* of 28 February 1855 suggested that the City clergy should seek out the inmates of banks and warehouses so that the churches in the Square Mile would be filled again. The only church open for daily prayers was St Bartholomew the Great, and it was difficult to discover when the other churches held services. Only two parishes in the centre of the City, St Andrew-by-the-Wardrobe and St Stephen, Coleman Street, made use of their buildings on Sundays but parish churches on the fringe of the City like St Botolph, Aldgate, and St Botolph, Bishopsgate, had sizeable Sunday congregations. There were certainly too many church buildings. At the time of the Great Fire in 1666 there were 109 churches of which 89 were destroyed. Not all were rebuilt, but 79 were open in 1700. Seventeen were pulled down in the nineteenth century and in the 1920s a commission suggested demolishing a further nineteen. Today there are 39 churches open for business in the Square Mile and, as Canon John Halliburton has pointed out, they are an outward and visible sign that the divine indwells the temporal and that the Church belongs to the market place. 'The City churches are of vital importance as signs of the divine involvement whatever practically they may do.'

Blomfield suggested that in principle he had no objection to City churches being closed and their ornaments and fabric used elsewhere, but it was difficult to put this into practice. Many of the churches were architectural masterpieces so any attempt to close them would be met with much opposition. The *Guardian* was opposed to any closures and in its issue of 14 June 1854 it pointed out that in England there was room for 58% of the population in church buildings but in the City there was room for only 35% of the local inhabitants. Blomfield did not know what to do. On 13 February 1855, London clergy meeting at Sion College were told by him that he intended to set up a Commission to enquire into the state and requirements of the metropolitan parishes, but his illness and retirement prevented this happening.

Too many or too few?

The committee of the Building Fund continued to meet for eighteen years under the Bishop's watchful eye, and during his episcopate nearly two hundred churches were built and endowed and over £0.5m (£15m) was raised. The expenses of the committee only amounted to £5,100 (£193,000) over the eighteen years of its life. Despite this magnificent effort it has been estimated that only a third of what was necessary was completed, because during the same period the population of London increased by over 600,000 people and all the new churches together could only seat 318,000. Nothing daunted the Bishop and in the year before his retirement he made an unsuccessful attempt to get Parliament to close several redundant City churches so that he could divert their endowments elsewhere. In the same year he proposed another church building fund, offering to give £25,000 (£750,000) himself, but it was now too late, his episcopate was over. His ardour did not however cool – on 27 April 1855 he told the Revd T. Thigo that Alderman Cubitt had agreed to build at his own expense a church on the Isle of Dogs. Cubitt had also given a site for a parsonage house, so would Thigo accept the incumbency? He declined the offer, so the Revd William John Caparn was appointed and stayed sixteen years. Other churches like St Philip, Earls Court Road and St John the Evangelist, Glenthorne Road, Hammersmith, were also planned by Blomfield but consecrated by his successor. Until 1834 the whole of Hammersmith was part of the parish of Fulham with a chapel of ease, St Paul's, in Hammersmith. Another church was needed, so in 1851 the Bishop called a meeting to raise funds for St John's, assign it a district and appoint a curate. He licensed a school for worship and the new building with 800 sittings opened in 1859.

Unlike Peel, Blomfield believed that if a church was built in a distressed area everything else would follow. In many places he was proved right. In 1847 Haverstock Hill had no church or schools but eight years later a large church had been built, day and infant schools for 400 children had been opened and a visiting Society, Ragged schools, libraries for 'Instruction in Both Worlds', and an 'Assistance in Confinement Society' were established. The same was true of Mile End where two years after the consecration of St Peter's Church, a District Visiting Society, Lying-in charity, two large schools and a Lending Library had been established. The church remained in use until the 1970s when it was closed, remaining derelict for twenty years. It was opened briefly for an all-day memorial service for Colin Winter, a former Bishop of Damaraland and a local resident. In June 1999 the London and Henley, an investment and development company proudly reported that having purchased the building it had constructed thirty-seven apartments on five floors, the smallest flat being valued at £67,000. 'Such stained glass as there was, was beyond repair but the conversion has new windows with red glass panels to pay homage to the past'.[9]

Church attendance even in the poor areas was by no means low, particularly by today's standards. Victorian respectability demanded attendance at Divine Service, and the census of Sunday 30 March 1851, the evening of which was wet, revealed that out of a total population of 18m people, 7,261,032 had attended a service that day in church or chapel. This would cause great rejoicing today, but at that time people were shocked that so few had attended a service in the Church of England.

Figures for London were very encouraging: they are shown in table 2:[10]

Table 2. *Attendance figures for some London (not City) churches in the 1851 census*

Church	Morning	Afternoon	Evening
Holy Trinity, Stepney	453 + 133S	–	468 + 130S
West Hackney Parish Church	1750 + 230S	480	1400
St Luke, Old Street	1000	1000	1000
St Mary, Hornsey	707 + 29S	417 + 8S	–
All Saints, West Ham	743 + 289S	–	690
St James, Paddington	1300 + 200S	–	500
Holy Trinity, Marylebone	1443 + 133S	582 + 7S	1305
St Luke, Chelsea	1274	782	1623
St John, Westminster	970 + 307S	524 + 340S	1169
St James, Piccadilly	1283 + 74S	682 + 72S	943
St Mary, Bryanston Square	1500 + 120S	500 + 120S	1200
Portman Chapel	200 + 150S	400 + 50S	1260
Holy Trinity, Islington	1620 + 210S	–	–
Christ Ch. Turnham Green	330 + 138S	–	380 + 36S
St Michael, Chester Square	1228 + 45S	515 + 12S	930 + 25S
St Mark, Hamilton Terrace	1200	–	700
St John, Hampstead	1144 + 256S	500 + 256S	900
St Michael, Highgate	1300	500	1000
St Martin-in-the-Fields	1500	750	1300

Figures given are for congregations, with Sunday School attendance where applicable S = scholars

Criticism of the Bishop's building programme came from all sides, especially from those incumbents who saw members of their congregation leaving to attend one of the new churches. The rector of Stepney complained that the mother church of St Dunstan would lose all its more respectable members, and he was joined in his complaints by clergy whose endowments were cut. Blomfield listened to all opposition, and wherever possible he altered his plans if they were unfair or wrong. There are however three valid criticisms. Firstly, many of the new churches were built hurriedly, so they soon fell into disrepair. St Jude, Bethnal Green, completed in 1846, was by 1869 in a very bad state. A strong wind blew in several windows and so many tiles had fallen off the roof that the rain poured in. Nothing was done for twenty years owing to lack of funds. The architecture of the new churches was disappointing, with an English romantic tradition, chancels and rood screens returned, but no new adventures in church building were tried. Blomfield considered that 'the Norman or Lombard style, with round arches, to be better suited to small ecclesiastical buildings than the pointed or early English'. He took a great interest in these details and told the Revd W Wilson, vicar of Walthamstow, that 'the steps to the altar in his new church were inconveniently steep and that the lower windows were disproportionately small'.[11] Secondly, the Bishop tended to think a church was still the centre of community life in London whereas often it was not, and certainly would not become so in years ahead. Thirdly, Blomfield wanted to create several small parishes complete with schools, halls and all the attendant societies, whereas it might have been cheaper and more in line with current London life to build one big parish church such as St Mary, Portsea, and staff its daughter churches from a central pool of clergy. Blomfield refused to countenance any more proprietary chapels in the diocese and told those who wanted to give money that they should support parish church appeals. His enthusiasm for the 'magic of masonry' was infectious and other bishops followed his example. In the 1850s and 1860s Bishop James Prince Lee built 110 churches in his new diocese of Manchester, and Samuel Wilberforce built 106 churches in the Oxford diocese before moving to Winchester in 1869.

Some of Blomfield's churches bear his image still. St Stephen, Rochester Row, financed by the generosity of Angela Burdett-Coutts in 1850 has a column the capital of which is adorned with eight heads including the Baroness, Blomfield and Queen Victoria. In St Paul's Knightsbridge, the Bishop's carved head glares down from the sanctuary roof, no doubt still expressing his disapproval of what goes on there.

The Bishop travelled great distances by carriage to visit his new parishes, using the time to write sermons and speeches. On Wednesday 22 July 1840 he journeyed to Barkingside to consecrate Holy Trinity Church, which had been erected by the generosity of local farmers at a cost of £3,000 (£120,000). 314 of the 472 sittings were free. Five parishes have since been carved out of the original district, but it still has a population of 16,000.

Blomfield left a legacy of far too many church buildings in London. They were often badly endowed, and many incumbents had to apply to the Ecclesiastical Commissioners for help. Working on the mistaken principle that if you open more pubs you sell more beer, he could not know that the decline in belief would leave many churches empty and unwanted. Some fell down of their own accord, Hitler's bombers destroyed many, but even today there are too many churches in the diocese of London costing a great deal of money and absorbing energies of clergy and laity which would be better employed in projects of pastoral care or evangelism. Some standing empty are an eyesore to the local community. Others have been sold for secular purposes. Government policies over the last twenty years have meant that parochial church councils have not been able to undertake projects for the homeless or other high risk, vulnerable groups, so that the outlook in London could be bleak. Can the 60,000 women and men on electoral rolls in the diocese maintain their many church buildings much longer? It took a great deal of courage and vision for Blomfield to build the churches; it will take even more to close them.

The Bishop is thus remembered with mixed feelings for his building programmes, but T. S. Eliot has written of him:

> I send you now one who accomplished much
> In time of drought and desolation.
> Blomfield, Bishop of London,
> Builder of many churches.
> One who was usually right
> And never intimidated, never disheartened,
> Displaying equal justice.
> Blomfield who built in a time which was no better than this.

Chapter Eight

Bishop of the Empire

The chief sign of life in the Church is a missionary spirit.
To this rule there is no exception.

S. C. Carpenter

It will make quite a revolution in the dinners of New Zealand;
tete d' Eveque will be the most récherché dish and there will be
cold clergyman on the side table.

Sydney Smith on hearing of the consecration of
George Augustus Selwyn

At his enthronement Blomfield was reminded that by an Order in
Council of 1634 he now had pastoral care over those British possessions overseas which had no bishop of their own. This meant that he
was virtually the Bishop of the British Empire, for in 1824 there
were only five colonial bishoprics – Nova Scotia, Quebec, Calcutta,
Jamaica and Barbados. The situation was ridiculous and intolerable,
because the Bishop had no legal jurisdiction outside England and no
means of inquiry into what was going on. One of his predecessors,
Bishop Sherlock, had tried unsuccessfully to appoint two or three
bishops 'for the plantations' in 1751; 'Sure I am that the care [of
overseas churches] is improperly lodged: for a bishop to live at one
end of the world and his church at another must make the office very
uncomfortable to the bishop and useless to the people'.[1]

Blomfield was determined that change should come, and soon after
his enthronement he said, 'Each colony must have not only its
parochial and district pastors, but its chief pastor to watch over and
guide and direct the whole. An episcopal church without a bishop is a
contradiction in terms. It is not enough just to send out missionaries
and build schools and churches.' He had recently received a letter
from a clergymen on the far side of British North America complain-
ing of the little attention which his Lordship paid to 'this part of his

diocese'. The Bishop was also much alarmed at the influence which Nonconformists were achieving in the colonies and felt that, had the Church of England been quicker off the mark in providing bishops, clergy and churches, they would not have gained so much ground.

Most of the missionary work until this time had been done through the Church Missionary Society and the Society for the Propagation of the Gospel. Neither of these could provide bishops for the new areas being opened up, because they lacked the necessary authority and financial backing. Blomfield was able to supply the authority, but for the first twelve years money remained a problem, so only five new colonial bishoprics were founded during this time: Australia (subsequently Sydney), Madras, Bombay, Newfoundland and Toronto. On 24 April 1840 Blomfield addressed a letter to Howley, suggesting that a new approach to missionary work be adopted. He pointed out that the old system of sending out missionaries followed later by a bishop must be reversed; every Christian community abroad must have its own bishop, and he proposed the setting up of a Colonial Bishoprics Fund to facilitate this plan. Two months later SPCK gave him £10,000 (£400,000) and SPG £7,500 (£300,000). His open letter to Howley finished with a flourish:

> If the Church of England bestir herself in good earnest and put forth all the resources and energies which she possesses, and for the use of which she must give account, she will in due time cause the reformed episcopal Church to be recognised, by all the nations of the earth, as the stronghold of pure religion, and the legitimate dispenser of its means of grace; and will be a chosen instrument in the hands of God, for purifying and restoring the other branches of Christ's holy catholic Church and of connecting them with herself, as members of the same mystical body, in the way of truth, in the unity of the Spirit, and in the bond of peace.[2]

The Anglican Communion was being born.

Ever practical, the Bishop realised that no government money would be made available, and the missionary societies could only give limited help – in 1833 SPG's expenditure had exceeded its income by £12,000 (£500,000) and the Society for the Conversion of Negro Slaves reported it had many more applications from intending missionaries than it could provide for. CMS did, however, vote £600 (£23,000) a year to endow a bishopric in New Zealand (subsequently Auckland) and the wise, good and brave George Augustus Selwyn was consecrated in Lambeth Palace as its first bishop, with a diocese extending from latitude 50° South to latitude 34° North (instead of

South). This mistake gave him a further 4,000 miles including the Melanesian Islands to oversee. Blomfield was soon to change his mind about CMS, which until then he thought was hostile to episcopal government. Characteristically he sent their Governing Body a clause to insert in their Constitution which asked that 'all questions relating to matters of ecclesiastical order and discipline, respecting which a difference shall arise between any Colonial Bishop and any Committee of the Society, shall be referred to the Archbishops and Bishops of England and Ireland whose decision thereon shall be final'. After much discussion the Governors agreed and Blomfield joined the Society. Not everyone supported these moves. Sydney Smith considered that the spread of Christianity in India would produce a revolution and rejoiced that the Government there made things difficult for missionaries.

On 24 April 1841 a large public meeting was held at Willis's Rooms in London and the Bishop spoke eloquently in favour of setting up and endowing many new bishoprics in the colonies. £12,000 (£500,000) was raised at the meeting, the Queen Dowager giving £2,000 (£80,000). Blomfield and the two archbishops each gave £1,000 (£40,000) and later Angela Burdett-Coutts contributed £35,000 (£1,500,000) to endow the sees of Cape Town and Adelaide. During the next seventeen years, until his death in 1857, twenty new colonial bishoprics were founded and a further six sees were created out of existing ones. The colonial sees founded during Blomfield's episcopate are: 1835, Madras; 1836, Australia (later Sydney); 1837, Bombay; 1839, Newfoundland and Toronto; 1841, New Zealand (later Auckland); 1842, Antigua, Gibraltar, Guiana and Tasmania; 1845, Colombo and Fredericton; 1847, Adelaide, Cape Town, Melbourne and Newcastle; 1849, Rupert's Land and Victoria (Hong Kong); 1850, Montreal; 1852, Sierra Leone; 1853, Grahamstown and Natal; 1854, Mauritius; 1855, Singapore, Labuan and Sarawak; 1856, Christchurch (New Zealand). Until 1849 South Africa had been part of the diocese of Calcutta, so Indian bishops would occasionally visit Cape Town to confirm and ordain, but in 1847 Robert Gray, a Tractarian, was consecrated as Bishop of Cape Town. Over the next twenty-five years he carved three further bishoprics out of his diocese: Grahamstown, Natal and St Helena. Between 1825 and 1841, the number of colonial clergy increased from 290 to 652 and by 1852 there were 2,000 communicants in Sierra Leone so in that year Blomfield consecrated a native, Vidal, as the first bishop there.

In 1842 the Bishop asked his diocesan clergy to give their collections on Palm Sunday to the fund and this produced over £8,000 (£320,000). A few months later, in the absence of Howley due to illness, he presided over the consecration of the new Bishops of Antigua, Guiana, Barbados, Gibraltar and Tasmania. The bench of bishops issued a statement that they would now take charge of the Fund, which appeared to Thomas Arnold a retrograde step as it might mean the propagation 'to the end of the earth' of the 'Popery of Canterbury',[3] because the Archbishop, not the Prime Minister, would now make the necessary appointments. This did not mean that Blomfield withdrew his influence from beyond London: he continued to be the bishop of any clergyman not in one of the new dioceses, and often spoke out on matters affecting the colonies. Sometimes he could be too vigorous, and once was asked by John Hobhouse MP to be less outspoken about idolatrous practices in India as it embarrassed the Government. Hobhouse in his youth spent three months in Newgate Gaol for attacking the privileges of the House of Commons, so it was an odd criticism for him to make. The Bishop pointed out that he could not remain silent and thus countenance idolatry. Something needed to be put in its place, and if the Established Church did not do it the Dissenters would. It was time the East India Company took its Christian responsibilities seriously.

Despite these successes the Bishop never tired of sounding a note of warning to the missionary societies. He pointed out that it is foolish to place all our hopes in the instruments used to bring about the Kingdom (churches, school, societies etc.). We must instead look 'to the Hand which alone can wield them with success ... If our endeavours are to be in any measure successful it can only be by the direct and continued influences of God's Holy Spirit'.

The Colonial Bishoprics Fund was a great success and in fifty years it collected and spent £840,000 (£33,500,000) on fifty-five new bishoprics. Bishop William Broughton, the first Australian bishop, who had nearly three million square miles to oversee, said Blomfield's name would always be venerated in his country for this work. The *Guardian*, never kind to Blomfield, grudgingly admitted that his achievements for the church overseas deserved to be written on his tomb in letters of gold, realising that it was largely due to the Bishop that a new episcopate was created in the Anglican Church in the nineteenth century. It now contained bishops who were not part of an Established Church, but whose links with England remained strong, and this new episcopacy continued to expand so that at the first Lambeth Conference ten years after Blomfield's death 144 bishops were invited and 76 attended. Today at Lambeth Conferences the English bishops are a small minority – the Church of England has become a world-wide Church.

The Jerusalem bishopric

One further question relating to the Church overseas concerned Blomfield, and that was the controversy concerning the Jerusalem bishopric. It was founded in 1841 by the King of Prussia, who considered that there ought to be a Protestant representation in Jerusalem led by a bishop in the Apostolic succession. In June 1841 he sent an envoy, Chevalier Ernest de Bunsen, to England to discuss the matter. The Lutheran Church in Prussia was firmly under the control of the King, whose position was close to that of a lay primate, and although it had bishops it did not claim to stand in the Apostolic Succession. Howley and Blomfield had long discussions with Bunsen and it was eventually agreed to go ahead with the scheme, England and Prussia taking it in turns to nominate the bishop. He would be empowered to ordain any Germans who would subscribe to the Thirty-Nine Articles and the Confession of Augsburg, minister to Protestants only and have oversight of the English congregations in Syria and Palestine. He was also to maintain friendly contacts with other Christian communions, particularly the Orthodox – the rights of the Patriarch being officially recognised.

No Protestant communion had a representative in Jerusalem so the plan received much support. Ashley and the Evangelicals thought it would begin the conversion of the Jews, Gladstone agreed to become a Trustee of the inevitable Fund, and Court and Government led by Peel thought it would provide a balance to Russian and French influence in the Holy Land, so a Bill was prepared to legalise the scheme. Blomfield said it was not necessary to consult the Syrian bishops or any other bishops, as their jurisdiction was not recognised by the Church of England. It would also, he thought, of course bind the English and Russian churches closer together.

A meeting of bishops held in August 1841 approved the plan, but later several bishops, who had not been there, attacked it. Blomfield told them they were too late: they should have attended the meeting. The Tractarians vigorously opposed the scheme – Gladstone, having changed his mind and Newman, supported by *The Times*[4] were loud in their opposition. In their view the King of Prussia was a heretic and his church, which did not possess the Apostolic Succession, was no church at all. Michael Chandler in his *Life* of Liddon reminds us that to begin with Pusey saw the scheme 'as a means of introducing episcopacy into German Protestantism and believed that to be a good idea'. Liddon devotes several pages in his *Life of Pusey* to this subject, saying that Pusey 'strongly failed at first to see what principles were involved but eventually joined in condemning it.' Newman was so disturbed by the scheme that Gladstone later claimed that it had finally driven him out of the Church of England.[5]

Strangely enough, no voice was raised in opposition when the Bill authorising the bishopric passed through Parliament. Two difficulties of the scheme were seized upon by the critics: the practice of the Catholic Church not to have more than one episcopate within the same territorial limits; and secondly, the constitutional difference between the two churches. Supporters of the scheme pointed out that the new bishoprics being founded throughout the world were already embracing bishoprics of other denominations. Moreover, Jerusalem was unique, as it was a free city for all Christian communions. Anyway, relations with the Orthodox would be cordial; if there would be any quarrel it would be with the Roman Catholics. The second point was more serious. Objectors felt that any plan to co-operate with a church that did not possess the Apostolic Succession might look as though Anglicans were jettisoning this belief, and this would seriously endanger relations with both Roman Catholics and Orthodox. This caused some clergy great concern, but not all Anglicans attached such great importance to the Apostolic Succession, and Blomfield himself spoke slightingly of it. Bunsen added fuel to the fire by saying that Anglicans do not have to believe in Apostolic Succession as a strict article of faith, quoting Article XXIII as evidence, and pointing out that many distinguished writers, such as Hooker, Wake, Andrews, Taylor and Stillingfleet counte-nanced the orders and sacraments of foreign non-episcopal Protestant churches. Many people accused Blomfield of pushing the Bill through too quickly, but he carefully considered the difficulties involved and consulted his brethren at every step (even if he did tell Gladstone that it didn't much matter what they said). He came to the conclusion that the advantages were greater than the disadvantages, and on 7 November 1841 he consecrated the new bishop.

The character of the men chosen to be the first bishops of Jerusalem ensured the see's early death after only three episcopates. Michael Solomon Alexander, the first bishop, consecrated by Blomfield and the Bishops of Rochester and New Zealand, was unequal to his task and had no knowledge of the Eastern Church. He was an Anglican born in Breslau and by race a Jew. His consecration moved Blomfield to tears: 'The establishment of a Hebrew bishop was more important and more efficient for promoting Christianity among the Jews than all the other means employed'.

His successor, Samuel Gobat, was a deacon who was priested then almost immediately consecrated. Personalities killed the bishopric, rather than opposition at home which had been largely silenced by

F. D. Maurice, whose *Three Letters to the Revd W Palmer* gave a calm and reasonable defence of the scheme. Samuel Wilberforce found this 'unanswerable'. There was, he thought, not the slightest suspicion of an inclination to say, 'Episcopacy is immaterial, let us fraternise.' He suspected that the lack of valid orders in the Lutheran Church was the reason for establishing contacts with other churches, and he wondered if Frederick William was hoping to get 'his future bishops ordained in Palestine in order to co-operate with us'.[6]

When Joseph Barclay, the third bishop, died in 1881 there was much opposition from men like Dean Church and Canon Liddon of Saint Paul's to the vacancy being filled, but after six years Archbishop Benson appointed the Archdeacon of Rangoon, George Blyth, who was forbidden to proselytise among Eastern Christians, and the Lutheran element of the scheme was quietly dropped.[7]

Chapter Nine

Education

Soap and Education are not as sudden as a massacre,
but they are far more deadly in the long run.

Mark Twain

Education with religion is the greatest good which man can bestow
on man; education unless grounded upon religious principles may be
a curse instead of a blessing.

British Critic, 1827

Preaching charity sermons was an episcopal pastime in the early nine-teenth century, and on Sunday 22 June 1828, just before his translation to London, Blomfield preached on behalf of the Society for the Improvement of Prison Discipline and for the Reformation of Juvenile Offenders. He suggested that the schools of the National Society which had been founded in 1811 had reduced juvenile crime, and thus the government should consider supporting them as a less expensive and more effective method of crime prevention. Warming to his theme and hoping to influence ratepayers, he indicated that 'a moderate expenditure, bestowed on the education of poor children, might be the means of curtailing and rendering unnecessary the cumbrous and costly machinery of punishment which is now employed to constrain, or to crush, as useless or noxious members of society those who have become so for want of early instruction and discipline'. The Bishop thus joined churchmen who for several years had been calling for parliamentary support for schools. Always prag-matic and prophetic, Blomfield now entered the fray. Not all bishops and clergy agreed with him, as some considered it particularly dangerous to teach the poor how to read and write. They might be influenced by the writing of anti-establishment figures like Thomas Paine whose *Rights of Man* sold 200,000 copies in 1792. (The Church is 'set up to terrify and enslave mankind and monopolise power and profit'.) Who knows where this might lead? Would it make the poor dissatisfied with their lot? 'The people at large', wrote the Revd Stephen Cassan, 'have no business with minds', and even Cobbett asked why a ploughboy should be taught to read and write, as these would be useless accomplishments for mounting a carthorse. Lord Melbourne said he did not believe in education 'because the Pagets got on so damn well without it'.[1]

One of Blomfield's predecessors, Bishop Beilby Porteus, (Chester 1776, London 1787–1808), had been a consistent supporter of charity and Sunday schools, saying these would bring the union of manual labour and spiritual instruction. He reassured the clergy and by the time of Charles James's episcopate most people realised that ignorance must be defeated, and that it is a basic human right to read and write. In 1807 Porteus and the bishops defeated a government move to establish a national system of education because they felt that the clergy, not local magistrates, should control schools; but no one pointed out that for generations the parochial clergy had not taken this function seriously. Sixty years would have to pass before clergy were forced to relinquish their control.

Some charity schools founded in the eighteenth century had been very effective indeed, but there were too few of them. Typical was the Sir John Cass School founded in Aldgate, City of London, by the haughty, wealthy and reserved Alderman Cass who in 1709 opened a three-storey building close to St Botolph's Church. With an eye for business he opened shops on the ground floor, a school room for fifty boys and forty girls on the first floor, and in the basement burial vaults which were for sale. These proved a mixed blessing as workmen had to remedy the 'intolerable stench arising therefrom'. The school was refounded in 1748 after a long legal wrangle over Cass's will and it still exists on two sites today. In 1818 Henry Brougham's enquiries revealed that 168,000 boys and girls were educated in such schools, and 53,000 in local dame schools.[2] In the belief that good behaviour and social harmony flowed from biblical teaching, the curriculum was always headed by religious instruction.

Manners and morals were also inculcated in the Sunday school movement which had been founded by Robert Raikes in the early 1780s. He wrote up his experiences in the *Gentlemen's Magazine* so the idea quickly spread throughout England. By 1787 he claimed that a quarter of a million children were attending and thirty years later Brougham's figure was 452,000. Sunday schools were particularly popular because they cost little and did not interfere with the working week.

Joshua Watson, aged 43, a successful wine and spirit merchant and a devout layman, abandoned his office in Mincing Lane and called a meeting on 16 October 1811 to discuss elementary education, or rather the lack of it, in places like London and other large cities. This was the beginning of the National Society for the Education of the Poor in the Principles of the Established Church, which soon became known as the National Society. Encouragement was given to incumbents to open their own parochial schools. Money was raised so that grants could be given to these new schools, but certain conditions had to be fulfilled: instruction must be given in the liturgy and catechism, attendance at church was required, and no books were allowed except those published by SPCK. Later these strict controls were relaxed, as was the plan for older children to teach younger children, although Dr Arnold was later to adapt this monitorial system at Rugby where prefects had a share in the running of the school. In London the Society bought land and established schools, one of which was in the Ely Chapel, Holborn, now St Etheldreda's Roman Catholic church. By 1815 every diocese was consulting the Society and 100,000 children were in its schools. Twenty years later the number was nearly a million.

In 1833 the Government for the first time gave what became an annual grant for building schools – £20,000 (£600,000) which was split between the National Society with 690 schools which received £11,000, and the British and Foreign School Society with 196 schools which received £9,000. The latter, founded five years earlier than the National Society, wanted an interdenominational approach to education without an attachment to the Established Church. It attracted Dissenters and many liberal Anglicans, and occasionally the two societies presented problems at parish level. Charlotte Bronte's *Shirley*, written in 1849, describes rival school feasts where the column of church schoolchildren, 'priest-led and woman officered', its band playing 'Rule Britannia', marches at quick step down the narrow village lanes, scattering the column of dissenting children and their pastors, who raise a feeble hymn and then turn tail.

Six years later a Committee of Council with a full-time secretary, Dr Kay, was set up to administer the grant, but he incurred the wrath of the bishops by suggesting that the civil power should control the education of England. Churchmen, including Blomfield, felt that the Church of England must maintain control over education, and their attitude probably delayed universal education by many years. The main bone of contention was control, and in July 1833 John Roebuck MP introduced a plan into the Commons for secular state education with local school districts to be controlled by democratic bodies. Short of stature, and a disciple of Jeremy Bentham and J. S. Mill,

Roebuck never doubted that savagery and unreason could be defeated by education. He was known as 'Tear 'em', because of his radical opinions expressed with a vehemence which often shocked his Bath constituents. Like his proposal to curtail the power of the House of Lords, his education plans were opposed by Whigs and Tories, and so had to be dropped. Peel said that if the Church was excluded from education, it would be an end of the Church and ultimately an end of all religious feeling. Blomfield had led the attack on Roebuck's plans by presenting a petition signed by 5,048 people who opposed the idea of secular education, and it is probable that he had considerably influenced his friend Robert Peel. In his Charge of 1834 the Bishop once again said that 'the education of poorer classes ought to remain in the hands of the parochial clergy', but he did ask that subjects such as history, geography and science should be introduced to widen the curriculum. The poor should be educated upon the same principles and in the same way as the rich, and he told the London clergy to ask the National Society for funds to establish church schools in their parishes.

The inevitable parliamentary committee was now appointed, but its Report issued in 1838 suggested that the present arrangements continue with an increased grant to the two societies. Two years later the Bishop reported that only one child in fourteen was attending school in Westminster, and one in twenty in Bethnal Green, and in a sermon in St Martin-in-the-Fields Blomfield once again said that education without religious instruction is null and void. 'We are desirous of expanding and cultivating the mind; but we are more solicitous about the training and preparation of the soul ... we bear in remembrance that man is not only an intellectual being but a moral agent ... man has a soul to be saved as well as a mind to be enlightened.' The following year the Bishop, horrified at the Committee of Council's plans to inspect all schools and to set up a non-denominational college for teachers, spoke at a meeting in Willis's Rooms. He condemned those who divided education into secular and religious, pointing out that religion is of the essence of education. The Reformation and Act of Uniformity had given the clergy authority to educate the people of England, so they must be allowed and enabled to do it.

Opinions varied concerning the way ahead. The Central Society, a secular organisation, attracted few but vocal supporters. The main division, as Owen Chadwick points out, was therefore not between religious and secular education but between two different notions of religious education.[3] Some, like the British and Foreign Schools Society, wanted a general religious instruction not controlled by the

Established Church, but some wanted church schools and dissenters' schools. In 1839 Lord John Russell proposed an increase in the grant paid to the two societies to £32,000 on the condition that they submit themselves to inspection by representatives from the Committee (the equivalent of a modern Ministry of Education). Everyone agreed that inspection was necessary and some pointed out that if public money was used then the public had a right to know if it was spent wisely. Bishop Wilberforce said it was a wedge that would open the way for all the rest of the secularists' ideas. John Allen, a priest who had been ordained by Blomfield, was asked to be an inspector and immediately went to Fulham Palace for advice. He found the Bishop in full dress waiting for his carriage to take him to the Privy Council where the Queen was to announce her forthcoming marriage to Prince Albert. The Bishop was gruff in manner and gave him no help, saying it had nothing to do with canonical obedience. Allen reminded him that at his ordination the Bishop had said he should come to him if he ever needed advice. Relenting, the Bishop told him, 'You know well that I disapprove of the whole scheme of Government education'. 'Then my mind is made up,' said Allen, making for the door; the Bishop called him back. 'Stay, if we *are* to have school inspectors, it will be better to have good men than bad ones. Perhaps you had better accept it.'[4]

Lord John Russell wanted to establish 'normal' schools which would give general religious education to all students, but those who were members of any particular church would receive instruction from their ministers. Dr Kay, who had changed his name to Kay-Shuttleworth, was secretary of the Committee and ensured that no bishop sat on it. Blomfield was furious and, according to Dr Biber, made one of his finest speeches in the Lords attacking the plans. After years of suggesting that education would cut the crime rate, he quoted a French report which suggested that crime had increased in areas of widespread education, but this, he pointed out, was because there was an absence of religious instruction in that particular area. The Bishop went on to quote the chaplain at a new prison in Clerkenwell who thought that educated criminals were the most wily and depraved. The Bishop looked anxious, and ended his speech by suggesting that education founded on religion would indeed be a weapon against social disorder, 'and by far the cheapest as well as the most effective measure of police which any Government can adopt'. Clerical supervision was, he said, essential, and the Government had a duty to provide its Established Church with funds for schools. If they gave dissenters a grant, it must be on a charitable not a legal basis. Russell later noted that Blomfield had suggested to him that Church and State must not fight over education, 'we should only injure one another'. The Prime Minister agreed to a meeting at Lansdowne House with the Archbishop of Canterbury and the Bishops of London and Salisbury. There he and Lord Lansdowne accepted the proposal whereby the inspectors of the National Society schools would send their reports to the bishops as well as to the Committee.

Blomfield still could not face up to the inevitable fact that the government should be the educator of the nation's children by founding its own secular schools, but in 1846 he received some information which should have made him change his mind. Mr T. Burgess had studied seven large parishes in the London diocese; the statistics which he found are shown in table 3.[5]

Table 3. *Church School provision in seven London parishes in 1846*

Parish	Population	Number of Church Schools	Children
St Marylebone	138,164	31	6,103
St Pancras	129,763	21	3,571
St Anne, Soho	16,480	3	274
St George, Hanover Square	66,453	24	2,399
Whitechapel	34,053	13	1,696
St James, Piccadilly	37,398	8	1,276
Shoreditch	83,432	12	2,558

He had included a few schools of other denominations but no private schools. In these seven parishes alone Mr Burgess reckoned that there were between 20,000 and 30,000 poor children without any educational facility, and suggested that fifty new schools were needed which would cost an average of £800 (£32,000) each exclusive of sites and fittings – a total of £40,000 (£1,600,000). No doubt the National Society and private individuals would help, but what was the Bishop going to do about it? Blomfield was shocked by the scale of the problem and immediately promised a personal donation of £500 (£20,000), an annual subscription of £25 (£1,000) and said the Diocesan Board of Education which he had founded in 1839 would take the matter seriously. However, he pointed out that its annual income from subscriptions was very disappointing – £4,000 (£160,000) – so he wondered if such a plan was possible.

In the country at large a few clerical voices were now raised to demand a system of state education. Bishop Longley said that the defence of the realm was not left to voluntary contributions, nor should the education of children be. Bishop Thirlwall of Salisbury wanted a clear separation of Church and State in education, and Walter Hook, the vicar of Leeds, in an open letter to the Bishop of St David's in 1846, estimated that there were 2m children who were not being educated in England and Wales. To put them in schools, he said would cost 25s (£50) a head each year. Half could be raised by fees and donations, but half must come from local or national government. He suggested that local clergy should visit these schools two mornings a week, and that the children be encouraged to attend church.

Meanwhile the debate about control of schools continued. Archbishop Howley had reached an agreement with the Government in 1840 which said that inspectors would be allowed into church schools, but could be vetoed by the bishop. Blomfield, with characteristic cunning, arranged for the Revd F. C. Cooke, Secretary of the London Diocesan Board of Education, to be inspector for London. The grant given to the two societies continued to rise, from £40,000 (£1,800,000) in 1842 to £125,000 (£5m) in 1848. The new Whig government of 1846 was determined to take more control of education, insisting that the incumbent should be in charge of religious instruction, but hand over the day-to-day running of his school to a parish committee of management. Incumbents were incensed by this, but had little power to resist. In the absence of Convocation the annual meeting of the National Society became the forum where fury and anger were ventilated. Some clergy were frightening in their opposition. The vicar of East Brent, Somerset, refused all state grants for his school and wrote to the inspector, 'My dear Bellairs, I love you very much but if you ever come here again to inspect I will lock the door of the school and tell the boys to put you in the pond'.[6] Meanwhile Kay-Shuttleworth founded a teacher training college at Kneller Hall which had no links with the Church, although he did appoint as principal a future Archbishop of Canterbury, Frederick Temple who was well known for his liberal views.

On 4 March 1850 Blomfield, supported by the Archbishop of Canterbury, asked the Government to appoint a Select Committee of the Lords to inquire into the workings of the Committee of the Privy Council, which by now had become the equivalent of a modern Department of Education. Lansdowne on behalf of the Cabinet was not sympathetic, but in 1851 the government grant to denominational schools was increased yet again to £150,000 (£6m). By 1858 it had become £663,435 (£26m). Resentment continued and one of Blomfield's archdeacons, Sinclair of Middlesex, expressed his alarm at the amount of influence wielded by the Committee, criticising their 'vast machine of inspectors, reports and pensions'. The Church had made an unsatisfactory bargain, yielding the maximum of power for the minimum of aid.[7] The following year the Committee, attempting to please the protesters once more, ruled that management committee members must be Anglicans and that bishops would have the power to dismiss teachers.

The census of 1851 showed that, of the 10,595 schools receiving state aid, 81% were Anglican and they instructed 76% of the 1,048,851 children being educated. The London Board of Education only had 363 schools, but Blomfield had sanctioned a plan by which the London clergy, assisted by their laity, held evening classes for young men in science, art and literature. Thus 800 students, who included shop assistants and clerks, were being educated in seventeen London parishes. Today's London Guildhall University, whose Business School is now one of the largest in Europe, regards Blomfield as one of its founders. The Revd Charles Mackenzie responded to the Bishop's call by establishing evening classes in Greek, Latin, Hebrew, English, Maths and Drawing at Crosby Hall, Bishopsgate. In 1861 these were reconstituted as the City of London College and over the next twenty years the College pioneered the introduction of commercial and technical subjects.

In his final Charge of 1854 Blomfield admitted that 'Our systems of education have not yet effectually reached that class that stands most in need of instruction – the very poorest'. He pointed out that most children left school before the age of 11, and nearly all by 13, so attendance often averaged only 4 years. In 1845 a third of the male and a half of the female population of the United Kingdom were illiterate. By 1871 it was 19% and 26%.[8] The Bishop made yet another appeal for funds for his newly-established Metropolis Schools Fund, which he hoped would tackle the problem of the 60,000 children in London not yet receiving education. The Fund was hindered by the Bishop's retirement, but it did build schools for 12,000 children.

Henry Mayhew in his massive survey, *London Labour and the London Poor* (1851), hardly mentions education, reckoning that only one in ten of the costermongers he met could read. Education to them meant a complete knowledge of the art of buying in the cheapest market and selling in the dearest. 'There are few lads whose training extends beyond this. The father is the tutor who takes the boy to different markets, instructs him in the art of buying, and when the youth is perfect on this point, the parent's duty is supposed to have been performed'. In his Charge, Blomfield agreed to support the establishment of free ragged schools in Bethnal Green for the poorest of the poor. Enrolment in a National Society school involved a small fee, so the Bishop thought that 'many little Tradesmen and Mechanics would send their children to a National school if the most destitute and ragged children went elsewhere'.

It is a tribute to church leaders like Blomfield that by the end of his episcopate there were so many children in church schools and Sunday schools receiving basic instruction in the three Rs. When at last the Education Act of 1870 provided free education for all up to the age of thirteen, the Church controlled 11,874 schools, and it was not until the turn of the century that attendance at state schools reached the number of those at church schools. Today there are 151 church schools in the diocese of London, all but one voluntary aided. There are 16 secondary schools and 135 primary schools, so Blomfield's legacy to the present London Diocesan Board for Schools is considerable. Between them these schools educate nearly 50,000 pupils, but they are not distributed evenly across London. Westminster has three secondary and nineteen primary schools, Tower Hamlets two secondary and nine primary but Hounslow only one secondary and two primaries. This probably reflects the priorities of Blomfield and his fellow Victorians.

It remains a disgrace, however, that in 1850 no bishop, including Blomfield, was prepared to demand that a ten-year-old should by law be in school instead of working in a shop or factory. The bishops stopped short of proposing a solution or policy 'that might have made them appear genuinely interested in the total welfare of the labouring masses they endeavoured to reach'.[9] By standing in the way of compulsory state education for seventy years the bishops and members of the National Society and the British and Foreign Schools Society delayed what was inevitable, gave the government a reason for inertia and denied thousands of children their basic right of education.

Chapter Ten

Gorham and the Bishop of London

How can a priest twice judged unfit for cure of souls by the church,
be put in charge of souls at the sentence of the civil power without
overthrowing the divine office of the church?
Archdeacon H. E. Manning to Robert Wilberforce,
26 February 1850.

The Duke of Wellington's last act as Prime Minister was to appoint
Henry Phillpotts to the See of Exeter, where he remained for thirty-nine
years carrying 'Tory principles of the extreme right into every aspect of
affairs'.[1] His predecessor, who only reigned for six months, was
hurriedly translated to Bangor to make way for this combative man who
had in his youth contemplated studying law; this might explain why he
spent nearly £30,000 (over £1m) on some fifty lawsuits during his
career. Phillpotts was originally anti-Roman Catholic, but Wellington
persuaded him to support emancipation and afterwards he was often
sympathetic to the Catholic insights of the Oxford Movement. In 1846,
at the behest of the Tory Lord Chancellor, he instituted George
Cornelius Gorham, a fellow of Queens' College, Cambridge, into the
living of St Just in Penwith, in Cornwall. At Cambridge Gorham had
become an Evangelical, and the Bishop of Ely threatened to refuse him
ordination because of his views on baptism. Now his views surfaced
again when the Bishop of Exeter demanded an interview with a priest
who wanted to work with Gorham. Unlike many bishops, Phillpotts,
'the mitred termagant', regularly examined curates and incumbents
before appointing them, and in this case he had been shocked by
Gorham's advertisement saying he wanted an assistant 'free from
Tractarian error'. He rebuked him and ended one letter, 'I am with
sincere regret and pain in so subscribing myself, your grieved and
offended Overseer in the Lord'.[2]

Gorham, who had been ordained for thirty-six years, found his
new parish in Cornwall uncongenial to his family, so asked the Whig

Lord Chancellor, Lord Cottenham, for a living nearer a town. In August 1847 he was offered Brampford Speke, which was close to Exeter and had a population of 400. The relationship between the Bishop and incumbent was already in an inflammable state, and four months later Phillpotts refused to appoint until he had examined Gorham. The enquiry was held for four days before Christmas, and fourteen more hours' examination followed three months later. A total of 149 questions were put to Gorham and on 11 March the Bishop declared he was unable to proceed with the institution. A month later, in a circular letter, the rejected incumbent described the circumstances as a 'cruel exercise of episcopal power stretched beyond the boundaries of reason and decency', which was not surprising as his family were living in various homes and the children were not being educated. Everything focused on Gorham's view on baptism. Like all Calvinistic clergymen he held that the grace of regeneration was not granted in baptism; it came either before, as prevenient grace, or after, at conversion. Phillpotts said it was impossible to consider anyone baptised in infancy as unregenerate.

A decision of Sir Herbert Jenner Fust in the Court of Arches confirmed the validity of the Bishop's action although, as Professor Chadwick comments, Sir Herbert found himself ill-at-ease among the ramifications of historical theology. The language of the Prayer Book was uncompromising; after administering baptism the priest says, 'Seeing now that this child is regenerate', and the catechism states that the person is made 'the child of God and an inheritor of the Kingdom of Heaven'. The elderly Sir Herbert, who was carried into court by two footmen, agreed that the meaning of regeneration was imprecise, but judged that an infant is indeed regenerated in baptism. Costs were awarded to the Bishop.

Gorham immediately appealed to the Judicial Committee of the Privy Council, and the Queen decreed that the appeal should be heard by seven lay assessors sitting with the two archbishops, Sumner and Musgrave, and the Bishop of London – none of these three having a vote. Blomfield was unhappy about it all, and did not reply to the letter of invitation, but did arrive when the Committee met on 11 December 1849. Pleadings lasted until 18 December, when Phillpotts' lawyer, Edward Badeley, caused a stir by saying he laboured under a disadvantage, as the archbishops had already committed themselves to Gorham's views. He pointed out that Archbishop Sumner had given preferment to William Goode, the Evangelical vicar of All Hallows by the Tower, who shared Gorham's views, but His Grace said he had not read Goode's book on the subject which was as yet unpublished. Dr Chadwick says it is as well that Badeley was ignorant of a letter of support sent by Sumner to Gorham nearly two years earlier.[3] At the dinner following the hearing all the lay judges except Sir James Knight Bruce felt that the Arches ruling should be overturned, but the prelates asked for time to consider. A month later Blomfield, 'after much vacillation, half assenting, being on and off by turns against Gorham and against the Bishop, disagreeing with everybody and everything'[4] gave an opinion for Phillpotts, and the two archbishops for Gorham. Stephen Lushington, the only trained ecclesiastical lawyer in the court, said he had the greatest difficulty in understanding what Gorham taught, but went along with the majority. When the judgment was announced there was applause and cries of 'Bravo.' It was unclear whether the judgment was a definition of Anglican theology or not. If so, had it any authority?

Blomfield was greatly distressed by the controversy, but found himself praised and congratulated by the opponents of Gorham, who began to ask if he was a covert Puseyite. Gladstone told him he was courageous and a protector of weaker men, but the Bishop replied that he had gone into the enquiry with an anxious desire to make peace and to find a compromise which 'might not greatly displease either class of churchmen although it might not satisfy either extreme'. However, when he found that Gorham was 'nullifying the sacramental character of baptism from the outward visible sign he could not concur in any judgment which should declare such an opinion to be within any allowable latitude of interpretation of the Articles and liturgy of the Church'.[5]

The Bishop of London was not usually at his best when discussing doctrine, preferring less abstract subjects such as bathhouses or bishoprics in Barbados. Brought up as an old-fashioned High Churchman, he was suspicious of Evangelicals and Tractarians who each tried in vain to get his support. The *Record* observed that 'he can speak smoothly as well as harshly to men of all shades and parties, differing from the Evangelical in principle or the Tractarians only in degree.' It was obvious to the Bishop that regeneration meant different things to different people. Tractarians thought it was the new birth spoken of in scripture, Moderates thought it meant embracing a new life in the fellowship of believers, and Evangelicals considered its blessings dependent on repentance and faith. Blomfield told Gladstone that by baptismal regeneration one becomes a child of God in the sense that God no longer regards one with displeasure but with favour, and this carries with it the remission of sins, but the final efficacy of these privileges only results if one grows in grace. More than the sacrament of baptism is needed.

Most bishops would now have let the matter drop, but not Blomfield. In his sixth Charge, delivered the following November to the London clergy, he gave his reasons for opposing the majority decision which had supported Gorham. He reasoned in clear, positive and forcible terms for the Church's acceptance of the doctrine of regeneration for all infants at baptism. He found Gorham's assertions 'wholly irreconcilable ... with the plain teaching of the Church of England and the Church Universal in all ages.'[6] The Judicial Committee had misunderstood Gorham's position which said that children are never regenerated by baptism, and this was dogmatically opposed to the doctrine of the Church of England. Of course regeneration does not invariably take place in unbelieving or impenitent adults, the Charge continued, but Gorham's real errors were ignored by the Committee. He had contradicted church teaching that an infant is made in and by baptism a member of Christ and not before or after baptism as he had suggested. The Prayer Book, which is a guide to doctrine as well as devotion, the Scriptures, and the Articles, all prove Gorham wrong. Baptism does not ensure a place in Heaven, but by it a person is brought to a state of salvation.

Toward the end of the Charge, Blomfield told his clergy that the confusion surrounding the sacrament is to a large extent the result of careless and irregular administration: services are rarely held in public, so few understand what baptism means. Ministers have mutilated or adapted the Office to suit a particular occasion, they have thrust the font into a corner of the church out of sight of the congregation, they have disregarded the rubrics, and they have left the catechism unexplained.[7] Is it any wonder that there is confusion? Perhaps the Gorham case will recall people to the true meaning of the sacrament. The result of years of neglect is that a clergyman who 'precisely and dogmatically' opposes the Church's doctrine can, by a decision of the highest tribunal, hold office in the Church. This is a disgrace. Gladstone was delighted with the Charge, saying it was 'not the last, I trust, and surely not the least but the greatest in the line of services as long and as bright as adorns the name of any of the prelates of modern times; an act of faith and courage'.

What alarmed most people about the judgement had little to do with doctrine; rather they were scandalised that a secular committee was enabled by law to reverse a decision on doctrine made by a Church Court. As early as 1846 Blomfield had seen the warning light, and had regretted his support for the changes in the law fourteen years earlier which had caused this situation. A Commission on which Blomfield sat had recommended that the Privy Council replace the High Court of Delegates as the supreme court of appeal in ecclesiastical matters, because only seven cases had come before the Court of Delegates since 1586. At Phillpotts' instigation Blomfield made three attempts in the late 1840s to rectify the situation by law, and in 1850 he tried again, having first called a meeting of twenty-five bishops on the 6th February at London House to advise him. When he introduced his Clergy Proceedings Bill in the Lords, the *Guardian* described his speech as a 'learned and masterly statement of the whole subject'.[8] Blomfield said that a question of fundamental principle was at stake: the Church must be able to discharge its functions without let or hindrance. The Court of Delegates should be reconvened and consist of the two archbishops, three senior bishops, the Lord Chancellor, the Dean of Arches, the judges of the Consistory Court of London and the Regius and Lady Margaret Professors of Divinity at Oxford and Cambridge. As the two ecclesiastical judges were 'spiritual persons' there were to be only two laymen on the Court, and Lord John Russell felt that this would alienate the laity from the Church. Several eminent men agreed with him, including Prince Albert, most of the Whig peers and the Editor of *The Times* newspaper. The Bill received its second reading in the Lords on 3 June 1850, Blomfield speaking persuasively and well. 'The Bishop spoke with more than his usual lucidity and force. His clear, grave tones interrupted for several moments towards the close by strong emotion, conveyed his speech to every part of the House'. It was not enough. The Government opposed the Bill and it was lost, 84–51. The Bishop was disappointed and decided to redirect his energies to reviving Convocation which would act as the Church's parliament.

Meanwhile in July Phillpotts threatened solemnly to excommunicate anyone who instituted Mr Gorham, but the following month the new incumbent broke open the church door at Brampford Speke and preached his first sermon to a large and lively congregation. Phillpotts refused to appoint a curate and wrote to the churchwardens commanding them to listen carefully to what their new vicar said in the pulpit. He also sent a pamphlet outlining the true doctrine of baptism to every house in the parish. One wonders what the inhabitants made of it all.

Blomfield was disturbed and disappointed by the whole affair, not because a bishop had been overruled in his own diocese, but because a Court decision, approved by evangelicals and valid in law, meant that a clergyman holding Calvinistic or uncertain doctrine on the subject of baptism could not be excluded from the ministry of the Church. As F. W. Cornish has said, 'It has been called by some the charter of religious freedom, by others a soul-destroying judgment. It extended the bounds of comprehension; it did nothing to settle the principles of comprehension'.[9]

Chapter Eleven

Last days

The Bishop of London's dinner invitations read
'The Church of England and Mrs Blomfield request the pleasure . . .'
Canon Sydney Smith.

I never got anything I asked for and I never asked for anything I got.
Bishop Blomfield.

Unfortunately for Charles James both archbishops decided to live to a great age. Howley succeeded to St Augustine's chair in 1828 on the death of Manners Sutton who was 'without genius or learning to make him angular or unpleasant'. In twenty-three years at Canterbury he had never given a Charge to his clergy, but did publish *Some British Species of Orobanche.** After fourteen years at Canterbury, in 1842, a rumour circulated that Howley had died of Asiatic cholera, so Peel who was holidaying on the grouse moors, immediately offered the archbishopric to Blomfield[1], but Howley recovered and lived a further six years. He was a gentle, kind, meek man, but Lord Brompton thought him 'a poor creature'; Gladstone described him as 'gentle among the gentle, mild among the mild'. Dr G. K. A. Best denies that he was a puppet pulled by Blomfield's strings, but William Bowles compared Blomfield to Howley as the 'wisdom of the serpent' to the 'harmlessness of the dove'. Son of a Hampshire vicar, Howley was a thrifty man who left an estate of £120,000 (£5m). Things are different now. When Lord Runcie of St Albans died in 2000 he left an estate valued at £40,000 net. Dr Chadwick describes Howley as 'a man of strong principle and quiet courage, fond of looking at both sides of a question. Men claimed that he had never been young. He was a lamentable speaker and perpetually lost the right words, visibly groping for the wrong. Making a speech at a

*Orobanche: root-parasite plants such as broomrape.

girls' school he could not think how to address them: 'my dear young friends – my dear girls – my dear young catechumens – my dear Christian friends – my dear young female women'.[2] After his death *The Times* said, 'It can scarcely be said that what fell from his lips ever deserved to be called a speech'. Small wonder that Blomfield for two decades was archbishop in all but name, but the two men were always firm friends, and Charles James never forgot he owed his position to his old mentor.

In York the Honourable Edward Vernon had already been living in Bishopsthorpe for twenty-one years when Blomfield moved to London, and he was to remain there a further nineteen. Described by Lord Esher as 'a sumptuous prelate' because he was Lord Vernon's youngest son, he changed his name to Vernon Harcourt in 1831 on inheriting the Harcourt estates. A simple, insignificant, reticent man, he could occasionally be arrogant. When the famous tenor John Braham sang at the York Festival the Archbishop sent him several letters advising him how to sing. The story was relayed with great merriment by Braham's daughter, Lady Waldegrave, in all the London drawing-rooms. In matters ecclesiastical he deferred to the Bishop of London. Whilst on the Ecclesiastical Commission he remarked, 'Till Blomfield comes we all sit and mend our pens and talk about the weather'. In October 1847 in his ninety-second year he fell into a pool at Bishopsthorpe when a wooden bridge collapsed. 'I think we've frightened the frogs', he said, but he too had been shaken, and five weeks later he faded away. Lord John Russell acted quickly. Maltby of Durham refused the archbishopric so Thomas Musgrave, Bishop of Hereford, was appointed.

The following year, on the day before his eighty-third birthday, Howley died. The Prime Minister considered three names and Blomfield, now aged sixty-one, was not among them. After only eleven days it was announced that the scholarly, pious Bishop Sumner of Chester had been appointed. A year earlier, Blomfield had slipped on a polished floor at Osborne House while visiting the Queen. He bruised his right eye and temple, his eyelids refused to close, and facial paralysis set in shortly afterwards. His speech became slurred, so that he was unable to speak in public for several months. He never fully recovered, and his handwriting considerably deteriorated. The *Guardian*, on the day after Howley's death, said that if the Prime Minister wanted an independent, able Primate, Blomfield was the natural choice; Russell, however, correctly thought that the Bishop of London's health would continue to decline, and he would therefore not be able to fulfil the obligations of the archbishopric. It was a great blow to the Bishop's pride. A few months later, he told Gladstone that his health was 'quite established' except for an affliction of his face which prevented him from preaching or officiating at services. People noted he was less cheerful and his hand continually moved to his cheeks. He became depressed and less able to withstand the criticisms which were being heaped upon him. Being passed over for the archbishopric had further added to his gloom. He now became less patient with criticism, and said he felt his grip on church affairs slackening. In May 1850 he was seriously ill, and in that July he mourned the loss of his friend Wordsworth and the sudden death of his colleague, Peel. Matters were not helped when two years later, feeling decidedly unwell, he with Dean Milman had to stand at the west door of St Paul's Cathedral for well over an hour waiting for Wellington's coffin to be taken down from the huge funeral car. An icy November wind blew through the Cathedral so that many of the 10,000 mourners sitting in specially-constructed stands put their hats on. The mechanism of the car had failed. Lord Anglesey complained that he had never been so cold in all his life. The Bishop now realised he could no longer cope with the huge amount of work undertaken in Fulham Palace. His health improved but in the autumn of 1853, aged sixty-seven, he had an attack of hemiplegia which the doctors connected with his fall six years earlier. On 16 January 1855 his friends noticed he spoke in a much lower, feeble voice at the consecration of St Andrew's Church, Thornhill Square, Islington. In July he made what was to be his last speech in the House of Lords. His eyesight began to fail, so he decided to visit a German eye specialist while he was visiting the English congregations on the continent. He spent the summer of 1855 at Grafrath, near Düsseldorf, where Dr Leuw saw him regularly and suggested a less stressful life. 'Not possible,' said the Bishop, who had just come from preaching to a large and attentive congregation in Bonn. Tired and worn out by the colossal load he had carried, he now found it hard to withstand the insults thrown at him. Liddell, vicar of St Paul's, Knightsbridge, later said he found it easier to stand up to Bishop Tait, as it had always given him intense pain to quarrel with Blomfield who now took opposition as a personal insult. Others were kinder. Sydney Smith, after the controversy caused by the Dean and Chapter Bill, met the Bishop to discuss points at issue 'with temper and caution', and then parted amicably. 'I like the Bishop and I like his conversation. The battle is ended, and I have no further quarrel with him and the Archbishop but that they neither of them ever ask me to dinner.' He was now a 'good boy' and asked Greville to 'take an opportunity to set him right and exhort him, as he has gained the victory, to forgive a few hard knocks'.

Returning to England on 22 October 1855, the Bishop, after preaching at Fulham parish church, had another attack of paralysis which robbed him of the use of his left side. He went to Hampstead for Christmas, and Thomas Ainger, the vicar of Hampstead, brought him Communion and all the family received the sacrament. The energetic Ainger was greatly admired by Blomfield as in his twenty-two-year incumbency he had enlarged his church, helped to found schools and a dispensary and provided new churches in the area around Hampstead. After a visit to Brighton the Bishop returned to Fulham, still helpless. The archdeacons of London and Middlesex now had to bear the heavy diocesan workload as there were no suffragan or assistant bishops. Twenty years earlier, Archdeacon Hale had asked him to create suffragan bishops but was told, 'I do not agree with you now – I may do so when I am three score'. Now it was too late. Dr Robert Todd, an old friend of the Bishop and professor of medicine at King's College Hospital, which he and Blomfield had helped establish in 1840, was summoned to Fulham and declared the Bishop to be very seriously ill. Samuel Wilberforce told Gladstone, 'the prospect as to London' was 'most gloomy', and the following March he called at Fulham Palace and noted in his diary,

Saw him, very low, very affecting state, spoke of himself as dying. I certain to succeed him and no one to whom he could more happily entrust his diocese. About himself his keen sight of past sins; no hope but simply in Christ's sacrifice for him. A great struggle between conscience and faith. 'Pray for me'. A most affecting sight in one so good.[3]

The two men now only 69 and 50 had been friends for many years. A report, possibly apocryphal, says that the young Samuel had gone to the Chapel Royal to hear the Bishop preach. As there were no other worshippers they decided to go for a walk in St James's Park and the friendship began. In 1842 Peel, the Prime Minister, had consulted Blomfield about Wilberforce's future. J. W. Croker, a Privy Councillor who lived at Alverstoke where Wilberforce was incumbent, thought Samuel one of the best preachers in England and 'of very deep yet cheerful piety but wanting in aplomb and dignity which we see for instance in the Bishop of London'. Wilberforce had been made Dean of Westminster, then, three years later much to Blomfield's delight, Bishop of Oxford. He was the only bishop present at Blomfield's funeral.

Towards the end of his time Blomfield's patience ran out. In his 1846 Charge he condemned the efforts of those intent on reviving the opinions and practices of the Roman Church. It perplexes and unsettles 'sensitive and imperfectly instructed consciences who desire absolute authority ... This is especially the case with females, the natural constitution of whose minds disposes them to rest upon the authority of others; while livelier sensibilities are more easily excited and satisfied by an aesthetic and ceremonial form of religion'. One wonders what Harriet Martineau said about that. The 1850 Charge went further when he attacked excessive ritualism, singling out for particular condemnation the books of devotion where

> a propitiatory virtue is attributed to the Eucharist, the mediation of the saints is spoken of as a probable doctrine, prayer for the dead urged as a positive duty and a superstitious use of the sign of the Cross is recommended as profitable; add to this the secret practice of auricular confession, the use of crucifixes and rosaries ... and it is manifest that they who are taught to believe that such things are compatible with the principles of the English Church, must also believe it to be separated from that of Rome by a faint and almost imperceptible line.

Nothing vague or uncertain about these words, and Dr Pusey was stung to publish his *Letter to the Bishop of London* saying he had been misrepresented and that his books of devotion had great theological and spiritual strength. Blomfield and Pusey were regular correspondents. Soon after his arrival in London he had sent Pusey, who had requested his opinion, two letters, each nine quarto pages, covered in closely written criticism and comments about his book on German Rationalism. Pusey was not greatly pleased but did make some alterations to the text.

In his last Charge, 1854, delivered in the early days of the Crimean War, the Bishop congratulated the nation because all classes were working together in goodwill and mutual kindness. He felt proud that the Church was helping the poor by attending to their temporal wants, providing education and thereby introducing them to the Christian faith. Then, unknowingly, he threw down a challenge to his successor. The population of London was increasing by 40,000 each year, so the shortage of clergy and buildings would continue. We must increase resources to maintain additional curates, he said, and then suggested a way to bring in more money, which we now call stewardship. 'I am inclined to believe that much might be done towards raising funds by collecting very small weekly or monthly subscriptions from the poorer members of our Church through the agency of well-organised associations'. He then referred to a Dr Baylee and the Liverpool Working

Men's Church Association where two thousand subscribers paying 1d to 6d a week raised several thousands of pounds for new churches. Why could this not be done in London?

Retirement

Bishop Sumner was asked to take the 1856 ordination in St Paul's because although Blomfield had regained his speech after his stroke the previous October he was still far from well. The great weight of pastoral care and administration was now too heavy for him to bear so, ever the innovator, the Bishop decided to retire, but as no bishop had done this since the Reformation a parliamentary Bill would be needed. He pointed out that he could not afford to leave without a substantial pension, as during his episcopate he had provided for every needy cause, and thus neglected his own family. He had rebuilt part of Fulham Palace at a cost of £2,000 (£80,000) so he asked for £6,000 p. a. (£240,000), a third of his income, to cover his costs and insurances. There was an immediate outcry: as no clergy had pensions, why should the Bishop of London? A bishop was also a peer of the realm, so would he keep his seat in the House of Lords? The *Record* suggested a general Bill to deal with episcopal retirements, particularly as Maltby of Durham also wanted to retire, but this would have taken several years to implement and the need was pressing. Two old men felt they could no longer preside over their dioceses – who would want to keep them in office against their will? Palmerston, the Prime Minister, was sympathetic, and agreed to sponsor the Bishops of London and Durham Retirement Bill, the latter being given £4,500 p. a. (£180,000) and Blomfield £6,000 p. a. (£240,000). The *Guardian* was not impressed, saying, 'the transaction has not that lofty character with which episcopal acts should properly be impressed'. It savoured of the solicitor rather than the saint.

There was much opposition to the Bill, which also allowed Blomfield use of the Fulham estate for his lifetime. Many were apprehensive because Palmerston and the Whigs would now be able to appoint two senior bishops. Some Prime Ministers enjoyed this power but some did not. Melbourne once remarked, 'Damn me, another bishop dead'. The Lord Chancellor, Lord Cranworth, a school friend of Blomfield, introduced the Bill into the Lords and explained why it was necessary. He pointed out that the surplus revenues of the two sees would provide ample retirement pensions, and a general measure was impossible because the new episcopal stipends fixed by the Commission left no money for pensions. The Archbishop of Canterbury, Sumner, reminded their Lordships that if the Bishop of London had been less charitable during his reign he would have no need to apply for help. Phillpotts of Exeter could not see why there was so much hurry, as the confirmation season was over. Lord Redesdale wanted to delay the Bill for three months as it was a hasty and partial measure; Lord Derby, however, said £6,000 represented the income of 60 curates but the Bishop was worth every penny. The Bill became law, and Blomfield resigned all his dignities, except the deanery of the Chapels Royal, because the Queen said she would like him to keep a connection with the Royal House. He had enjoyed preaching in the Chapel Royal but in 1849 had ended his special confirmation services which were held there for the sons of the nobility. At Fulham, with tears in his eyes, he signed the necessary document, and soon letters and Addresses of affection poured in. 'It is almost worth resigning to find so much kindness from one's friends', he remarked. Replying to the archdeacons and clergy he recalled the sacred bond which had united them with him for twenty-eight years and thanked them for their many kindnesses. 'Let me add that I am not conscious of having ever allowed any difference of opinion on matters not affecting the foundation or the essential doctrines of our holy faith, to influence my conduct towards any individual of my clergy, but that I looked only to his faithfulness and diligence in winning souls to Christ'. He said he had long felt that a younger, stronger man was now needed for London.

The *Guardian*, usually critical of the Bishop, reported that he had won preferment not by academic achievements, high though they were, nor by marriage, nor by political toadying, but by having a great aptitude for work. He had not always justified the hopes churchmen placed in him, nor had he 'supported with uniform consistency a course which we thankfully acknowledge to have been in the main rightly directed'. Very few however, could have steered the diocese through such difficult times, and 'few, surely, would on the whole have displayed so much impartiality, temper, and forbearance ... the Bishop has been firm'.[4] 'Of the Bishop of Durham we had rather not say much'. Blomfield's resignation was covered in one and three-quarter columns, Maltby's in three lines.

In October 1856 Blomfield asked his successor and his wife to stay at Fulham for five days. Archibald Campbell Tait, a Scot and Dean of Carlisle, had been brought up as a Presbyterian, and would later become Archbishop of Canterbury. When he was nineteen he visited London and asked to walk through Lambeth to see 'how I shall like the place when I get there'. Blomfield at school had said, 'I mean to be a Bishop', so obviously neither man suffered from a lack of ambition. Queen Victoria and most of her subjects had been horrified a few months earlier when five of Tait's six daughters had died from scarlet fever, and this may be one of the reasons why preferment to such a senior post came so quickly. In London he looked favourably on the Evangelicals but was bitterly opposed to ritualists, and the Public Worship Regulation Act of 1874 was the disastrous result. Four clergy were imprisoned. Like his predecessor he encountered trouble at St Paul's, Knightsbridge, and St Barnabas, Pimlico, where he withdrew the licence of the curate, William Poole, for hearing a woman's confession in a darkened vestry. After an appeal to the Archbishop of Canterbury the sentence was confirmed, and Poole was told that what he had done was 'most dangerous and likely to cause serious mischief to the cause of morality and religion'.[5]

Tait, born in 1811, had grown up in a Church threatened by disestablishment and subject to radical reform, so, after Blomfield's resignation and his appointment, he said he wanted to build bridges between the Church and the poor, and he himself went to preach outdoors in working-class areas, addressing omnibus drivers in Islington, costermongers at Covent Garden, and gypsies in Shepherd's Bush. Some London clergy, like Robert Maguire of Clerkenwell and his curates, followed his example, but they were not typical.[6] Tait was unknown on religious platforms, never having sat in Convocation, and he realised it would be difficult to follow a bishop who had so much energy, intelligence and eloquence, a man whose 'business habits and organising genius had gone far to change men's views of the English episcopate'.[7] He felt that Blomfield had settled the Church firmly on orthodox lines, free, as far as possible, from 'the taint either of Tractarian bigotry, or from the Arnoldian laxity of belief'.[8]

The Bishop lived less than a year in retirement at Fulham. His funeral took place on 11 August 1857, and a large number of clergy, including Liddell from Knightsbridge and Dr Biber, the biographer, joined neighbouring tradesmen assembled in the quadrangle of the Palace. At 12.30 the procession moved to Fulham parish church, where the Bishop was buried in the churchyard. Blomfield's archdeacons and his two chaplains were pall-bearers together with the rector of Hornsey. At the Bishop's request the service was 'simple and unadorned'. A memorial was erected at Fulham and later, thanks to subscriptions from friends, a recumbent effigy of the Bishop was placed in the north ambulatory of St Paul's Cathedral. *The Times* reported that the Cathedral was hung with black and presented an imposing appearance. It took the artist George Richmond seven years to craft the marble memorial of 'one of my early and very constant friends'. It was his first sculpture and he refused all assistance. Later he described the Bishop in a letter to his son Alfred Blomfield. 'In middle life one saw the warfare, as in later life the victory ... there was a touch of sadness underlying all that revealed itself when the face was in repose. The fire of life seemed to burn brighter and quicker than in other men, his very walk was significant of this – that short, firm and rapid step, with a sort of *I am ready* expression in it ... also the way he stood, erect, and resting equally on both feet, they well apart, often the hands crossed behind him, never languid, never reclining. He looked every inch a churchman, and, unbounded in his generosity to others, was severe really only to himself.'

After his death the three archdeacons, who had been working closely with him in the diocese, all praised his energy and ability. Archdeacon Sinclair said that an abruptness of manner hid a kind-hearted sensibility, which probably accounted for the popular error of supposing him to be a harsh, stern man. Archdeacon Hale called him 'one of the most simple-hearted of mankind, one of the firmest of friends', and likened him to St Paul, somewhat to the disadvantage of the saint. Both, he said, were scholars and founders of churches, both were pious, charitable, fearless and affectionate but St Paul, unlike Charles James, was a poor speaker.

The *Guardian*'s obituary notice does not do justice to the leader of the second Reformation in the Church of England and has an under-current of Tractarian disapproval of the Bishop's practical gifts. 'His career was eminently a practical one. His scholarship at Cambridge was second only to Dr Gaisford but after his elevation to the Bench it was subordinated to Church business. His failures can be traced to that excess of caution and absence of venture and enthusiasm which so preeminently distinguish a practical man. Two deeds deserve to be "written on his tomb in letters of gold" – the erection of the Bethnal Green churches and the creation of the colonial episcopate. Whereas there were 5 overseas bishoprics in 1840 now there are 25 and 6 more shortly to be founded. He had great powers of organisation and management'. The *Guardian* thought the great blot on his career was the Church Commission.

The Times praised his preaching, his simplicity in diction and skill in arrangement. The power of his voice, naturally melodious, enabled him to command the attention of even the largest congregations. His passion for business, accessibility and freedom from nepotism were also noted. The *Record* disagreed, as three years earlier it had condemned the Bishop for giving his son-in-law, John Smith, a parish in Acton, his nephew the Launton Rectory and his son the City living of St Andrew Undershaft. All three men were in Orders and suitably qualified, but the *Record*'s editor smelt corruption. Writing a few years later, Anthony

Trollope felt nepotism in bishops can be allowed unless it is too glaring. 'A bishop's daughter is supposed to offer one of the fairest steps to promotion which the Church of England affords.'

Thanks to Blomfield, his successor came to a diocese which had been reorganised and reformed. As Wilberforce remarked, the sole object of Blomfield's episcopate had been to increase the moral and spiritual efficiency of the Church of England, so the late Victorian bishops had come into a goodly heritage: they had much to thank him for.

Chapter Twelve

The man

He came in like a lion and went out like a lamb.
Harriet Martineau.

There are two well known preservations against ague,
the one is a good deal of care and a little port wine; the other is a
little care and a good deal of port wine. I prefer the former.
Charles James Blomfield.

The Bishop's days were well-planned and disciplined. In the summer he rose at 6 am, in winter 6.30 am. Until breakfast he read and studied the Bible, and perhaps prepared a sermon or wrote letters. He always tried to complete his Charges and Addresses well in advance, and usually read his sermons but delivered his speeches without notes. He was in great demand as a preacher and delivered hundreds of sermons, many of which were published. Most sermons at this time lasted at least an hour, so could not be prepared on the back of an envelope the night before; in 1824 Edward Irving preached the annual sermon of the London Missionary Society which lasted for three and a half hours, allowing two pauses for hymn-singing.[1] As there was no means of amplification, long addresses could be a strain on the vocal chords as well as on the ears. Looking at the Bishop's published sermons, I suspect they lasted for nearly an hour. Unlike his predecessor at London, 1787–1808, Beilby Porteus who, when asked to preach a charity sermon, said he only gave one a year and this and next years' were already promised, Blomfield felt that bishops should speak with authority and often. He had a dislike of men such as Bishop Stanley of Norwich, and Whately, Archbishop of Dublin, who, according to Greville, 'had a skimble-skamble way of talking as if he was half tipsy and thought the Church was founded upon liberty of conscience and the right of private judgement'. In 1842 the Bishop published three sermons, preached at St James's

Piccadilly, insisting on the divine authority of episcopal church government, and saying the bishops should speak clearly and directly to offer a sure foundation on which people could base their hopes of the hereafter. Despite believing in the divine institution of the Church, the Body of Christ, he reminded his hearers, in a sermon published after his death, not to put too much trust in the machinery and apparatus of societies, missionaries, churches and schools, giving them an efficacy not their own. Perhaps he was preaching to himself. 'We forget how utterly worthless and inefficient they are without the direct intervention of God himself.' Similarly, he points out that the connection with the State is important but not essential. Civil rights and privileges together with endowments are adventitious accidents. If they were done away with the Church would still continue; 'the Church might even be crippled in the exercise of its functions by the interference of the State. The State cannot create or destroy it.' He believed strongly that the Church is not simply a society formed on considerations of expedience for the purpose of mutual protection, encouragement and edification of its members. 'It is the appointed conduit through which the blessings of the Gospel flow in certain definite channels. It is the outward means of conveying to us the inward graces divided by the Spirit to every man.'[2] Bishop Wilberforce, who heard Blomfield preach on 'Flee youthful lusts', was 'affected to tears', but thought, 'He flings his head at you too much but otherwise has a very effective manner and is the best preacher in the London Diocese'. The Bishop said he had only once in his life preached extempore. One Sunday at Chesterford he walked over to Little Chesterford church to take the afternoon service, but on arrival found he had left his sermon at home. He had decided to preach on 'The fool hath said in his heart: there is no God', so he went ahead. As one parishioner left, he told Blomfield, 'I liked the sermon, but I can't say I agree with you. I think there is a God.'

Summers were spent at Fulham Palace, and he was 'generally settled' there from the beginning of October to the end of January. At other times he was at London House in St James's Square. Mornings were devoted to correspondence – at least thirty letters arrived each day. His copy books, now kept at Lambeth Palace Library, contain many letters to incumbents giving them instructions on various matters, but also several of a pastoral nature. Twice the Bishop wrote to Hardwicke, the Postmaster-General, about letter carriers, one asking him to employ a total abstainer known to him, and the other asking him to help financially a man who was now unable to deliver the early-morning letters in Fulham, and thus had seen his salary drop from 18s to 11s a week. Friday mornings were set aside for clergy interviews, when twenty to thirty men would wait to see him. Their needs were dealt with briskly and efficiently, even to the point of abruptness. The Bishop sat at one end of a table, with a notebook beside him in which he noted rapidly the subjects of discussion. Incumbents of the very large parishes were told that they could come at any time even if he had to travel to town specifically to see them. One of his diocesan clergy noted in his diary, 'When you go to a man of business keep to your business, finish your business and then go about your business'. On 17 November 1841, Chevalier Ernest de Bunsen called by appointment to show the Bishop his 100 pages in quarto, being the various liturgies proposed for the bishopric in Jerusalem. Work began at 8 am consulting the German original, and ended at 11 am. A short break was held for family prayers and breakfast. Blomfield corrected the text and made many observations which greatly impressed Bunsen, who later expressed astonishment at the morning's work. The Bishop's many appeals for church buildings and schools, and his interest in every aspect of Church and State reform, meant endless committee work, but he would brook no delays or drawn-out discussions. Decisions had to be reached quickly. In his obituary *The Times* noted that he had 'the most marvellous power of dispatching business'.

The same obituary noted that friendship was important to him, pointing out that he kept many of his friends from school and college days. 'His fund of anecdotes diffused a charm over the society of every circle which he entered'.[3] Puns were a particular pleasure. Sydney Smith, himself 'crackling away like a congenial bonfire of jokes and good sense and uproarious laughter, the baiter of bishops', said that Blomfield affected 'short, sharp sayings, seasoned ... sometimes with a little indiscretion'.[4] The Bishop tried to fill his home with interesting people, including Sir Henry Holland, the physician, Sir Walter Scott, Wordsworth, Hallam, Macaulay, and George Richmond, whose marble effigy of the Bishop is in the north ambulatory of St Paul's Cathedral. Throughout his life he had a streak of Puritanism, and cards were never allowed to be seen after dinner. In 1854, when the Great Exhibition moved to Sydenham, he joined Archbishop Sumner and the Bishop of Winchester in requesting that the nude statues be provided with fig leaves. The directors agreed, but doubted whether they could find enough leaves before the date of opening.[5] He disliked dancing and objected to hunting and shooting. 'Theatrical amusements' he considered not conducive 'to the ends of piety and morality'. He spoke French fluently, and could read German well. One of his recreations was music and he enjoyed attending concerts, but his chief interest was gardening. The gardens at Fulham Palace with their half-mile river frontage had been a show-place since Elizabethan days, and were a great joy to him. Howley had reorganised them, but Blomfield introduced the latest improvements and planted new and rare trees, including a *Cryptomeria japonica* and an *Eilanthus glandulosa* said to be the best specimens in England, which he would proudly, with his quick, firm step, take visitors to see. The Bishop spent £10,000 (£300,000) putting the estate back in order, altering the building, re-roofing it, adding several rooms and rebuilding one of the wings. He partially rebuilt and buttressed the south side of the Fitzjames courtyard in a Tudor style, putting his coat of arms above the central doorway and his motto, 'Vigilando et orando', 'watching and praying', in the guard-room. He raised the level of the water-meadows to stop flooding, and after his retirement was pushed there in a wheelchair to enjoy the river views. He tried living in Hampstead, then Brighton, but finally decided to remain at Fulham, and a year after his retirement he died in the Porteous Library, now a museum, where his bed had been placed so he could see the garden.

Having been one of the foremost classicists at the turn of the century, no doubt the Bishop would have liked to have kept up his studies, but it was not to be. While at Cambridge he had won several medals, and as a young Fellow of Trinity in 1809 had edited five of the seven plays of Aeschylus and founded a magazine, *Museum Criticum*, which lasted nine years. It brought to light neglected fragments and works by obscure authors, and published essays on Greek and Roman history. In one article Blomfield pointed out that if E. H. Barker's edition of Stephen's *Thesaurus* continued at the present speed it would run to fifty volumes, and take seventy years to publish. The author, who was well known for writing anonymous reviews which flattered his own books, was not pleased. In 1820 a tournament of scholars had taken place, when Barker took exception to an article written by Blomfield in the January edition of the *Quarterly Review*. He accused him of being a hypocrite with an 'utter disregard of truth and unblushing impertinence'. He attacked Blomfield's edition of Callimachus as being 'a motley mixture of old stubborn, stiff readings', with a deplorable want of critical acumen. The young Blomfield took up the cudgels with gusto, saying, 'I have not time for anything elaborate for this cur'. Barker replied by congratulating him on his appointment to St Botolph's, saying he hoped this meant he would no longer need to be the hireling of publishers, and indulging in low-minded spite. Such views were, however, rare and A. E. Housman, the classical scholar and poet, thought that 'our great age of scholarship which began in 1691 ended in 1824 with the successive strokes of doom which consigned Dobree and Elmsley to the grave, and Blomfield to the bishopric of Chester'. In 1836, while recovering from an illness, the Bishop had returned to Greek verse, but in 1840 felt he had no time for even 'the slightest libation to the Ausonian muse'. In his biography his son Alfred reports that the young Charles James had each day spent 'sometimes 16 – even 18 hours over his books'. This, together with the stressful nature of his work in Chester and London, meant that his health was never good. In 1836 he fell seriously ill, and his recovery was hindered when one of the horses drawing his carriage had a fit. Blomfield jumped out and seized the wheel of the carriage to prevent his wife being hurt. The incident left him incapacitated for several weeks, and on resuming work he received a congratulatory Address from the archdeacons and clergy. In thanking them he pointed out that he had not been idle in convalescence, but had translated the greater part of Gray's *Elegy* into Latin verse. He made a good recovery, and in July 1844 Peregrinus, in a letter to the *Christian Examiner*, described him as a 'round faced, fresh-looking, apparently well-fed personage'.

Family

We know very little of the Bishop's family life, which is hardly mentioned in the two tombstone biographies. In November 1844 he was greatly upset by the death of his mother, Hester. Writing to his wife he said, 'The loss of one dear friend makes us value those who are left more highly ... it is a great consolation to me to reflect upon your great and unvarying kindness to my dearest mother ... you were, in all respects, as a daughter'. His father, Charles, had died in 1831, and his mother continued to live in their house on Angel Lane in Bury St Edmunds with her unmarried daughter Elizabeth. She occupied herself by superintending the girls' Sunday school and in other good works, and she enjoyed visiting her children at Fulham, Stevenage, and Ealing once or twice a year. She had borne ten children, four of whom died at birth. She was buried in St James' churchyard in the same vault as her husband, which also contained the remains of their four children, and also the Bishop's son by his first marriage to Anna Heath. The estate of the Bishop's parents was valued at slightly less than £12,000 (£0.5m) in 1846, the house being worth £1,600 (£67,000). The Bishop erected a window in St Mary's Church, Bury St Edmunds, in memory of them, but this had to be replaced in 1914, a commemorative plaque being placed below the new window.

The Bishop's first wife, who had come from Norfolk to marry him in 1810, bore him six children of whom only one daughter survived, Maria, who in 1843 married the Revd Henry Brown, rector of Woolwich. Anna died after childbirth in 1818, and the following year, on 29 May at St George's, Hanover Square, he married a widow, Dorothy Kent, née Cox. Her father was a brewer and her mother was the daughter of the rector of East Bilney, Christopher Munnings, who came from a distinguished Norfolk family. Dorothy and Charles James had eleven children, one of whom died in infancy.[6] Their father took great pains to teach them Latin, Greek and the Scriptures. One of his daughters later recalled that the hour or half-hour before breakfast was the happiest time of the day, as he would patiently teach them without any angry words. Evenings were always 'cheerful' with much music and conversation.

The Bishop's fourth son, Arthur William, followed him to Trinity College, Cambridge and then, after graduation, set up an independent practice as an architect which, thanks to family connections, soon had many church projects on the drawing board. Three years after his father's death he married Caroline Smith, and they named the first of their two sons after the Bishop. Arthur was appointed architect to the Bank of England in 1883 and knighted six years later. In his church building and alteration work he favoured the English Perpendicular style and used modern materials such as iron in his screen for St Peter, Eaton Square (1895), and for the columns in St Mark, Marylebone (1871). His ecclesiastical output was considerable, and in London his most notable buildings include Sion College Library on the Embankment, which was opened by the Prince of Wales in 1886; the Royal College of Music; St John's Church, Wilton Road; St Barnabas, Bell Street; St Saviour, Oxford Street; and St James, West Hampstead. Only this last church still stands.

According to the journal *Ecclesiology Today*, his finest building is Privett parish church in Hampshire whose patron was George Nicholson, a gin-maker of Bow, East London, who had bought the local manor house. One of his sons and three of his workers had died after being overcome by gin fumes, and the church is a magnificent high Victorian Gothic memorial to them. It is now preserved by the Redundant Churches Fund. Arthur died suddenly in 1899, and was buried near his country house in Broadway.

In his book *A Suffolk Family*, the Bishop's grandson notes that his father's generation were 'a clever family and witty but the massive ability of their father did not descend to that generation. It was said of us in the old days at Fulham that if as a family we could have stuck together we might have gone far but like the bundle of sticks in

Aesop's Fables we preferred to remain disunited. The Bishop's widow lived for thirteen years after his death, dying on 12 February 1870 at Richmond, her estate amounting to £8,000 (£360,000).

Blomfield thought that children should be acquainted with God from an early age, so family prayers were all-important. It was necessary 'that servants should be present, as they were much occupied during the greater part of every day in the necessary duties of their station ... Family prayers brought them all to a proper sense of equality and fellowship.'[7] Those in the higher walks of life should set an example as men were quick to imitate their betters. In a sermon on Humility he admitted the necessity of social distinctions, but deplored Christians who treat servants with 'haughty coldness'. The sin of pride, he thought, was less prevalent as one descended the social ladder and there is more humility amongst the poor, as there was also 'certainly more of charity, according to their means'.[8] The Bishop wrote a *Manual of Family Prayers* in 1824 which ran into seven editions. Such books, written by seventeenth-century Anglican divines like Robert Nelson, had fallen into disuse, so the Bishop was one of those responsible for restoring their place in Victorian households. His book appointed prayers for morning and evening, and special prayers for times of sickness and bereavement.

His clergy

Being the only bishop in the diocese, Blomfield relied heavily on his archdeacons to help him appoint and then superintend the huge number of clergy under his care. William Hale had been at Blomfield's side for over thirty years, as a curate at Bishopsgate, then as his chaplain at Chester and London. In 1839 he was made Archdeacon of St Albans. Soon moving to the Archdeaconry of Middlesex, then in 1842 to the more lucrative Archdeaconry of London, he was only nine years younger than the Bishop. In 1847 Blomfield gave him the rich living of St Giles Cripplegate, which he held with the archdeaconry. The two men must have liked each other, though they had little in common. Hale was a staunch Tory and an opponent of reform, particularly disliking the plan to abolish burials in towns which made the Bishop remark, 'I have two archdeacons with different tastes, Sinclair is addicted to composition and Hale to decomposition'. John Sinclair came to Blomfield's notice when he was secretary of the National Society. The Bishop made him one of his examining chaplains, and in 1842 gave him the wealthy living of St Mary Abbots, Kensington, realising he was one of the new breed of ecclesiastical administrators. With Blomfield he began the task of subdividing the area into fourteen manageable districts, and was rewarded by being made Archdeacon of Middlesex. Single-minded and unmarried, he combined both jobs for over thirty years. In the mid-1840s he established rural deaneries in the London area, telling the clergy that at their meetings they should avoid publicity, maintain the rules laid down by the Bishop, discuss practical subjects of pastoral concern and be extra careful when they were unanimous. That would suggest extreme views!

The situation was not changed greatly by the boundary alterations of 1845, when an effort was made to make the diocese coterminous with the metropolis north of the river. Sadly, an opportunity was lost to create one diocese, or possibly an archbishopric, north and south of the Thames. London now gained eight parishes in Kent: Charlton, Deptford, Eltham, Greenwich, Lee, Lewisham, Plumstead and Woolwich; but it retained only nine Essex parishes: Barking, Chingford, East and West Ham, Little Ilford, Leyton, Walthamstow, Wanstead and Woodford. The rest of Essex was transferred to Rochester, and London also lost its parishes in Hertfordshire and Buckinghamshire. The abolition of certain Peculiar jurisdictions also brought into Blomfield's care parishes in the City of London formerly comprising the Archbishop of Canterbury's Peculiars of the Arches, and several parishes in Middlesex and Surrey which had formed the Archbishop's Peculiar of Croydon. The 1863 London Diocese Act, and the 1875 Diocese of St Albans Act, removed the Essex, Kent and Surrey parishes, and in 1877 by an Order in Council the Diocese of London was confined to the County of Middlesex including the Cities of London and Westminster; this remains the situation today.[9]

Blomfield's clergy regarded him with mixed feelings. Incumbents who had seen their stipends slip downwards because of the Bishop's efforts on the Ecclesiastical Commission could not be expected to like him, but it is interesting that between 400 and 500 clergy in the Diocese said his was a vigilant, able, conscientious and affectionate administration, and when he retired he left behind 'a large body of clergy and laymen deeply impressed with the value of [his] guidance and sympathy'. They recognised his bold, ready and powerful assertion of the Church's rights and claims in Parliament, and recognised their obligation 'for the promptitude, patience and assiduity with which all our applications for advice and assistance have been met'.[10] He had tried to improve their lot, and had even pondered on how they might retire. In a letter to a layman of 27 October 1841 he said he doubted whether the suggestion of creating a kind of college for old and worn out incumbents would work. Nothing short of a strict monastic rule would prevent a scandal. He did not elaborate on what sort of a scandal he had in mind. He warmed to the suggestion of a pension fund, but thought that too much money was needed for new churches and for the stipends of clergy, so that money could not be raised for pensions. 'I believe it is what we shall come to in time ... I once endeavoured to establish a fund to which all incumbents should be bound to subscribe and from which their widows and in some cases themselves if disabled might receive pensions ... but the attempt failed.'

Blomfield's involvement with Church and State affairs at national level undoubtedly meant that his clergy suffered from a lack of pastoral care. However, he tried to keep a close watch on his parishes and his letter books at Lambeth Palace contain many written to clergy in need. The phrase 'it is my decided opinion', occurs frequently. He paid particular attention to churchwardens' replies to the Visitation queries of himself and the archdeacons. Whereas Bishop Osbaldeston had asked seven questions in 1762, Blomfield in 1842 asked his clergy eighteen questions covering fabric of the church, number of worshippers and scholars, weddings and baptisms, and ended by enquiring, 'Are there any special circumstances which appear to you to impede progress of religion in your parish?' Some clergy caused him great concern. Joshua King, the incumbent at St Matthew, Bethnal Green, since 1809, was a particular thorn in his flesh, leaving parish affairs to his curate and a disabled clergyman living in the parish. For twenty years the Bishop tried to get King to take an interest but he failed; he considered declaring the living vacant but decided against it. His nephew, Bryan, one of the joint secretaries of the Bethnal Green Churches Fund, could not have been more different. In 1842, he became rector of St George-in-the-East, a parish which had 154 brothels in its boundaries. He was joined by Charles Lowder fourteen years later, and the two men were among the greatest of London's slum priests. The riots there in opposition to Tractarian practices caused much violence and publicity at the end of the 1850s.[11]

Ray, the perpetual curate of Canvey Island, only held services once a fortnight, but after prolonged correspondence agreed to change to weekly. The island was always accessible, said the Bishop, except during a violent storm, and if mud was a difficulty a change of clothing and boots could be kept in a house on the island.

Blomfield admired hard-working clerics like Sir Henry Dukinfield of St Martin-in-the-Fields, who was a pastor with particular care for the poor, and in 1842 he offered him St Mary Abbots, Kensington, which he refused because of ill health. In 1845 he gave a prebendal stall in St Paul's to James Endell Tyler, incumbent of St Giles-in-the-Fields and a friend of Newman. His parishioners, who included many lawyers, wanted to name a street after him but modestly he only allowed them to use his middle name. Tyler took seriously Baptist Noel's call to preach in the streets, but felt he would be more at home in his National schoolroom which was 'pretty large' and in the midst of much ignorance, poverty and vice. Accordingly on Thursday evenings he held a Scripture class which drew about three hundred attentive listeners. Workmen came in their aprons and the hour fled by. 'Wishing to avoid any excitement', there was no hymn-singing. His successor, Samuel Garratt, spent much of his time with the large Irish community in London, and asked Blomfield if he could conduct parts of his services in Irish. The Bishop told him the law forbade it, then 'looked up with a kindly smile and said "I will tell you what I would do if I were you. I should have the service all the same, only you must not say that the Bishop of London gave you leave".' Garratt later wrote, 'The kindly and sensible advice gave me a lesson for life'.[12] Most observers, then and now, would be surprised by the adjective used twice to describe the Bishop.

Blomfield demanded high standards. Of one clergyman, Mr Veitch, he wrote 'a laborious man, above the average, but a coarse man who smokes cigars and has other habits which commonly belong to a smoking clergyman'. He insisted that the Revd W. W. Berry, vicar of Stanwell, should have an assistant curate if he also held the chaplaincy of a workhouse which was 'a parish in itself'. He drew the attention of John Mills, vicar of Holy Trinity Paddington, to the lack of a third service on Sundays. It was the only Paddington church and very populous, so Blomfield thought two services inadequate. In 1846 he seemed harsh in his treatment of Mr Harvey who was chaplain of Genoa, Frankfurt and Antwerp. The Consul at Antwerp had closed the church, so Blomfield called Harvey home and licensed him to a curacy at Thaxted. Harvey declared that the doors of London House were closed against him, and that 'he was overridden by the mitred priestcraft of Charles James'. The *Liverpool Courier*, commenting on the case, said that it was such behaviour by bishops that filled conventicles, and the *Family Times* on 24 October 1846 suggested that the Bishop rarely came into contact with his inferior brethren without giving them offence.

Nathanial Woodard would have agreed. Ordained aged 30 in 1841 by Blomfield he was given sole charge of the new district of St Bartholomew, Bethnal Green with the promise he would be the first vicar when the church was consecrated. Woodard had changed his evangelical views and at Oxford became convinced of the catholicity of the Church of England and formed a friendship with Frederick Oakeley. After two years, in May 1843, a parishioner complained to the Bishop about a sermon he had preached on the confession of sins. Blomfield read the text, which does not survive, and told Woodard he would not be appointed the first incumbent, 'I consider your sermon ... to be erroneous in point of doctrine and highly dangerous as to the effects which it is likely to produce upon poor educated people. I give you full credit for devotedness and zeal and am deeply concerned that you should have adopted opinions and notions which are likely to mar the good effects of your many excellent qualities.'

On 1 August Blomfield pointed out that Woodard had clearly spoken of auricular confesson as a duty, saying that all the sins of the people should be known to the minister. Over the next few months the Bishop refused to change his mind, even after an interview at which his son-in-law, the Revd C. B. Dalton, was told 'to sit in a corner and hear what passed'. Woodard, hurt and angry, pointed out that with three young children he would not be able to find a job. He declined, however, to recant his opinion that 'a priest had power to convey God's pardon to penitent sinners', and denied he had been in the habit of visiting a Roman Catholic Establishment in Poplar.

The Bishop stood firm, but did agree to license him as curate of St James', Clapton. Woodard felt this to be a step down and after a short time left London to take a curacy at Shoreham, Sussex, where he founded Lancing College and the Corporation of Schools which bears his name. Somewhat surprisingly Blomfield wrote to him asking him to open schools in London.[13]

Another furore surrounded the Revd Charles Kingsley, rector of Eversley in Hampshire, who in 1851 was invited to preach at St John's Church, Charlotte Street, on 'The Message of The Church to Labouring Men'. He is known today for his children's book *The Water Babies* and for his emphasis on muscular Christianity. (His cure for drunkenness was a daily cold bath; 'with a clean skin in healthy action, and nerves and muscles braced by a sudden shock, men do not crave for artificial stimulants'.[14]) Kingsley was at this time causing a stir by embracing what came to be known as Christian Socialism, hence the invitation to preach on this subject. In the sermon he said he approved of the Mosaic law which forbade the permanent sale of land. Just as Kingsley was about to say the final prayer, the incumbent, Mr Drew, rose in the reading desk, and said it was his painful duty to point out that much of what the preacher had said was dangerous and untrue. A dignified silence followed, but someone asked for the text of the sermon, and the next day several papers led attacks on the 'Apostle of Socialism'. Blomfield read these with horror, and wrote immediately to Kingsley forbidding him to preach again in London. Kingsley replied respectfully, asking His Lordship to read the sermon. Letters of support flowed into London House, and a huge rally of working men on Kennington Common expressed their rage and sympathy. Kingsley was regarded as a traitor to his class and even he himself began to doubt when his meetings were attended by 'bearded men, vegetarians and other eccentric persons'. One even wore a straw hat and blue plush gloves.[15] Blomfield carefully read the sermon and wrote asking Kingsley to visit him at London House. The prohibition was withdrawn.

Charles Greville, the diarist and historian, thought Blomfield 'an agreeable man in society, good humoured, lively, a little brusque in his manner', and one who could sing a duet with a lady of an evening. He thought him intemperate and imperious, and relates his dealings with William Capel, a disreputable good-for-nothing parson, brother of Lord Essex and rector of Watford. The Bishop appointed a curate who was not welcomed by Capel, and on one Sunday there was an unseemly race for the reading desk at church. Refusing to pay his curate, Capel was summoned to the Hertford Assizes. Uncharacteristically Blomfield had not prepared his case, so the incumbent won, costs of £1,000 (£30,000) being awarded against the Bishop. Some years later Blomfield agreed to preach a charity sermon at Watford and afterwards dined at the vicarage and stayed the night. Capel, much to the surprise of the Diocesan, came down to breakfast in an old grey dressing gown and red slippers. When asked later by a friend how all this came about, Capel replied that at the trial 'I gave him a good licking and that made him civil. We are very good friends now.'[16]

The letter books reveal that a written agreement was made with the directors of Van Diemen's Land Company to employ a Mr Knight as chaplain. The company reneged on this and the Bishop had to find the stipend himself. On his return to England to become a curate of Brightling the man took to drink; eventually £10 notes were sent to Knight, and Blomfield helped him to get pupils when he began work as a tutor.[17]

Two incumbents who gave the Bishop much pleasure were William Champneys and Thomas Dale. Champneys was thirty when in 1837 Blomfeld appointed him to St Mary, Whitechapel, which had a population of 30,000 and was one of the very poorest parishes in the diocese. Known for his practicality and friendliness, he was probably one of the most effective slum parsons, founding twenty day, ragged and Sunday schools, opening three churches and employing thirteen Scripture Readers. An Evangelical and friend of Lord Shaftsbury, he was concerned with social issues and later became Dean of Lichfield. On Blomfield's retirement he said he had disagreed several times with the Bishop but had always been listened to with the same fixed and earnest attention. The Bishop was a mixture of firmness and kindness. One of Champneys' curates, Dr Spencer, went as incumbent to an equally poor parish, St Matthew, St Marylebone, in 1853 and remained there nearly forty years. With never more than one curate, he visited his 8,000 parishioners regularly but never lived in the parish, which was full, he said, of turbulent and ignorant Irish. Thomas Dale was made vicar of St Pancras in 1846 and stayed until he left to be Dean of Rochester in 1861. The parish had 150,000 inhabitants and Blomfield admired the way this old-fashioned High Church Evangelical tackled his work. In 1852 Dale asked the Bishop whether his senior curate could be made the incumbent of a nearby vacant parish, but was told it had been promised to someone else. A second letter was dispatched to Fulham Palace expressing the greatest regret so, by return, the Bishop gave in, saying, 'I wish the appointment to be considered as much yours as mine so I will appoint your curate'.

A Transitional Figure

When Trollope published his fourth novel, *The Warden*, 1855, it was soon realised that Archdeacon Grantley's three sons, Charles James, Samuel and Henry were thinly disguised portraits of Blomfield, Wilberforce and Phillpotts of Exeter. Sam was soft and gentle, attractive in his speech, cunning and not beloved by his brothers. Henry was brilliant, courageous, game to the backbone, rejoicing not in his friends but in the multitude of his foes. Charles James

> was an exact and careful boy. He never committed himself . . . was mindful not to mix too freely with other boys. He had not the great talents of his younger brothers but he exceeded them in judgement and propriety of demeanour; his fault, if he had one, was an over attention to words instead of things; there was a thought too much finesse about him . . . he was too fond of a compromise.

Disraeli also borrowed the Bishop of London for a character in his novel *Tancred*, (1849), where he appears as the favourite bishop of Tancred's mother.

> He combined a great talent for action with very limited powers of thought. Bustling, energetic, versatile, gifted with an indomitable

perseverance and stimulated by an ambition that knew no repose. With a capacity for mastering details and an inordinate passion for affairs. He could permit nothing to be done without his interference and consequently was perpetually involved in transactions which were either failures or blunders. He was one of those leaders who are not guides ... Placed in a high post in an age of political analysis the bustling intermeddler was unable to supply society with a single solution. Enunciating second hand, with characteristic precipitation some big principle in vogue as if he were a discoverer, he invariably shrank from its subsequent application the moment that he found it might be unpopular or inconvenient. All his quandaries terminated in the same catastrophe – a compromise.

Harriet Martineau, the Unitarian writer, also had no liking for the Bishop, but in her *Biographical Sketches* grudgingly admits he worked hard, despite being very wealthy and the fount of too much patronage. 'We believe that to the last it was uncertain to everybody what his church views really were.' He should be a lesson to those who appoint bishops that 'Greek scholarship is of little consequence in these days in comparison with clear and honest convictions, ripened judgement in ecclesiastical matters, liberal views, inflexible courage and decision and unquestionable disinterestedness.'

Not one of these writers knew Blomfield well, so their judgements are superficial. His clergy respected but did not love him, and were often perplexed by his desire not to join any church party. The Evangelicals, who grew in number during his episcopate, thought him too Tractarian, the liberals resented his treatment of F. D. Maurice, and the Tractarians thought him a persecutor.

Ten years after Blomfield's death Anthony Trollope, in a series of articles in the *Pall Mall Gazette* compared and contrasted the bishops of George III and Victoria. The former wore aprons and wigs around which there was 'an odour of pious decorum', the absence of which meant that much of the episcopal awe had departed. The dress of the upper classes had become simpler in the early days of the century, and Blomfield had unsuccessfully tried to persuade George IV to sanction the disuse of the episcopal wig. William IV took a different view, and wigs disappeared, Blomfield being one of the first bishops to stop wearing one. In reply to Blomfield's remark, 'I find my episcopal wig a serious encumbrance', the King sent a message: 'Tell the Bishop he is not to wear a wig on my account. I dislike it as much as he does, and should be glad to see the whole Bench wear their own hair.'[18] Howley wore his in church till his death, and George Murray, Bishop of Rochester, wore his wig outside church until he died in 1860. Trollope regretted that aprons were only now worn in a shorn degree, and 'lawnsleeves themselves do not seem to envelop the occupant in so extensive a cloud of sacred millinery as they did in the more reverent days of George IV' when bishops were wealthy ecclesiastical barons living like great lords in palaces, drawing their income from territorial domains. By the middle of the century the Ecclesiastical Commission had ended all that, so that a bishop 'is paid his simple salary of £5,000 a year – quarterly, we suppose – and knows not and recks not of leases'. It was a very different ecclesiastical world, and Blomfield had lived through it all and been responsible for many of the changes. The middle classes were emerging and religion began to replace the irreligion of the Regency. England was settling down to prosperity, family values and prayers, philanthropy and religious discussions, which were to last for a hundred years. Peace descended, with the exception of the Crimean War in the middle of the century which shook the confidence of England, and was at its height when Blomfield retired. On 31 December 1854, Greville wrote in his *Memoirs*, 'almost everybody is in mourning, and grief and despair overspread the land ... our army is perishing before the walls of Sebastopol'.

David Newsome reminds us that the Victorians' sense of duty 'was unbending and they showed little sympathy for weakness and none at all for idleness'. They possessed an extraordinary faith in the power of the human will, and they 'lived closer to the stark realities of life than later generations who have developed both a protective technology and a sensibility to insulate themselves against the horrors and vicissitudes that were part of Victorian life'. Their priorities often make ours look shallow and short-sighted, so much of their time and effort had to go into keeping alive.[19]

Blomfield's influence entered every part of national life, sacred and secular. The Established Church, thanks to his efforts, was reformed and made ready to face a modern world; the bishopric of London gave up most of its territories overseas as he helped found thirty-one new bishoprics. Within the diocese, churches were built so that new congregations under the leadership of an incumbent could worship God and serve the local community. He desperately wanted to show that the Church could be useful. Education and social issues such as housing, sanitation and poverty all received his attention, and he chaired, or was a member of, many of the committees which brought much-needed changes. Yet he remained deeply unpopular, and has been largely forgotten since his death. His gifts and talents were, however, acknowledged in his lifetime by a junior bishop who was once heard to say to him on a public platform, 'When I look round this vast city with its ever-increasing population, and consider the almost superhuman efforts which must be required to meet its spiritual needs, my first thought is that I am thankful that I am not Bishop of London. My second is, that I am thankful that you are'.[20]

Dr Biber's biography, which was published a year before Blomfield's death, is a solid, heavy read, but occasionally it comes alive. In his final chapter he compares the Church of England in 1828 to a vessel which having been long laid up is unexpectedly towed out in crazy, half-rigged and ill-found condition for active service in a tempestuous sea against a foe armed to the teeth. 'Leaks have to be stopped, timber repaired, ammunition purchased. Compass has to be mounted and rudder fixed and crew drilled in seamanship and gunnery – all in the face of the enemy.' Dr Howley, 'a prelate of great intelligence ... but of slow and hesitating mind and timorous temperament [is] called to take the helm', but summons his former chaplain to his side. Blomfield brings the vigour of youth and intellect, is eager and quick-sighted; bold and energetic. In thirty years everything is transformed and the enemy engaged.

Blomfield spent the last winter of his life at Fulham Palace. His health did not improve. He was still quite helpless and in great pain. Dr Biber's biography was read to him, and each evening his family met for prayers at the bedside. By the summer of 1857 he realised his time was short and he began to prepare himself for death, his meditations concentrating mainly on Psalm 51. He made several bequests, including a silver-gilt communion set to St Paul's Church, Bow Common. It consisted of a flagon, two chalices, two patens, and an almsdish which had formerly been used in Queen Caroline's chapel. At the beginning of the twentieth century they were recast into a large chalice and two patens, which were destroyed when the church was bombed in the Second World War.

On 4 August his old friend the vicar of Fulham, the Revd R. G. Baker, read the commendatory prayer. All his family were present in his bedroom, which had hanging on its walls paintings of some of his great predecessors: Ridley the martyr, Sandys, Grindal, Laud, Porteous and Howley. He took leave of his family and the following day, 5 August 1857, aged 71, he became unconscious, and at 5 pm his heart stopped beating.

Appendix

Some of the churches built in the present London Diocese during the episcopate of Bishop Blomfield. 1828–1856. Listed by the present deaneries.
> * denotes the building is still in use for Anglican worship.

1. **City of London**
   Holy Trinity, Gough Square 1837.
   > Demolished *c*. 1905. Parish merged with St Bride, Fleet Street

2. **Westminster (Paddington)**
   All Saints, Cambridge Place (Norfolk Square) 1846/7
   > Burnt down and rebuilt 1895. Demolished *c*. 1960
   Christ Church, Lancaster Gate 1854/5
   > Closed 1977. Demolished (except spire) 1978
   Holy Trinity, Bishop's Bridge Road 1844/6
   > Closed 1978. Demolished 1984
   *St James, Sussex Gardens 1841/3
   > Rebuilt 1881/2
   *St John, Kensal Green 1844
   *St John, Hyde Park Crescent 1830/31
   *St Saviour, Warwick Avenue 1855. Rebuilt
   *St Stephen, Westbourne Park 1855/6

3. **Westminster (St Margaret)**
   All Saints, Ennismore Gardens 1849
   > Now the Russian Orthodox Cathedral
   Christ Church, Broadway 1842/3
   > Demolished 1954
   Holy Trinity, Bessborough Gardens 1851
   > Demolished 1953

St Andrew (formerly St Mark), Ashley Place 1853
>   Demolished *c.* 1953
*St Barnabas, Pimlico 1850
*St Gabriel, Warwick Square 1852
St Luke, Berwick Street 1837/9
>   Demolished
St Mary the Virgin, Vincent Square 1835
>   Demolished
*St Matthew, Great Peter Street 1849/51
St Michael, Burleigh Street 1831/33
>   Demolished 1905
*St Michael, Chester Square 1846
*St Paul, Knightsbridge 1843
>   Carved head of Bishop Blomfield in sanctuary roof
St Philip, Elizabeth Street
>   Demolished
*St Stephen, Rochester Row, 1850
>   Gift of Angela Burdett-Coutts. Blomfield's head is carved on the capital of the first column.

4. Westminster (St Marylebone)
*St Andrew, Wells Street 1846
>   Re-erected at Kingsbury 1934
St John the Evangelist, Charlotte Street 1845
>   Bombed 1945
St Luke, Nutford Place 1854
>   Demolished 1953
*St Mark, Hamilton Terrace 1847
St Matthew, St Marylebone 1851
>   Rebuilt 1878
St Stephen, Portland Town 1848
>   Demolished *c.* 1948. Now St John's Wood Parish
St Thomas, Portman Square 1857
>   Closed 1929

5. Hackney
*All Saints, Haggerston Road 1856
*Holy Trinity, Shepherdess Walk, Hoxton 1848
*St Barnabas, Homerton 1845/7
*St James, Hackney 1841
>   Now contains the Huddleston Centre
*St John of Jerusalem 1845/7
*St Matthias, Stoke Newington 1853

*St Peter, Northchurch Terrace, De Beauvoir Town 1845
St Philip, Dalston 1840
    Closed 1953

6. **Islington**
    *All Saints, Caledonian Road 1839
        Rebuilt
    All Saints, Skinner Street 1828/30
        Demolished *c.* 1869
    *Christ Church, Highbury 1848
    Holy Trinity, Cloudesley Square 1828
        Building still stands and is used by Pentecostal Church
    *St Andrew, Thornhill Square 1852
    *St John, Upper Holloway 1826/8
    *St Jude, Mildmay Park 1854/5
    *St Luke, West Holloway 1843
    *St Mark, Tollington Park 1854
    *St Mark, Myddleton Square 1828
    St Matthew, Essex Road 1850
        Bombed and not rebuilt
    St Paul, Balls Pond Road 1828
        Closed. Building still stands
    St Philip, Clerkenwell 1831/2
        Demolished

7. **Tower Hamlets**
    All Saints, Buxton Street, (Spicer Street) 1839
        Closed and demolished 1951
    *Christ Church, Isle of Dogs 1857
    Christ Church, Watney Street 1841
        Bombed and not rebuilt 1941
    Holy Trinity, Bow 1839
        Closed. Building still stands
    St Andrew, Bethnal Green 1840
        Closed and demolished 1958
    St Bartholomew, Bethnal Green 1842
        Closed *c.* 1979. Now apartments
    St James the Great (the Red Church), Bethnal Green 1844
        Gift of the Bishop's brother and sister.
        Closed *c.* 1985. Building now apartments
    *St James the Less, Bethnal Green 1840/42

St James, Ratcliffe 1838
>Bombed 1940, demolished 1951.
>Site now used by the Royal Foundation of St Katharine's Chapel

*St John, Bethnal Green, 1828

St John the Evangelist, Halley Street, Limehouse 1853
>Bombed 1940. Demolished 1956

St Jude, Whitechapel 1848.
>Demolished 1925

St Jude, Bethnal Green 1845
>Bombed and not rebuilt

*St Mary, Cable Street, 1850

St Mary, Spital Square (Wheler's Chapel) 1842
>Demolished 1911

St Mark, Goodmans Fields, Whitechapel 1839
>Demolished 1927

St Matthias, Bethnal Green 1846
>Closed. Demolished 1954

*St Paul, Bow Common 1856/8
>Bombed and rebuilt

St Paul, Dock Street, 1846
>Built to replace a floating church, the *Brazen*.
>Closed *c.* 1980. Building still stands

St Paul, Mill Hill 1833

*St Peter, Bethnal Green 1840/41

St Peter, Cephas Street 1838
>Closed *c.* 1980. Building stands, now apartments

St Philip, Bethnal Green 1841
>Closed. Demolished 1954

St Simon Zelotes, 1846
>Closed. Demolished 1953

St Thomas, Baroness Road, Bethnal Green
>Closed. Demolished 1953

St Thomas, Arbour Square 1838
>Bombed and not rebuilt 1941

8. Hammersmith and Fulham
*St John, Walham Green 1828
*St Mary, Hammersmith Road, West Kensington 1835
*St Peter, Black Lion Lane, Hammersmith 1829
*St Stephen, Shepherds Bush 1850

9.   Hampton
  *Holy Trinity, The Green, Twickenham 1841
  *St John the Baptist, Hampton Wick 1832
  *St Mary, Hampton 1839/41 (Rebuilt)

10.   Hounslow
  *Christ Church, Turnham Green 1843
  *Holy Trinity, Hounslow 1829/31
  *St John the Baptist, Isleworth 1856

11.   Kensington
  *Christ Church, Victoria Road 1850/51
  *St Barnabas, Addison Road 1829
  *St James, Norlands 1844/5
  *St John, Notting Hill 1845
  St Paul, Vicarage Gate, North Kensington 1855
        Bombed and Demolished *c.* 1946
  St Peter, Kensington Park Road 1855/57
        Demolished

12.   Chelsea
  *Christ Church, Christ Church Street 1839
  *Holy Trinity, Brompton 1829
  *Holy Trinity, Sloane Street 1832. Rebuilt 1890
  St Jude, Turk's Row, Chelsea *c.*1843
        Demolished
  *St Mary the Boltons, Kensington 1850
  *St Saviour, Walton Street 1839/40
        Closed 1997. East end now a worship centre, West end is
        apartments

13.   Spelthorne
  Nil

14.   Central Barnet
  *Christ Church, St Alban's Road, Barnet 1845
  *Holy Trinity, East Finchley 1846
  *St John the Apostle, Whetstone 1832

15.   West Barnet
  *All Saints, Church Walk, Childs Hill 1856

16. **North Camden (Hampstead)**
   *Christ Church, Hampstead Square 1853
   *St Mark, Regent's Park 1853
   *St Saviour, Eton Road, South Hampstead 1849/56

17. **South Camden (Holborn and St Pancras)**
   Christ Church, Albany Street 1837
       Closed, Building used by Antiochian Orthodox Church
   Christ Church, Endell Street 1844
       Demolished 1931
   Christ Church, Woburn Square 1831
       Demolished 1938
   *Holy Trinity, Clarence Way, Haverstock Hill 1850
   Holy Trinity, Gray's Inn Lane 1837
       Demolished
   Holy Trinity, Little Queen Street 1829/31
       Demolished
   *St Anne, Brookfield, Highgate West Hill 1853
   *St Mary Magdalene, Munster Square 1852
   *St Mary the Virgin, Eversholt Street 1852
   *St Paul, Camden Square 1847/9
       Demolished *c.* 1960. Small chapel exists today

18. **Enfield**
   *Christ Church, Cockfosters, 1839
   *Jesus Church, Enfield 1835
   St James, Edmonton 1849
       Closed *c.* 1980
   *St James, Enfield 1830/31
   *St Paul, Winchmore Hill 1828

19. **East Haringey**
   *Holy Trinity, Tottenham 1830
   *St Michael, Wood Green 1844

20. **West Haringey**
   *St James, Muswell Hill 1842
   *St Michael, Highgate 1832

21. **Brent**
   *St John the Evangelist, Wembley 1846

22/23.Ealing
   *St John, Southall 1837
   St Mary, Hanwell 1842

24. Harrow
   *All Saints, Harrow Weald 1845
   *Holy Trinity, Northwood 1852

25. Hillingdon
   St John, Uxbridge 1837

Other Churches

   *St Philip, Earls Court Road. In 1849 a temporary church
   (Upper Room) was established at the corner of Warwick
   Gardens and Pembroke Gardens in the parish of St
   Barnabas, Addison Road. Its vicar, Francis Hessey put
   forward a plan for a permanent church in 1856. St Philip,
   Earls Court Road was opened in 1858.

   *St John the Evangelist, Glenthorne Road, 1859. Plans and fund
   raising begun in 1851.
   *Holy Trinity, Manchester Road, Isle of Dogs, 1857. Plans
   drawn up in 1854.

London Highways named after Bishop Blomfield

   Blomfield Street, EC2
   Bloomfield Terrace, SW1 (incorrect spelling!)
   Blomfield Road, W9
   Blomfield Villas, W2
   The latter two are situated on what was the See of London's
   estate in Paddington.

Notes

Notes to Introduction

1. Owen Chadwick, *The Victorian Church*, pt. 1 p. 133.
2. *Census of Great Britain in 1851* (1854), p. 90.
3. R. A. Soloway, *Prelates and People*, p. 22.

Notes to Chapter One: The challenge of London

1. A. Blomfield, *Memoir*, vol. 2, p. 180.
2. *The Times*, 17 January 1829.
3. D. M. Lewis, *Dictionary of Evangelical Biography 1730–1830*, vol. 1, p. 111.
4. *ibid*, p. 277.
5. E. Churton, *Joshua Watson*, vol. 2, p. 318.
6. Owen Chadwick, *The Victorian Church*, pt. 1, p. 328.
7. R. A. Soloway, *Prelates and People*, p. 237.
8. Lord Shaftesbury, Article in *Quarterly Review* (1847), vol. 82, pp. 147–52.
9. Venetia Stanley, *High Society*, Viking Publishing (1998), p. 280.
10. Horace Mann, *Census of Great Britain 1851: Religious Worship Report* (1854), p. 300.
11. F. Sheppard, *London 1808–1870*, p. 239.
12. *ibid*, p. 240.
13. E. Beresford Chancellor, *Life in Regency and Early Victorian Times*, p. 17.

Notes to Chapter Two: Preparation for power

1. Richard Girling, *Sunday Times*, 22 February 1998.
2. E. V. Blomfield, *An Account of Blomfield Families*, pt. 1, p. 40.
3. Sir Reginald Blomfield, *A Memoir of C. J. Blomfield*.
4. C. Smyth, *Simeon and Church Order*, p. 52.
5. J. Morley, *Life of Gladstone*, vol. 1, p. 28.

6. Saul David, *Prince of Pleasure*, p. 360.
7. R. T. Blomfield, *A Suffolk Family*, p. 15.
8. Clive Dewey, *The Passing of Barchester*.
9. A. Blomfield, *Memoir*, p. 76.
10. *ibid*, p. 79.
11. *The Times*, 21 May 1825.
12. *Hansard*, new series XIX, p. 124.
13. *ibid*, p. 174.

Notes to Chapter Three: Early days in London

1. Owen Chadwick, *The Victorian Church*, pt. 1, p. 134.
2. Venetia Murray, *High Society*, p. 81.
3. Denys Forrest, *St James's Square*, p. 127.
4. Roger Fulford, *George IV*, p. 258.
5. James Garrard, unpublished thesis on Archbishop Howley, University of Oxford.
6. Gordon Huelin, *King's College London 1828–1978*, p. 4.
7. F. Maurice, *Life of F. D. Maurice*, vol. 2, p. 176.
8. *The Times*, 10 May 1830.
9. A. Blomfield, *Memoir*, p. 114.
10. David Cecil, *The Young Melbourne*, p. 260.
11. L. G. Mitchell, *Lord Melbourne*, p. 14.
12. Saul David, *Prince of Pleasure*, p. 56.
13. BM Add MSS 38303 fol. 27, The Duchess of Kent to Blomfield, 13 March 1830.
14. C. Hibbert, *George IV*, p. 777.
15. G. H. Sumner, *Life of C. R. Sumner*, p. 2.
16. D. Cannadine, *The Invention of Tradition*, ed. Hobsbawn and Ranger (1983), ch. 4.
17. R. A. Soloway, *Prelates and People*, p. 148.
18. C. Hibbert, *Queen Victoria* (HarperCollins, 2000).
19. D. Cannadine, *op. cit*. p. 114.
20. Both pictures are illustrated in Christopher Lloyd's *The Paintings in the Royal Collection* (1999), pp. 298, 299.
21. R. A. Soloway, *op. cit*. p. 245.
22. *The Times*, 16 June 1832.
23. G. E. Biber, *Bishop Blomfield and His Times*, p. 144.
24. *The Times*, 24 October 1831.
25. *Hansard*, 3rd series, vol. XII, (1832) col. 267–270.
26. Owen Chadwick, *op. cit*. pt. 1, p. 32.
27. L. G. Mitchell, *op. cit*. p. 145.

Notes to Chapter Four: A social conscience

1. Unpublished sermon quoted by Biber, p. 129.

2. *Hansard*, (1832) p. 985.
3. E. L. Woodward, *The Age of Reform 1815–1870*, p. 434.
4. J. B. Sumner, *Treatise on the Records of the Creation* (1816), vol. 2, p. 92.
5. R. A. Soloway, *Prelates and People*, p. 172.
6. *ibid*, p. 174.
7. CJB, Letter copy book 358, p. 25, Lambeth Palace Library.
8. David Thomson, *England in the Nineteenth Century*, p. 203.
9. R. A. Soloway, *op. cit.* p. 166.
10. W. A. Cobbett, *A History of the Protestant Reformation in England* (1829).
11. A. Blomfield, *Memoir*, p. 70.
12. Roy Porter, *London*, p. 262.
13. S. Halladay, *The Great Stink of London*.
14. *Hansard*, (1842) LXIII p. 199.
15. *Hansard*, 3rd series CXXV, p. 408.
16. Roy Porter, *op. cit.* p. 269.
17. R. A. Soloway, *op. cit.* p. 215.
18. *Hansard*, LXXXVII (1846), p. 107.
19. David Newsome, *The Victorian World Picture*, p. 83.
20. Hugh Miller, *London Cemeteries*, p. 8.
21. *ibid*, p. 11.
22. *Hansard*, 3rd series, (1850) CXXXV, p. 410.
23. B. J. Richardson, *The Health of Nations*, vol. 1, quoted in Brose, p. 95.

Notes to Chapter Five: Church reform

1. G. K. A. Best, 'An appraisal of Establishment', in *Anglican–Methodist Relations*, ed. W. S. F. Pickering (1961).
2. cf his sermon 'The nature of the Church and the duties of its members', quoted in Brose p. 8.
3. Peter Virgin, *The Church in an Age of Negligence*, p. 43.
4. *ibid*, p. 14.
5. A. Blomfield, *Memoir*, vol. 1, p. 21.
6. Olive Brose, *Church and Parliament*, p. 39.
7. Owen Chadwick, *The Victorian Church*, pt. 1, p. 48.
8. Virgin, *op. cit.* p. 54.
9. G. E. Biber, *Bishop Blomfield and His Times*, p. 168.
10. *ibid,* pp. 140, 141.
11. A. B. Webster, *Joshua Watson, The Story of a Layman*, p. 86.
12. Blomfield, *Charge* of 1836, pp. 18, 44.
13. Virgin, *op. cit.* p. 163.
14. *ibid*, p. 211.
15. *ibid*, p. 161.
16. G. K. A. Best, *Temporal Pillars*, p. 298.
17. Blomfield, *Charge* of 1838, p. 24.

18. Sydney Smith, *Collected Works*, p. 617.
19. G. K. A. Best, *op. cit.* pp. 300–2.
20. David Cecil, *Melbourne*, p. 32.
21. C. Thorp, Charge to the clergy of the archdeaconry of Durham, 1838, p. 5.
22. R. Bagot, Charge to the clergy of the diocese of Oxford, 1838, p. 7.
23. P. J. Welch, 'Bishop Blomfield', unpublished PhD thesis, p. 205.
24. *The Croker Papers*, ed. L. J. Jennings, vol. 2, p. 265.
25. S. C. Carpenter, *Church and People*, p. 99.
26. J. T. Middaugh. *The Reform of the Church of England 1830–1841*, pp. 265–9.
27. Sydney Smith, 'First Letter to Archdeacon Singleton', *Collected Works*, vol. 3, p. 311.
28. *ibid,* pp. 342, 343.
29. For a full account of their discussion, cf Best, *Temporal Pillars*, pp. 331–47 .
30. P. J. Welch, *op. cit.* p. 244.
31. R. Blomfield, *Memoir*, p. 131.
32. G. E. Biber, *op. cit.* p. 150.
33. In 1948, the Commissoners merged with Queen Anne's Bounty, and thus possessed assets of £210m, a third of which came from the Bounty.
34. L. G. Mitchell, *Lord Melbourne*, p. 18.
35. C. Hibbert, *Wellington*, p. 350.
36. *The Greville Memoirs*, vol. 3, p. 162.
37. BM Add MS 40503 fol. 306, Blomfield to Peel, 12 March 1842.
38. Owen Chadwick, *op. cit.* pt. 1, p. 106.
39. P. J. Welch, 'Blomfield and Peel', in *Journal of Ecclesiastical History*, April 1961.
40. W. Sinclair (ed.), *Thirty-Two Years of the Church of England.*
41. P. J. Welch, 'Revival of an Active Convocation', in *Journal of Ecclesiastical History*, October 1959, p. 195.

Notes to Chapter Six: In the Diocese

1. P. J. Welch, 'The significance of Bishop Blomfield' in *Modern Churchman*, December 1955, p. 5.
2. Blomfield to Pusey 18 September 1841, in Pusey House library.
3. A. Blomfield, *Memoir*, p. 85.
4. Anthony Trollope, *Pall Mall Gazette*, 1836.
5. Blomfield, letter to Bishop Wilson of Calcutta. A. Blomfield, *op. cit.* p. 226.
6. David Cecil, *Lord M*, p. 140.
7. P. Galloway, *A Passionate Humilty* (1999), p. 31.
8. *ibid*, p. 44.
9. P. Galloway and C. Rawll, *Good and Faithful Servants*, p. 6.
10. *ibid*, p. 54.

11. *Record*, 24 February 1851.
12. H. P. Liddon, *Life of Pusey*, vol. 2, p. 272.
13. P. J. Welch, unpublished thesis, p. 315.
14. A. Blomfield, *op. cit.* vol. 2, p. 58.
15. W. J. E Bennett, 'Farewell letter to the parishioners of St Paul's, Knightsbridge', 1851.
16. C. and F. Brookfield, *Mrs Brookfield and her circle*.
17. Lord Illchester, *Chronicles of Holland House*, p. 377.
18. F. Bennett, *The Story of W. J. E. Bennett*.
19. A. Blomfield, *op. cit.* p. 160.
20. Maria Trench, *Charles Lowder*, pp 58–60.
21. Owen Chadwick, *The Victorian Church*, vol. 1 p. 506.
22. P. Butler (ed.) *Pusey Rediscovered*, p. 223.
23. D. F. Cartwright, The Story of the Community of the Nursing Sisters of St John the Divine.

Notes to Chapter Seven: New Churches

1. R. A. Soloway, *Prelates and People*, p. 314.
2. M. H. Port, *Six Hundred New Churches*, p. 125.
3. H. P. Liddon, *Life of Pusey*, vol. 1, p. 329.
4. C. J. Blomfield, 'Reply to the Retirement Address sent to him by the London Diocesan Church Building Association' (1856).
5. *Guardian*, Blomfield's obituary, 12 August 1857.
6. cf Appendix.
7. Blomfield to G. R. Gleig, 18 November 1851.
8. Blomfield to Rhodes, 2 September 1837. Copy book 29 March – 28 September 1837.
9. *The Times*, 23 June 1999.
10. Mr Horace Mann's *Report on Religious Worship* (1851). cf Census of Great Britain, 1851, (13 & 14 Vict. c. 53).
11. Copy book 7 December 1839 – 8 January 1840.

Notes to Chapter Eight: Bishop of the Empire

1. Hawkins, *Documents relative to Colonial Bishoprics* (1855).
2. G. E. Biber, *Bishop Blomfield and His Times*, p. 280.
3. A. P. Stanley, *Life and Correspondence of Thomas Arnold*, p. 448.
4. *The Times*, 19, 26, 29 October 1841.
5. Michael Chandler, *The Life and Work of Henry Parry Liddon*, p. 60.
6. Ashwell and Wilberforce, *The Life of Samuel Wilberforce*, vol. 1, p. 202.
7. Chandler, ibid pp. 62, 63.

Notes to Chapter Nine: Education

1. Owen Chadwick, *The Victorian Church*, vol. 1, p. 337.
2. R. A. Soloway, *Prelates and People*, p. 351.
3. Owen Chadwick, *op. cit.* vol. 2, p. 338.
4. Grier, *Memoir*, p. 87, quoted by Brose, p. 193.
5. T. Burgess, *Metropolis Schools for the Poor – A Letter to the Lord Bishop of London* (1846), p. 7.
6. Owen Chadwick, *op. cit.* vol. 1, p. 344.
7. *Guardian*, 24 May 1848.
8. David Newsome, *The Victorian World Picture*, p. 146.
9. R. A. Soloway, *op. cit.* p. 429.

Notes to Chapter Ten: Gorham and the Bishop of London

1. Owen Chadwick, *The Victorian Church*, vol. 1, p. 25.
2. G. C. B. Davies, *Henry Phillpotts*, p. 231.
3. For a full account see Chadwick, *op. cit.* vol. 1, pp. 256–71.
4. Greville, *Memoirs*, vol. 1, p. 210.
5. Blomfield to Gladstone, 11 March 1850.
6. A. Blomfield, *Memoir*, p. 121.
7. C. J. Blomfield, *Charge* of 1850, p. 36.
8. *Guardian*, 6 June 1850.
9. F. W. Cornish, *The History of the English Church in The Nineteenth Century*, vol. 1, p. 334.

Notes to Chapter Eleven: Last days

1. Ashwell and Wilberforce, *Life of Samuel Wilberforce*, vol. 2, p. 184.
2. Owen Chadwick, *The Victorian Church*, pt. 1, p. 11.
3. Ashwell and Wilberforce, *Life of Bishop Wilberforce*, vol. 2, p. 315.
4. *Guardian*, 9 July 1856.
5. Nigel Scotland, *John Bird Sumner*, p. 118.
6. J. Hollingshead, *Ragged London in 1861*, p. 31.
7. Davidson and Benham, *Life of Archbishop Tait*, vol. 1, p. 194.
8. *ibid*, p. 197.

Notes to Chapter Twelve: The Man

1. David Newsome, *The Victorian World Picture*, p. 143.
2. C. J. Blomfield, *Twenty-Four Sermons* (1857), p. 324.
3. *The Times*, 7 August 1857.
4. Sydney Smith, *Collected Works*, p. 338.
5. Owen Chadwick, *The Victorian Church*, pt. 1, p. 464.
6. See chapter 2.

7. C. J. Blomfield, 'A Sermon on the duty of Family Prayers', p. 19.
8. C. J. Blomfield, *Twenty Four Sermons*, p. 165.
9. cf the *Index to the London Diocesan Returns 1763–1900*, ed. Melanie Barber (1991), Lambeth Palace Library.
10. Address to the Bishop of London by the Archdeacons, Rural Deans and Clergy, 27 September 1856.
11. cf Owen Chadwick, *op. cit.* pt. 1, pp 497–501.
12. Michael Hinton, *The Anglican Parochial Clergy*.
13. Cf. Sir John Otter *Memoir of Nathaniel Woodard*, Bodley Head, 1926, pp. 10–31. I am grateful to the Revd John Hunwicke for drawing my attention to this.
14. Newsome, *op. cit.* p. 85.
15. Chitty, *The Beast and The Monk* (Hodder, 1974).
16. Greville, *Memoirs*, p. 112.
17. Olive Brose, *Church and Parliament*, p. 82.
18. Owen Chadwick, *op. cit.* vol. 1, p. 134.
19. David Newsome, *op. cit.* p. 264.
20. A. Blomfield, *Memoir*, vol. 2, p. 204.

Select Bibliography

Part One: Sermons, Addresses, Letters etc of Bishop Blomfield

The Bishop's papers, 1828–1856

73 volumes including 60 letter books, 8 volumes of loose correspondence and papers and 5 volumes of rural deans' returns and diocesan visitation returns. Formerly kept at Fulham Palace, they were transferred by the Church Commissioners in 1960 to Lambeth Palace Library. There is an index compiled and edited in 1986 by Dr Richard Aspin who was then the Assistant Archivist of Lambeth Palace Library.

Visitation Charges

To the Archdeaconry of Chester. Published by J. Mawman, London, May 1823.

To the clergy of London. July 1830, July 1834, October 1838, October 1842, October 1846, November 1850, 1854. All published by B. Fellowes, London.

Books and Pamphlets

Five lectures on the Gospel of St John, Lent 1822. R. Clay, London, 1823.

A Letter to Charles Butler . . . in vindication of English Protestants. J. Mawman, London, 1825.

The Christian's Duty Towards Criminals. The Philanthropic Society, London, 1828.

A Manual of Private Devotion. SPCK.

A Letter on the Present Neglect of the Lord's Day. Fellowes, London, 1830.

A Manual of Family Prayers. J. G. & F. Rivington, London 1833.

Proposals for the creation of a fund to be applied to the building and endowment of additional churches in the Metropolis. Fellowes, London, 1836.

Twelve lectures on the Acts of the Apostles. Fellowes, London, 1838.

A Letter to the Archbishop of Canterbury upon the formation of a fund for endowing additional bishoprics in the colonies. Fellowes, London, 1840.

Correspondence between the Lord Bishop of London, the Chaplain and

Congregation of the British Church Establishment in Madeira. Hatchard, London, 1846.

A Pastoral Letter to the Clergy of the Diocese of London. Fellowes, London, 1847.

Correspondence between the Revd W. J. E. Bennett and the Bishop of London. Westerton, London, 1850.

Printed Speeches in the House of Lords

On the Irish Church Bill, 24 August 1835, Fellowes.

On National Education, 5 July 1839, Fellowes.

On Ecclesiastical Duties, 30 July 1840, Fellowes.

On Appeals from Ecclesiastical Courts, 3 June 1850, Fellowes.

Printed Sermons

Sermon preached to the Sons of the Clergy, St Paul's Cathedral, 23 May 1822, Rivington 1823.

Sermon preached to the Society for the Propagation of the Gospel, St Mary le Bow, 16 February 1827, SPG 1827.

Sermons preached at St Botolph Bishopsgate, Fellowes 1829.

Sermon preached at the Chapel Royal at St James, Fellowes 1830.

Sermon preached at the Coronation of King William IV at Westminster Abbey, 8 September 1831, Fellowes 1831.

Sermon preached at the opening of King's College London, 8 October 1831, Fellowes 1831.

'The Uses of a Standing Ministry', Fellowes 1834.

'National Education', preached at St Martin-in-the-Fields, 18 February 1838, Fellowes 1838.

Sermon preached at the Coronation of Queen Victoria at Westminster Abbey, 28 June 1838, Fellowes 1838.

'The duty of prayer and intercession for our rulers', St James, Westminster, 1 July 1838, Fellowes 1838.

'The Light of the World', preached before the King of Prussia, St Paul's Cathedral, 30 January 1842, Fellowes 1842.

Three sermons in the church of St James, Westminster, Lent 1842, Fellowes 1842.

'The Manifestation of the Spirit'. St Mary's Cambridge, 3 July 1842, Fellowes 1842.

'God's ancient people not cast away', preached before the London Society for Promoting Christianity among the Jews, Fellowes 1843.

Twenty-four sermons on Christian doctrine and practice. Bell & Daldy 1859.

Part Two: Other published sources

Books published in London unless otherwise stated

Ackroyd, Peter,

Dickens.
Sinclair Stephenson, 1990.

Ashwell A. R. and
  Wilberforce R. G.,

Life of The Right Reverend Samuel Wilberforce, 3 vols.
John Murray, 1880/82.

Barnes, G.,

Stepney Churches.
Faith Press, 1967.

Bell, Alan,

Sydney Smith.
Clarendon, Oxford, 1980.

Bennett, F.,

The Story of W. J. E. Bennett.
1909.

Beresford Chancellor, E.,

Life in Regency and Early Victorian Times.
Batsford, 1926.

Best, G. F. A.,

Temporal Pillars.
Cambridge University Press, 1964.

Biber, G. E.,

Bishop Blomfield and His Times.
Harrison, 1857.

Blomfield, A. F.,

Memoir of Charles James Blomfield, 2 vols.
John Murray, 1863.

Blomfield, E. V.,

An Account of the Blomfield Families.
Printed privately, 1950.

Blomfield, Reginald,

A Memoir of C J Blomfield.
Printed privately, 1935.

Blomfield, R. T.,

A Suffolk Family.
Chiswick Press (printed privately), 1915.

Brookfield, C. and F.,

Mrs Brookfield and Her Circle, 2 vols.
1874.

Brose, Olive J.,

Church and Parliament.
Oxford University Press, 1959.

Butler, P. (ed.)   *Pusey Rediscovered.*
                              SPCK, 1983.

Carpenter, S. C.,   *Church and People 1789–1889.*
                              SPCK, 1933.

Cartwright, D. F.,   *The Story of the Community of the Nursing.*
                              Sisters of St John the Divine.
                              Faith Press, 1968.

Cecil, David,   *Lord Melbourne.*
                              Constable, 1955.

Chadwick, Owen,   *The Victorian Church*, Pts 1 and 2.
                              Adam & Charles Black, 1966.

Chandler, Michael,   *The Life and Work of Henry Parry Liddon.*
                              Gracewing, Leominster, 2000.

Church, R. W.,   *The Oxford Movement 1833–1835.*
                              Macmillan, 1900.

Churton, E.,   *Memoir of Joshua Watson.*
                              Oxford, 1861.

David, Saul,   *Prince of Pleasure.*
                              Little, Brown & Co., 1998.

Davidson, R. T.   *Life of Archbishop Campbell Tait*, 2 vols.
  and Benham, W.,   Macmillan, 1891.

Davies, G. C. B.,   *Henry Phillpotts, Bishop of Exeter 1778–1869.*
                              SPCK, 1954.

Dewey, Clive,   *The Passing of Barchester.*
                              Hambledon Press, 1991.

Ellesworth, L. E.,   *Charles Lowder and the Ritualist Movement.*
                              Darton, Longman & Todd, 1982.

Forrest, Denys,   *St James's Square.*
                              Quiller Press, 1986.

Fulford, Roger,   *George IV.* 1935.

Galloway, Peter and   *Good and Faithful Servants.*
  Rawll, Christopher,   Churchman, Worthing, 1998.

Garrard, James,
'Archbishop Howley'.
Unpublished PhD Thesis, Oxford University, 1992.

Gash, Norman,
Sir Robert Peel.
Longman, 1976.

Greville, Charles
Memoirs. ed. L. Strachey and R. Fulford. 1938.

Halliday, Stephen,
The Great Stink of London.
Sutton, 1999.

Healey, Edna,
Lady Unknown.
Sidgwick & Jackson, 1978.

Hibbert, Christopher,
The Making of Charles Dickens.
1967.

Hibbert, Christopher,
Wellington.
HarperCollins, 1997.

Hibbert, Christopher,
Queen Victoria.
HarperCollins, 2000.

Hinton, Michael,
The Anglican Parochial Clergy.
SCM, 1994.

Hollingshead, J.,
Ragged London in 1861.
Smith Elder, 1861.

Huelin, Gordon,
King's College, London 1828–1978.
King's College, 1978.

Ilchester, Lord,
Chronicles of Holland House.
John Murray, 1937.

Jennings, L. J. (ed.),
The Croker Papers and Diaries of J W Croker.
John Murray, 1885.

Lewis, D. M. (ed.),
Blackwells Dictionary of Evangelical Biography 1730–1860, 2 vols. Oxford, 1995.

Liddon, H. P.,
Life of Edward Bouverie Pusey, 4 vols.
Longman, Green & Co., 1893.

Mann, Horace,   *Census of Great Britain, 1851. Religious Worship Report*, 1854.

Martineau, Harriet,   *Autobiography*, 3 vols.
                                 1877.

Mathieson, W. L.,   *English Church Reform.*
                                 Longmans, 1923.

Maurice, F.,   *Life of Frederick Denison Maurice*, 2 vols.
                                 1884.

Millar, Oliver,   *The Victorian Pictures in the Collection of H. M. The Queen.*
                                 Cambridge Univ. Press, 1992.

Miller, Hugh,   *London Cemeteries.*
                                 Avebury, Amersham, 1981.

Mitchell, L. G.,   *Lord Melbourne 1779–1848.*
                                 Oxford University Press, 1997.

Morley, J.,   *Life of William Ewart Gladstone*, 3 vols.
                                 Macmillan, 1903.

Newsome, David,   *The Victorian World Picture.*
                                 John Murray, 1997.

Overton, J. H.,   *The English Church in the 19th Century.*
                                 1894.

Parker, C. S. (ed.),   Sir Robert Peel – Private Papers, 3 vols.
                                 John Murray, 1891–1899.

Port, M. H.,   *Six Hundred New Churches.*
                                 SPCK, 1961.

Porter, Roy,   *London.*
                                 Hamish Hamilton, 1994.

Prestige, L.,   *Pusey.*
                                 Philip Allan, 1933.

Read, Donald,   *Peel and the Victorians.*
                                 Blackwell, 1987.

Reynolds, Michael,   *Martyr of Ritualism, Father Mackonochie of St Alban's Holborn.*
Faber & Faber, 1965.

Scotland, Nigel,   *The Life and Work of John Bird Sumner.*
Gracewing, Leominster, 1995.

Sheppard, Francis,   *London 1808–70.*
1971.

Sinclair, W. (ed.),   *Thirty-Two Years of the Church of England.*
1874.

Smith, Charles Nowell, (ed.),   *Letters of Sydney Smith,* 2 vols.
Oxford, 1953.

Smith, Sydney,   *Collected Works.*
1850.

Smyth, C.,   *Simeon and Church Order.*
1940.

Soloway, R. A.,   *Prelates and People.*
Routledge & Kegan Paul, 1969.

Stanley, A. P.,   *Life and Correspondence of Thomas Arnold.*
Ward Lock, 1890.

Stanley, Venetia,   *High Society.*
1998.

Sumner, G. H.,   *The Life of the Right Rev. C. R. Sumner.*
John Murray, 1872.

Thomson, David,   *England in the Nineteenth Century 1815–1914.*
Penguin, 1950.

Trench, Maria,   *Charles Lowder.*
New York, 1883.

Trollope, Anthony,   *Clergymen of the Church of England.*
Chapman & Hall, 1866 (reprinted by the Trollope Society).

Varley, E. A.,   *The Last of the Prince Bishops.*
Cambridge University Press, 1992.

Virgin, P.,   *Sydney Smith.*
                             HarperCollins, 1994.

Virgin, P.,   *The Church in an Age of Negligence.*
                             James Clarke, 1989.

Webster, A. B.,   *Joshua Watson, The Story of a Layman,*
                             1771–1855.
                             SPCK, 1954.

Welch, P. J.,   'Bishop C. J. Blomfield'.
                             Unpublished PhD Thesis, University of
                             London, May, 1952.

Welch, P. J.,   'Bishop Blomfield and the Development of
                             Tractarianism in London' in
                             Church Quarterly Review Oct–Dec 1954.

Welch, P. J.,   'The Significance of Bishop C. J. Blomfield' in
                             Modern Churchman, 1955.

Welch, P. J.,   'Anglican Churchmen and the Establishment
                             of the Jerusalem Bishopric' in
                             Journal of Ecclesiastical History, Oct 1957.

Welch, P. J.,   'The Revival of an Active Convocation of
                             Canterbury (1852–55)' in
                             Journal of Ecclesiastical History, Oct 1959.

Welch, P. J.,   'Blomfield and Peel. A Study in Co-operation
                             between Church and State, 1841–1846' in
                             Journal of Ecclesiastical History, April 1961.

Welch, P. J.,   'The Difficulties of Church Extension in
                             Victorian London', in the *Church Quarterly
                             Review*, July–September 1965.

Woodward, E. L.,   *The Age of Reform 1815–1870.*
                             Oxford, 1938.

Papers and Periodicals

The Times
British Critic
Punch
Guardian
John Bull
Quarterly Review
Hansards Parliamentary Reports
Reports of His Majesty's Commissions for Building and Promoting the Building of Additional Churches in Populous Places. London 1821–24
Report on the Poor Law 1834
Report on the Sanitary Conditions of the Labouring Population 1842

Index